Discovering the Limits of European Integration: Applying Grounded Theory

DISCOVERING THE LIMITS OF EUROPEAN INTEGRATION: APPLYING GROUNDED THEORY

KERRY E. HOWELL

Nova Science Publishers, Inc.
Huntington, New York

Senior Editors: Susan Boriotti and Donna Dennis
Office Manager: Annette Hellinger
Graphics: Drew Kane and Jennifer Lucas
Information Editor: Tatiana Shohov
Book Production: Latoya Clay, Cathy DeGregory, and Lynette Van Helden
Circulation: Anna Cruz, Ron Hedges, Andre Tillman Ave Maria Gonzalez and Evelyn Woodberry

Library of Congress Cataloging-in-Publication Data

Howell, Kerry E.
Discovering the limits of European integration: applying grounded theory / Kerry E. Howell.
p. cm.
Includes bibliographic references and index.
ISBN 1-56072- 843-4
1. Europe--Economic integration. 2. European federation. 3. European Union. 4. Conflict of laws--Europe--Case studies. 5 Conflict of laws--Insurance--Europe. 6. Insurance, Life--Law and legislation--Europe. I. Title.

HC241.H69 2000 00-061652
337.1'42--dc21 CIP

227 Main Street, Suite 100
Huntington, New York 11743
Tele. 631-424-6682 Fax 631-424-4666
e-mail: Novascience@earthlink.net
Web Site: http://www.nexusworld.com/nova

Printed in the United States of America

CONTENTS

LIST OF TABLES & FIGURES

LIST OF ABBREVIATIONS

ABI	Association of British Insurers
BIIC	British Insurers International Committee
BIPAR	Bureau International des Producteurs D'Assurance et des Assurances
CAP	Common Agricultural Policy
CEA	European Insurance Committee
CET	Common External Tariff
COREPER	Committee of Permanent Representatives
DG	Directorate General
DTI	Department of Trade
EC	European Community
ECB	European Central Bank
ECOFIN	Council of Economic and Finance Ministers
ECSC	European Coal and Steel Community
Ecu	European Currency Unit
EDC	European Defence Community
EEC	European Economic Community
EFTA	European Free Trade Area
EMI	European Monetary Institute
EMU	Economic and Monetary Union
EP	European Parliament
ERM	Exchange Rate Mechanism
ESCB	European System of Central Banks
EU	European Union

FIMBRA	Financial Intermediaries Managers and Brokers Association
GATT	General Agreement on Tariffs and Trade
GDP	Gross Domestic Product
GNP	Gross National Product
IGC	Intergovernmental Conference
LAUTRO	Life Assurance and Unit Trusts Regulatory Organisation
MEP	Member of the European Parliament
NATO	North Atlantic Treaty Organisation
NTB	Non-Tariff Barrier
OCA	Office De Controle des Assurance
OCI	Officer of the Commission for Insurance
OJ	Official Journal of the European Communities
PIA	Personal Investment Authority
QMV	Qualified Majority Voting
SEA	Single European Act
SEM	Single European Market
TEA	Treaty on European Union
UK	United Kingdom
UN	United Nations
WTO	World Trade Organisation

ABOUT THE AUTHOR

Dr Howell has a Ph.D. in Political Science and is a Senior Lecturer and Jean Monnet Associate in the Business School at Anglia (Polytechnic) University. He has a number of publications which include: *European Union Governance: Sub-National interests, Supranationality and the Life Insurance Industry (1999); Using Interest Groups in the European Union: The Case of the Life Insurance Industry (1999). Virtue, Virtu, the Categorical Imperative and the Civic Constitution: Defining Corporate Governance (2000).*

FOR GEMMA & MATTHEW

ACKNOWLEDGEMENTS

I would like to acknowledge the guidance and comments made by Gerard Dickinson, Henry Ellis, Wyn Grant, Justin Greenwood, Philip Hardwick and Kevin Moloney on earlier drafts of the study. I appreciate the support of the Worshipful Company of Insurers and Association of British Insurers and the participation of a number of European institutions and interest groups. Finally, I would like to acknowledge the support and encouragement of my family and friends.

PREFACE

Overall this work aims to discover the limits of European integration. To accomplish this the study uses grounded theory methodology to deal with some of the problems with European integration theories and international relations. Furthermore the idea of European Union (EU) is investigated in relation to Kantian and Hegelian thought which again allows a re-assessment of European integration and its limitations. The rationale for the study was provided by the rapidity of change that has taken place over the last fifteen years. As European integration intensified the theories that informed and explained the process became questionable. Theories previously discarded especially neo-functionalism, needed revisitation and re-assessment. This study provides such a re-assessment and through an empirical study reaches conclusions and makes generalisations regarding the process and limitations of European integration.

As noted, through grounded theory methodology and an empirical study of the European life insurance this work investigates the extent of sector involvement in the European Union's decision-making processes. Through this empirical study it critically analyses philosophical and theoretical understandings of European integration. Grounded theory methodology is illustrated by the study in the following ways. First, through the open coding (conceptualisation, categorisation and dimensionalisation) of individual Member States' life insurance regulations the study formulates a regulation table and matrix. Further coding and a survey of Member State life insurance industries, refined and verified the matrix. This investigation raised questions as to how the legislative differences (that underpin regulatory structures) between Member States may be resolved. Secondly, through an interview programme, sub-categories emerged and process was verified and illustrated through a series of models. The tables, models and the matrix provide the building blocks of the substantive theory. Thirdly, the matrix and models fitting together around the core category of European integration illustrate axial coding. The core category is identified through selective coding and is the category around which sub-categories are integrated. Axial coding draws all parts of the analysis together: it is the pivot or the axis of theory building. Finally, substantive theory is formulated through grounded theory techniques in relation to a number of formal theories e.g. neo-functionalism and intergovernmentalism; this allows a re-assessment of European integration and a clearer understanding of its limitations.

Chapter One reviews the literature relating to grounded theory, integration theory, insurance and the European Union (EU). Chapter Two explains grounded theory methodology in relation to the concepts of *self-interest* and *common interest.* Initially, through inductive and later deductive procedures, a substantive theory is constructed by which our understanding of formal theories e.g. neo-functionalism, intergovernmentalism and the European integration process may be enhanced. The methodology considers that the most important aspect of research is not explanation but understanding. Thus, the work does not wish to prove or disprove existing formal theories: it simply wishes to comprehend them and consider how they may further our understanding of the European integration process. The work also recognised the deficiencies of the formal theories in respect of their application to the EU alone (or Eurocentricity) and considers that in this context they are substantive theories themselves[1].

Initially, Chapter Three adds to the discussion regarding theory initiated in the methodology chapter. It provides an analysis of integration theory, by comparing functionalism, neo-functionalism, realism and intergovernmentalism and indicates how Kantian and Hegelian political philosophies underpin these. The chapter illustrates the complexity of integration theory and its relationship with four main theoretical schools. It

[1] Substantive theory is built through grounded theory processes (and the research itself) to allow an analysis and further the understanding of or formal theories in the process of European integration. Both substantive and formal theories are defined further in the methodology chapter below.

argues that functionalism is peace-oriented and has much to teach us about non-violent means of solving international problems. The chapter concludes that the EU decision-making process, through the use of interest groups, is a means of overcoming turbulence and consequently intensifies European integration.

Chapter Four provides the foundations of the substantive theory through the construction of a regulation matrix. Through grounded theory techniques of *categorisation*: *conceptual labels*; the emergence of *properties* and *characteristics*; and *dimensionalisation* the chapter illustrates the differences between Member State life insurance industries' legislation. Substantive theory is formulated through *code*, *theoretical*, *operational notes* and *diagrams*. The matrix posits convergence, which illustrates the creation of a Single European market (SEM) through harmonisation. To this initial analysis (through further coding and categorising), the results of a survey are added. Frequency tables, cross-tabulations and chi-squared tests are used to assess the extent of sector involvement in the creation of the Third Life Assurance Directive and subsequent regulatory environment. This provides the initial stages of the substantive theory and sets up a number of questions that are addressed in the following chapters.

Chapter Five identifies the core category of European integration and investigates the problems and questions indicated by the axial coding. The conclusions drawn from selective coding indicate that to fully understand the process of European integration it would be necessary to undertake a series of interviews. The interviews were undertaken with individuals involved in the creation of the Third Life Assurance Directive and provide an understanding of how the categories formulated in the previous chapter may be negotiated and compromised. Indeed, the interview questions were formulated on the basis of the open and axial coding outcomes. Finally, through the emergence of sub-categories the chapter adds to the substantive theory by developing a decision-making model, which gives some insight into the formal theories.

Chapter Six makes generalisations regarding the process indicated in Chapters Four and Five, investigates the concept of spillover and the part this may play in European integration. The chapter adds to the substantive theory through the construction of a spillover model, which provides an understanding of spillover processes in the EU. The chapter investigates spillover and considers whether it plays a part in the creation of a SEM in financial services. This is accomplished through an analysis of EU financial services legislation. The chapter argues that there is a distinction between horizontal and vertical spillover and intergovernmental and neo-functional spillover[2]. It also contends that the revival of supranationality has given an impetus to the integration process. Furthermore, the part life insurance plays in the process of integration, and the difficulties in creating the Third Life Assurance Directive are explored. The chapter concludes that the integration of financial services is intrinsically tied to the success of Economic and Monetary Union (EMU), and that even though neo-functional spillover is an important process it can only take European integration so far without further intergovernmental spillover in the form of further treaties.

Chapter Seven sets out a substantive theory which illustrates the extent to which the formal theories are at work in the process of European integration and how far sectors, through interest groups and the Commission, dictate the limits of European integration. Additionally, there is an analysis of intergovernmentalism and nationalism and the extent to which these accepted norms are historical realities. Finally, the work attempts to identify the limits of European integration by using Hegelian and Kantian philosophies. It attempts to bridge the theoretical gap between international and regional integration theories, which has implications for the limitations of the European integration process. Through the amalgamation of theory and practice and an analysis of the interaction between formal and substantive theory the limits of European integration are investigated and a number of conclusions drawn.

[2] Neo-functional spillover is part of the integration process in that legislation in one area spills into another. Intergovernmental is where one treaty necessitates further treaties and where the neo-functional process pushes for further integration through the harmonisation of specific legislation which will eventually necessitate further treaties.

INTRODUCTION

No conclusion of peace shall be considered valid as such if it was made with a secret reservation of the material for a future war (Kant, 1995; p 95).

Grounded theory suggests that there is an over-emphasis on verification theory and wishes to demote the idea that the discovery of relevant concepts and hypotheses are *a priori* to research. Furthermore, grounded theory can be based on pragmatism (Dewey, 1950) in the context of *symbolic interaction* (see Mead, 1962; Blumer, 1962; 1969). Symbolic interaction is distinct to human beings because it is part of what makes us human, rather than simply reacting to human action we interpret or define them (Blumer, 1962). Mead (1962) argued that the ability to react to self was the central mechanism of existence. "This mechanism enables the human being to make indication to himself of things in his surroundings and thus to guide his action by what he notes. Anything of which a human being is conscious . . . he is indicating to himself. . . . The conscious life of the human being . . . is a continual flow of self indications" (p 180). Fundamentally, " . . . the formation of action by the individual through . . . self-indication always takes place in a social context" (p 183).

One now regularly takes an impartial and general standpoint in observing and evaluating one's own conduct . . . (however) . . . The organised community or social group which gives to the individual his unity of self may be called the generalised other which is the attitude of the whole community (Blau, 1952; pp 162-163 authors brackets).

Symbolic interaction presupposes the following:

a. The individual has a self and an amalgamation of interpreted selves encompasses society.
b. Individual action is constructed through interpreting the situational context.
c. Groups and collective action incorporate the alignments of individual actions that are formulated through interpreting the actions of others.

Consequently, research should be pursued with this in mind, interpretations of situations change as individuals change (this includes the researcher and the researched). Indeed, with the knowledge that pure objectivity cannot be attained the research may be more objective i.e. any analysis that does not accept subjectivity can never be objective. Grounded theory attempts to understand social patterns on the basis of symbolic interaction and construct social theory.

Grounded theory looks to the generation of theory through comparative analysis and does not attempt to undermine theory but improve it. Effectively, " . . . a theory's only replacement is a better theory" (Glaser and Strauss, 1967; p 28). "Grounded theory is based on the systematic generating of theory from data, and itself is systematically obtained from social research. Thus the grounded theory method offers a rigorous orderly guide to theory development that each stage is closely integrated with a methodology of social research" (Glaser, 1978; p 2).

Fundamentally, research should be approached with an open mind and as much objectivity and distance as is possible. However, it is acknowledged that such objectivity is difficult, as everyone has subjective tendencies. Indeed, the recognition of subjectivity is a necessary element of dealing with it. This may be considered to encompass theoretical sensitivity which is initially gained by entering the research " . . . with as few predetermined ideas as possible, especially logically deduced, *a priori* hypotheses" (Glaser, 1978, p 3). Such enables the researcher to remain sensitive and " . . . record events and detect happenings without first having them filtered through and squared with pre-existing hypotheses and biases" (ibid).

This is what may be labelled foresight or that which allows the researcher certain expectations of what may be discovered. As does the background or environment (fore-structure) which indicates possible ways of questioning

(Heidegger, 1978). Stern (1994) argued that grounded theory was an interpretative method and underpinned by " . . . phenomenology, that is methods that are used to describe the world of the person or persons under study" (p 213). Grounded theory involves the " . . . soliciting of emic viewpoints to assist in determining the meaning and purposes that people ascribe to their actions" (ibid, p 110).

This study argues that the objective of grounded theory is an attempt to understand reality through social constructions and an attempt at objectivity through recognising the subjectivity of the researcher and researched in terms of their interpretative nature.

The subject matter of the investigation is European integration theory. The work constructs a substantive theory through grounded theory techniques to allow further comprehension of formal theories e.g. neo-functionalism and intergovernmentalism, which provide explanations of European integration processes. From the late 1960s until the mid-1980s when one discussed European integration one usually emphasised intergovernmentalism. "Neo-functionalism and intergovernmentalism were contending theories of European integration in the 1960s but by the 1970s intergovernmentalism appeared to have carried the day, until in the 1980s the single market programme and the Single European Act led to a revival of neo-functionalist explanations" (George, 1994; p 1).

This work wishes to enter the debate and seeks to illustrate the extent to which neo-functionalism or intergovernmentalism may be at work in the process of European integration. An analysis of a service sector (the life insurance industry) has been undertaken in respect of its relationships with the EU decision-making institutions. It is considered that through *self-interest*, national life insurance industries attempt to create a market in their own image. Through compromise a single market is formed, European integration taken a step further and this enhances the welfare of Europeans in general. Fundamentally, in the perpetuation and evolution of the human species, *self-interest* and *mutual assistance* work hand-in-hand.

The research began with a series of preliminary interviews with UK life insurance companies and the Association of British Insurers (ABI). These gave an idea of the UK sector's understanding of Europe and allowed the compilation of a questionnaire. Interviews were later undertaken in Brussels, Paris and London where individuals involved in the decision-making processes were asked to comment on their part in the creation of the Third Life Assurance Directive.

A major survey of the European life insurance industry provides an understanding of that industry in terms of how it approaches the EU, how it ascertains national self-interest in terms of market conditions, and the extent of compromise in the creation of the Single European Market (SEM). Less extensive surveys were made of European and national interest groups, the European Parliament and Permanent Representatives.

Inductive investigation allows an overall picture of the EU and SEM to be established; subsequently this allowed deductions about the European integration process. Through the induction-deduction aspects of the grounded theory methodology, further understanding of European integration is established.

The work explores whether the EU is *supranational* and whether this supranationality, in tandem with *spillover*, is part of the integration process. The renewed pace of the European integration in terms of the SEM, monetary union and the implications this has for political union raised new questions about its limitations. Furthermore, the work investigates how far interest groups and industries are either the willing or unwilling creators of European economic and political union and to what extent *self-interest* creates peace and welfare in Europe and ultimately the Kantian 'civic constitution'? Indeed, because of the renewed pace of European integration theoretical explanations need to be reassessed.

Neo-functionalism went into decline with the slowing up of the integration process. Now the pace has quickened, it may be possible to discern elements of neo-functionalism, in relation to intergovernmentalism, at work in the evolving SEM and EU. This work intends to determine the extent of neo-functionalism in the re-vitalised European integration process. Keohane and Hoffman (1990) emphasised the need for a theoretical framework for the evolving EU and indicated that neo-functionalism may provide this. However, they do point out that further empirical research is necessary. This work aims to provide a part of that research and in the process attempt to discover the limits of European integration.

Chapter One

Reviewing the Literature

The ultimate philosophy and the hierarchy of preferences invite discussion rather than proof or refutation; analyses of present facts or prognostications about facts to come, alter with the unfolding of history and the knowledge we acquire of it (Aron, 1985; p 236).

Introduction

This chapter overview's the literature that the study has drawn on in building a substantive theory and an understanding of European integration processes. The literature review is broken down into three subject areas, which provide the overall underpinning of the work. The areas covered incorporate: the methodology literature; integration theory literature; and life insurance and EU literature.

Methodology Literature

Grounded theory suggests that there is an over-emphasis on verification theory and wishes to demote the idea that the discovery of relevant concepts and hypotheses are *a priori* to research. For further see (Glaser and Strauss, 1967: Glaser 1978: Charmaz. 1983: Strauss. 1987: Strauss and Corbin. 1990:

Corbin and Strauss, 1990; Glaser 1992; Strauss and Corbin, 1994; Stern, 1994; Melia, 1994; Annells, 1996).

Glaser and Strauss (1967) draw on the pragmatist school, particularly Dewey (1950) and Mead (1962). Dewey (1950) considered that theory cannot answer questions "... unless we are willing to find the germs and roots in matters of experience" (p 12). Furthermore, grounded theory can be based on *symbolic interaction* (Mead, 1962 and Blumer 1962; 1969). Symbolic interaction is distinct to human beings, it is part of what makes us human because we "... interpret or define each other's actions" (Blumer, 1962; p 179) rather than simply reacting to them. Furthermore, humans have and are able to act towards self. Mead considered that the ability to react to self was the central mechanism of existence. "This mechanism enables the human being to make indication to himself of things in his surroundings and thus to guide his action by what he notes. Anything of which a human being is conscious ... he is indicating to himself ... The conscious life of the human being ... is a continual flow of self indications" (ibid p 180).

Grounded theory aims to generate theory in a social context through comparative analysis. It does not attempt to undermine theory but to improve it. Effectively, " ... a theory's only replacement is a better theory" (Glaser and Strauss, 1967; p 28).

Guba and Lincoln (1994) considered that grounded theory is *postpositivist*, while, Annells (1996) contends that our understanding of grounded theory is based on an "... awareness of the method's ontological, epistemological and methodological perspectives" (ibid; p 379) and that these may be broken down into four paradigms of enquiry. These are *positivism, postpositivism, critical theory* and *constructivism*. Indeed, that one's understanding of methodology and consequently grounded theory is determined by one's metaphysical assumptions. Grounded theory involves the "... soliciting of emic viewpoints to assist in determining the meaning and purposes that people ascribe to their actions" (Guba and Lincoln, 1994; p 110). "Grounded theory methodology incorporates ... assumption(s) ... concerning the human status of actors whom we study. They have perspectives on and interpretations of their own and other actors' actions. As researchers we are required to learn what we can of their interpretations and perspectives" (Strauss and Corbin, 1994; p 280 author's brackets). This study considers that this is the basis of grounded theory: an attempt to understand reality through social constructions and an attempt at objectivity through recognising the subjectivity of the researcher and researched in terms of their interpretative nature.

"The purpose of grounded theory . . . is to build theory that is faithful to and illuminates the area under study" (Corbin and Strauss, 1990; p 24). As noted above, Glaser and Strauss (1967) considered that grounded theory was concerned with two types of theory: substantive and formal (conceptual); theory allows hypotheses and substantive concepts to emerge from the data, so analysis may identify concepts relevant to understanding the data. "In discovering theory, one generates conceptual categories or their properties from evidence; then the evidence from which the categories emerged is used to illustrate the concept. The evidence may not . . . be accurate beyond doubt . . . but the concept is undoubtedly a relevant theoretical abstraction about what is going on in the area studied" (Glaser and Strauss, 1967; p 23).

The object of research, according, to Strauss and Corbin, " . . . in a grounded theory study is a statement that identifies the phenomenon to be studied" (1990, p 38). However, this does not mean that qualitative and quantitative data are incompatible. "In many instances both forms of data are necessary - not quantitative to test qualitative but both used as supplements, as mutual verification and most important for us, as different forms of data on the same subject, which when compared with each other generate theory" (Glaser and Strauss, 1967; p 38).

Glaser and Strauss (1967) emphasised that generating theory was accomplished through the collection, coding and analysis of the data and that as far as possible these three operations should be undertaken together. These areas should interact continually, from the beginning of the investigation to its end. The separation of these areas hinders theory generation whereas set ideas stifle it. In this study the aim is to generate a substantive theory in relation to intergovernmentalism and neo-functionalism and investigate them with regard to their applicability as general theories of integration and their relevance to the EU.

Integration Theory Literature

The main aim of this work is to rediscover and assess formal theories relating to European integration e.g. neo-functionalism and intergovernmentalism. The study considers that these developed out of functionalism and realism which were themselves based on the Kantian concept of the international civic constitution (Kant 1995, see *Idea for a Universal History With a Cosmopolitan Purpose* pp 41-53 and *Perpetual Peace* pp 93-115) and Hegelian interpretations of the state and recognition (Hegel, 1967). Indeed the study argues that Hegelian recognition can provide a bridge between realist and functional understandings of integration. To discover the limits of European integration it is important to understand how these theories have been adapted and the direction that on-going debates have taken.

Furthermore, the basis of European integration may be identified in early Greek thought. Aristophanes (1970) personified Peace as a Goddess who is released from confinement by the " . . . farmers, merchants, labourers, craftsmen, aliens, visitors" (pp, 233-34). Peace was buried but through working together, through the integration of activity, Peace is freed from her incarceration. This identifies people working together, in ancient Greece to form a pan-hellenic state and an integrated and peaceful environment.

There have been a number of commentators who have written in the realms of international relations and integration theory and discussed how they are informed and underpinned by realism, functionalism, intergovernmentalism and neo-functionalism. For further see (Bulmer 1993; Claude 1956; George 1994, 1995; Groom and Taylor 1975; Haas 1958, 1964, 1968, 1971, 1975, 1976; Heathcote 1966; Hoffman 1966; Keohane and Nye 1990; Keohane and Hoffman 1990, 1991; Lindberg 1963 1967; Lindberg and Scheingold 1970, 1971; Moravsik 1991, 1993; Mitrany 1943, 1944, 1965, 1970, 1975, 1975a, 1975b, 1975c; Nye 1971, 1971a; Pentland, 1973; Rees 1992; Sandholtz and Zysman 1989; Sandholtz, 1994; Schmitter 1969; Schmitter and Streeck, 1994; Sewell 1966; Sweeny 1984; Taylor 1968, 1968a, 1983, 1971; Wallace, Wallace and Webb 1977; Wallace 1990; Webb 1983). However, in general the debate revolved around neo-functionalism and intergovernmentalism and which of these is most precise in describing the process of European integration.

The initial proponents of neo-functionalism were Haas (1958) and Lindberg (1963). However, they both to reconsidered their understandings of neo-functionalism because of the re-assertion of the nation-state in the 1960s. Indeed, the actions of De Gaulle during the 1960s, illustrated the deterministic nature of neo-functionalism and the absence of a dependent variable[1] (Heathcote, 1966). This led to ten years of debate and the displacement of neo-functionalism as a plausible theory. Yet, because of the impetus the SEA and the Maastricht Treaty created, commentators are once again turning their attention to neo-functionalism. Indeed, Rees (1992) commented that the recent developments in Europe " . . . have led to renewed interest in theories of integration, especially neo-functionalism" (p 13).

The modern understanding of functionalism[2], in the realms of international relations, is commonly attributed to David Mitrany. Additionally, the ideas of federalism[3] were re-formulated over the same period in history

---

[1] The dependent variable regarding European integration relates to some sort of end result. Neo-functionalism does not propose an end. It does not draw borders around Europe nor give it a specific form. It is a peaceful process pursuing a peaceful end. However, the material aspect of the end is uncertain. In this context the limits of European integration are unidentifiable.

[2] Functionalism is the means by which change toward a goal of international collaboration is brought about; it is illustrated through organisations which would be designated a specific task that would evolve as functional needs changed. The system incorporates the premise of peaceful co-operation. The outcome may be a pluralist international community where national control is marginalised through functional linkages, or more extreme, where the nation-state disappears and is replaced by functional rationality. This is where organisational patterns are undertaken at the most rational level i.e. either continental, international or local. Effectively, functionalism is a process of internationalisation in terms of politics and the assurance of peace, whereas decisions, are carried out at the most rational or functional level. Functionalism does not adhere to the concept of constitution or regionalism. In Kantian terms, it pursues the concept of 'Perpetual Peace' without a civil constitution at regional nor international level. Mitrany considered that human beings have no concept of what the end result of integration should encompass, so why invent one? Kant may be perceived as functionalist in terms of his pursuit of world government or internationalisation. However, he may be considered federalist in terms of his wish for a constitution.

[3] Federalism, is based on the concept of peace and is premised on the Kantian ideas of both the civil constitution and 'Perpetual Peace'. Federalism may be understood in

(see Hodges, 1972) and in themselves provide a strand of neo-functional thought[4]. This work provides an analysis of neo-functional ideas that emanate from functionalism and federalism. Functional theories have also been posited by Claude (1956) who builds on Mitrany's work (1943) and considers international organisation as a process; and Sewell (1966) who attempts to verify a functional process through an analysis of the World Bank. Haas (1958) proposed a concept of incrementalism which was based on his study of the European Coal and Steel Community (ECSC); this placed an emphasis on 'functional integrationalism' (Burton, 1975). Indeed, through his study of the ECSC Haas developed neo-functionalism (Haas 1958, 1964, 1968, 1971). Puchala (1972) allegorically compares European integration with the story of the blind men and the elephant, " . . . each blind man concluded that the elephant had the appearance of the part he touched . . . each had gained enough evidence from his own experience to disbelieve his fellows and to maintain a lively debate" (ibid, p 267). Ultimately he provides his

terms of the development of European history. Initially, it may be seen as an ideal denied by the nation state between the French Revolution and the First World War. Secondly, the inter-war period where it allows an understanding of the European crisis; and finally in the post-war period where its application could overcome the European difficulties with the nation state and war. The difference between functionalism and federalism is that the former identifies a process: the latter an end in the federal state. Federalism provides for the enlargement of representative government; it allows administration to extend from one to many states. If one considers a world federation flowing out of European federalism then one may be indicating a neo-functional end in that supranationality is not an end in Europe but part of the process toward internationalisation.

[4] Unlike functionalism, neo-functionalism posits that integration is most easily to be realised in a regional setting. Functionalists conceded that a supranational state would keep peace at the regional level. However, it would also create a power bloc and this would not ensure peace at the international level. In this context Mitrany criticised European integration. Haas accepted Mitrany's criticism when he argued that regional integration may lead to a future world made up of fewer and fewer units, each unit with all the power and self assertion that we associate with classical nationalism (Haas, 1970). This provides an acceptance of the realist argument and indicates the difficulties created when theory lacks a dependent variable. Neo-functionalism is the interaction between interest groups and the new supranational centres of power in the pursuit of a new market environment. Limitations are difficult to identify.

"concordance system" (in which actors find it possible to harmonise their interests consistently) from which an analysis of the dynamics of international integration may be launched (ibid, pp 276-283). Taylor (1968) argued that there were two broad theories for understanding Europe: (a) federalist/neo-functionalist (b) technocratic/functionalist. However, he does not come to any conclusions about which is the most useful, but does clarify some aspects of integration theory. Nye (1971) considered that neo-functionalism should be used as a means of understanding integration and making comparisons: that if it is freed from the characteristics that linked it specifically to Europe, it would be useful for analysing integration in other settings.

Neo-functionalism has also been influenced by systems theory (Easton, 1953) and envisages elites and interest groups that change their loyalties towards a supranational grouping, rather than national groupings alone. This is done to satisfy wants, preferences and interests that transfer into demands which in turn are transformed into decisions (Easton, 1965). Lindberg acknowledges this approach to the extent that there is a process by which "political actors" in different settings " . . . are persuaded to shift their expectations to a new centre" (Lindberg, 1976; p 6). He considered that as " . . . a contributor to the European integration literature I have more and more come to feel as if I were excavating a small isolated portion of a large, dimly-perceived mass, the contours of which I could not make out" (Lindberg, 1967; p 345).

In an attempt to overcome this Lindberg used Easton's model (Easton, 1965, 1965a) to provide " . . . a framework of logically consistent and integrated categories" (Lindberg, 1967; p 346). He concentrated on Mitrany's idea that there should be no final outcome and doesn't refer to a political community. However, in both Haas and Lindberg, there is a change of emphasis in respect of the institutions on which the interest group or sector makes its demands: the European Union.

Further understandings of neo-functionalism are based around Schmitter (1971) and his concept of integration, which he termed as, " . . . the process of transferring exclusive expectations of benefits from the nation-state to some larger entity. It encompasses the process by virtue of which national actors of all sorts (government officials, interest group spokesmen, politicians as well as ordinary people) cease to identify themselves and their future welfare entirely with their own national government and its policies" (Schmitter, in Lindberg and Schmitter, 1971; p 238).

Sweeny (1984) underpins the theoretical aspect of the EU with functionalism and defines it in terms of the distinction between the general will and the will of all. For functionalists, the general will resides with those concerned with the non-political welfare needs of all people. Webb (1983) argued that European integration had produced a policy-making system that was partially integrated, but that political integration was unlikely and neo-functionalism was obsolete. She suggested that only two realistic frameworks remained: intergovernmentalism and interdependence[5]. However, there are a number of different interpretations of interdependence (Rosecrance *et al,* 1977; Keohane and Nye, 1977; Cooper, 1977; Taylor 1980). The main problem with the theory is "... that it tends to ignore the relationship between *Gemeinschaft* and *Gesselschaft* that is found in any political process. The form which this relationship usually takes is the modification of perceptions of self-interest by such factors as emotional ties, preferences 'we feeling' or the identification of mutual values" (Taylor, 1980; p 373). This work questions the extent to which there has, or has not been, a shift in the EU from a pure *Gemeinschaft* toward the *Gessellschaft* (a shift from interdependence ground in intergovernmentalism toward integration through aspects of neo-functionalism). "In other words, the realisation that interests are mutual is expected to precede the procedural or constitutional arrangements, and interdependence is seen to involve a learning process by which decision-makers are brought to recognise common interests" (ibid).

Haas (1976) also identified such a process in his concept of turbulence where clashing perceptions create confusion and " . . . everything is up for grabs" (p 179). The complexity of the situation is not based on limited knowledge but on too much, " . . . turbulent fields are the existence of very large bodies of knowledge . . ." which "... provide certainty for parts . . ." but confuse the whole (ibid). Garrett (1992) considered the difficulties of co-operation and the problems of discriminating between outcomes but when he spoke of preferences he spoke of government preferences. Indeed, there was

---

[5] Keohane and Nye (1977) examined the basic principles of interdependence and considered that in general terms the theory accepted the *Gessellschaft* theory of society rather than the *Gemeinschaft*. The former stresses the management of the market place in which conflicting interests interact. The latter concentrates on consensus, stability and duty. It emphasises relationships between actors and considers that interests may be modified in respect of mutuality and preferred relationships.

little mention of interest groups. However, Garrett and Weingast (1993) indicate how interest groups provide the basis for shared beliefs and "focal points" (p 176) which assists in the creation of certainty and understanding, the outcome of which, is further integration. This area is also explored in Haas (1975) where knowledge and space are again questioned in relation to integration, as it is by Derrida (1992) with regard to the concept of Europe. What are the boundaries of Europe? What is Europe? Is it no more than a peninsula of Asia? These are important issues in discovering the limits of European integration. Should we indicate a designated land mass or leave the parameters open? Furthermore, Graubard (1963) posits the need for a new Europe. He questions the first forty years of the twentieth century with its conceptions of nationalism and the demise of socialist and liberal utopias. He argued that Europe should be optimistic and that " . . . the present efforts, seemingly chaotic, may in time be viewed as the uncertain strivings of an old society to renew itself, by taking what is best from its recollections of a not undistinguished past" (p 653).

More recently, Keohane and Hoffman (1990) provided an understanding of 'spillover' that distinguished between domains and sectors. They argued that successful spillover necessitates prior agreements among Member States in terms of the SEA and the Maastricht Treaty etc. This study has some sympathy with the framework posited by Keohane and Hoffman (1990) and attempts to adapt it through its study of financial services.

Mutimer (1989) revisits neo-functionalism and emphasises the importance of the SEA. He also argued that federalism was inappropriate when analysing the EU. However, he eventually dismissed neo-functionalism because " . . . even in amended form it is not sufficient" (ibid p 101). Pederson (1992) considered that intergovernmentalism should be combined with elements of neo-functionalism to enable a new framework of analysis. Keohane and Hoffman (1990, 1991) emphasised pooling sovereignty rather than transferring it from the Member States to supranational institutions. Moravcsik (1991, 1993 and 1998) whose analysis of the SEA provides evidence that the primary source of integration resides with the Member States themselves takes an intergovernmental stance. "Liberal-intergovernmentalism divides the EU decision process into two stages each of which is grounded in one of the classical integration theories" (Hix, 1999; p 15). Initially domestic actors demand European integration and as in neo-functionalism these ". . . actors have economic interests and compete for these interests to be promoted by national governments in EU decision-making" (ibid). Fundamentally, integration is driven by inter-state bargaining, states are unitary actors and supranational institutions have limited impact on outcomes (ibid). Sandholtz (1994) and Sandholtz and Zysman (1989) took a less intergovernmental perspective and argued that three groups reshaped the EU: industrial elites, EU institutions and Member State governments. Furthermore, Sandholtz (1994) investigated why Member States were prepared to give up their currencies and the sovereignty this entails. He argued that membership of the EU defines preference parameters and decisions. Intergovernmentalism alone failed to explain the impact that membership of the EU has on Member State preferences, interests and demands. Indeed, if European integration is to be fully understood a combination of approaches is necessary. Along with a call for more empirical studies this is a theme that has also been argued by Tranholme-Mikkelsen (1991), George (1994, 1995), Garrett and Tsebelis (1996), Gehring (1996), Richardson (1996a), Ugur (1997).

Through an empirical study of European integration over the late 1960s and early 1970s, Kirchner (1976) argued that the ". . . logic and forces outlined by Haas were generally found to be operative" (p 4). However, in a later work he contended that neither neo-functionalism nor intergovernmentalism adequately captured " . . . the existing overlap in decision-making between national and Community authorities, the sharing of joint tasks and interests, and the fusion of competencies between the national and Community level" (Kirchner, 1992; p 35). Pierson (1996) relied on neo-functional criticisms of intergovernmentalism and posits historical institutionalism as a means of understanding European integration[7]. Furthermore, Corbey (1995) amended neo-functionalism and argued that dialectical functionalism provided the impetus for European integration. Indeed, European integration is " . . . a process of action (decision to act) and reaction (response to integration). Progress is generated by the mutual interaction of the institutions of the EU, member states, and interest groups, Since integration proceeds in stages, the dialectics of the process has to be given more attention" (pp 262-63).

---

[7] Historical institutionalism is historical because things develop over time and institutional because this temporality is based in organisations through rules, structures and norms. Changes over time through changes in institutions or ". . . social processes understood as historical phenomenon" (Pierson, 1996; p 131).

Peterson (1995) considered that " . . . the gap remains wide between theoretical models which seek to explain broad patterns of European integration and those which seek to explain the EU's policy-making process" (p 69) However, the debate has turned toward governance through the arguments initiated by Keohane and Hoffman (1991), Marks (1993) and Marks *et al* (1996; 1996a). Questions were formed regarding the political order that is emerging in the EU and based on more general theories, policy-making investigated. Indeed, two theories predominate within the debate.

On the one side, functionalists and neo-functionalists have conceived of the process of institutional innovation as one of integration in which supranational institutions compromise state autonomy and sovereignty by shaping institutional competencies, resources and decision-making rules. On the other side . . . intergovernmental theorists have argued that member states and their executives continue to dominate decision-making in the European Community. . . . While they differ substantively, these contending accounts share a fundamental assumption about how to conceptualise the European Community. Both view the defining features of the outcome in terms of the relative role of supranational versus national institutions. They share a conception of the outcome of institution building in the European Community as varying along a dimension characterised by intergovernmentalism at one extreme and a supranational state at the other (Marks, 1993; p 391).

Hooghe and Marks (1997) link neo-functionalism (through supranational actors and interest groups) to multi-level governance and intergovernmentalism to state-centric governance. They conclude that the state-centric approach is not capable of fully explaining European policy making processes; that EU decision-making and policy-making are of a multi-level nature. Indeed, Marks *et al* (1996) provide an interesting interpretation of the present situation. "Multi-level governance does not confront the sovereignty of states directly. Instead of being explicitly challenged states in the European Union are being melded gently into multi-level polity by their leaders and the actions of numerous sub-national and supranational actors. State-centric theorists are right when they argue that states are extremely powerful institutions that are capable of crushing direct threats to their existence" (p 371). However, it is not necessary ". . . to argue that states are on the verge of political extinction to believe that their control of those living in their territories has significantly weakened" (ibid). (For a critical overview of

European integration theories and the current state of the debate, see Cram, 1997).

Interest group studies have been undertaken in an attempt to allow further understanding of European integration. The growth in the validity of the EU as a decision-making entity is made evident by the proliferation of interest group activity in aftermath of the SEA (Mazey and Richardson, 1992; 1993; 1996). Involved in the overview of the theories is the neo-pluralist and neo-corporatist schools (Schmitter, 1990; Streeck, 1989; Grant, 1990; Streeck and Schmitter, 1991; and Jordan 1991). There is also a strong emphasis on pluralism in the EU (Grant, 1989; Kirchner and Schwaiger, 1981; Sargent, 1987).

A number of theorists concern themselves with interest groups in general (Sidjanski, 1970; Averyt, 1975). Kirchner (1980) provided an analysis of the formation and development of interest groups at the European level and gives an indication of the characteristics of the groups and their interaction with the European decision-making bodies. He also provides an illustration of the top twenty-one interest groups at the European level, indicating in general terms how they attempt to influence decision-making in Europe (ibid, p 111). In more general terms there has been some analysis of interest groups in relation to the European Union (Lieber, 1974; Mazey and Richardson, 1992; Grant, 1995) each considering that further empirical work was necessary. Sidjanski (1970) proposed that groups establish themselves at the European level because they recognise a new centre of decision-making. As the EU began to affect certain interests, organisations congregated around the new institutions ". . . sometimes . . . prompted by invitation or even pressure from the Commission" (p 402). Following an empirical study of European decision-making processes Mazey and Richardson (1996) support the idea of interest group/Commission interaction and provide clear evidence that consultation and lobbying are prolific.

Hix (1994) pointed out that, even though they had the same ontological and methodological basis, there was a distinction between the way international relations and comparative politics theories analysed the EU. Indeed, he considered that theories of international relations were limited when analysing the internal politics of the community. "The international approaches may be appropriate for the studies of European integration. However, comparative politics are more appropriate for the analysis of European Community politics" (p 23). This study considers that both are applicable when analysing the EU. However, as the EU becomes more integrated, comparative politics will become ever more predominant. As European integration intensifies the debate will gradually move away from politics between states and turn toward European governance and politics within states. This slight shift may be identified through the governance arguments initiated by Hooghie and Marks (1997), Keohane and Hoffman (1991), Marks (1993), Marks (1995), Marks *et al* (1996) and Marks *et al* (1996a). As well as the shift toward debates around governance, this change has also been realised through the study of specific sub-national interests and their interactions with EU policy-making institutions. (see Camerra-Rowe, 1996; Coen, 1997; 1998; Greenwood *et al*, 1992; Greenwood and Cram, 1996; Greenwood, 1995; 1997; Mazey and Richardson, 1996; McLaughlin *et al*, 1993; McLaughlin and Greenwood, 1995; McLaughlin, 1995).

As noted above, in the international relations tradition there have been attempts to synthesise pluralist and realist theories like neo-functionalism and intergovernmentalism through multilevel governance (Hooghie and Marks, 1997). Furthermore, some commentators have considered that historical institutionalist arguments indicate that the EU " . . . is no longer simply a multilateral instrument, limited in scope and firmly under the control of individual member states" (Pierson, 1996; p 158). That Member State " . . . governments are not the only important decision-makers in the EU" (Garrett and Tsebelis, 1996; p 294). And the EU illustrates ". . . an emergent multitiered system of governance" (Pierson, 1996; p 158).

Overall there is now some agreement that " . . . a range of ideas are partial to explain the realities, dynamics and complexities of European integration" (Greenwood, 1997; p 242). Indeed, the amalgamation of ideas came about following the Single European Act (SEA), Qualified Majority Voting (QMV) and Member State uncertainty about where the reassertion of the SEM would lead them. The loss of the veto (in many areas) and uncertainty in the face of supranationality questioned the realist tradition " . . . of member states as rational utility-maximisers in interstate bargaining, jealousy guarding their sovereignty and calculating the limits to which sovereignty needed to be pooled for their own advantage" (ibid, pp 242-43). With the renewed emphasis on integration many realised that the EU was in the process of metamorphosis and that this would have " . . . major implications for the actors, the processes and the outcomes of policy-making at all levels in Europe: supranational, national and sub-national" (Marks *et al*, 1996; p 14).

This study implies that there is an amalgamation of international relations approaches to European integration processes in the form of multilevel and multi-tiered governance. Indeed, it argues that through an empirical study of the EU life insurance industry, insurance interest groups and EU policy-making institutions it can provide some generalisations regarding both governance and European integration.

Pool (1992) concluded that ". . . insurers are certainly much better organised as a pressure group than the other players in the insurance markets. Even they, however, have not always found it easy to arrive at a common perception of what a common market should mean for them" (p 11). The Commité Europèen des Assurances (CEA) was established in 1953 and for many years has acted on behalf of its membership regarding to European issues. The main objectives of European interest groups are two-fold. Firstly, they should ". . . promote the exchange of information and try to find common denominators" (Kirchner, 1980; p 109). And secondly, ". . . co-ordinate and exert pressure for adopted policies through the European organisations and the national affiliations on both the EC and the national government" (ibid).

Camerra-Rowe (1996) pointed out that different sectors undertake different strategies when it comes to lobbying European institutions. Indeed, firms often have an incentive to lobby directly. . . . However, it is rare for a firm, even a large one, to rely on one channel of representation" (ibid, p 6). As data presented by Coen (1997; 1998) verified, large companies do lobby the Commission directly. There is a high degree of lobbying strategies and activities undertaken by large companies in the EU. Indeed, there is evidence that ". . . this new lobbying activity is a function of of the changing regulatory competencies of the European Commission" (Coen, 1998; p 76). This provided the basis for a number of difficulties. Companies that lobby directly undermine the role of interest groups because the message they carry may not represent the whole sector. Also, they may have limited incentives to compromise their positions in the collective because they are able to lobby themselves. Finally, they may force the association to reach consensus, which may lead to the acceptance of the lowest common denominator and undermine the effectiveness of the interest group. However, it is evident that sub-national activity exists through large companies lobbying the EU institutions directly. Yet even though ". . . single firm representation is heard, the firm concerned is usually told that the Commission would wish to explore the issue further by talking to the interest group concerned in order to ensure that it gets a more representative opinion" (Greenwood, 1997; p 4). Furthermore, even though there are a number of interest groups from separate Member States, competition gives way to co-operation through resolving issues at the EU level (Browne, 1990). This is achieved by moving the ". . . analysis from the domain level to the issue level in order to provide a common substantive context for elite/pluralist interpretations" (ibid, p 477). This is echoed by Coen (1998) who considers that through issue based politics the Commission has ". . . institutionalised its bargaining position with business and has created a form of 'elite pluralism' . . . (which) requires that firms develop . . . pan-European political alliances in exchange for access to restricted entry forums" (p 77, author's brackets).

The European insurance industry is mainly made up of medium-size enterprises, which in general lack the political weight and resources to undertake direct action in Brussels (although the nature of the EU insurance industry is gradually changing through mergers and acquisitions). However, these companies are still small in relation to the larger multinationals. As a result, both national and European interest groups have a greater influence on the Commission and their membership. Companies need to accept the interest group's ". . . policy position even if it does not take account of their particular interests because they cannot effectively represent their own views. As a result, and paradoxically, the more fragmented insurance sector was better able to undertake collective activity in pursuing Community policy" (Camerra-Rowe, 1996; p 21). However, even though the likes of Allianz could lobby directly, it only does so intermittently. This is because ". . . Allianz dominates the insurance sector. Because of its size, the national and the European trade associations have generally taken the views of the firm into account in drawing up policy positions" (ibid, p 19). Indeed, in some instances, Allianz's position on certain issues became the national association's position. This was verified by SMEs who took care not to contradict Allianz in the formulation of policy (ibid). Furthermore, a change in the position of a Member State interest group can also have an effect on EU policy. For instance during the early nineties the French interest group started to change its stance on regulation. It " . . . gradually swung to join the liberalising elements of the CEA . . . a position which has supported the European Commission . . ." (Vipond, 1995; p 107) regarding the Third Life Assurance Directive.

Browne (1990) questions whether organisations exist that integrate policy domains and issues within a domain. The provision of three generations of life assurance directives indicates a policy domain integrated in the domain of financial services and the Third Life Assurance Directive is an issue within this policy domain (p 484). The Third Life Assurance Directive is a narrow issue and this brought about success. Indeed, the CEA is concerned with other issues relating to the policy domain of insurance. However, other interest groups deal with other policy domains relating to banking, capital markets and pensions, which belong to the domain of financial services. In this way issues can remain narrow and successes more frequent (p 490). Furthermore, Browne (1990) considers that interest groups and other lobbying organisations create coalitions in terms of the goals they pursue. It is considered that the CEA is more integrated than those organisations identified by Browne (1990) because it has a policy domain that becomes more integrated as European integration intensifies. Indeed, the CEA has become an interest group with a developed issue identity.

"In order to be effective Euro-lobbyists, groups must be able to co-ordinate their national and EC level strategies, construct alliances with their European counterparts, and monitor changing national and EC policy agendas" (Mazey and Richardson, 1993; p 191). However, regarding their different cultures and understandings about what would be best for a SEM, how may this be accomplished? How are policy-domains and focused issues constructed? How do separate Member State industries overcome self-interest and work toward collective interest? These are issues that will be explored through out the study.

The insurance sector is considered to have a unified and influential interest group because companies are willing to accept interest group representation. Indeed, the Commission promotes interest group representation. However, it does prefer European-wide interest federations over representatives of individual or national organisations (OJ/93C 63/03). Furthermore, ". . . both the European Commission and the European Parliament frequently stress that they want to speak to European organisations" (Club De Bruxelles, 1994; p 96).

This study acknowledges the theoretical differences outlined above and aims to provide a greater understanding of the issues in an attempt to identify the limits of European integration. The above has given a summary of the main aspects of the theoretical literature to provide an understanding of the discussions regarding European integration theory. The main concern is to provide an understanding of the literature, point out how this work fits into the on-going debate and if possible, discover the limits of European integration.

LIFE INSURANCE AND EUROPE UNION LITERATURE

This work concentrates on the life insurance industry which has a number of interest groups at both the national level [Association of British Insurers (ABI) in the UK] and European level [Comité Européen Des Assurance (CEA)] and [Bureau International Producteurs Assurances et Reassurances (BIPAR)]. Through an analysis of the life insurance industry and the above interest groups it attempts an understanding of European integration processes in theoretical and practical terms.

The Treaties of Rome state that the " . . . liberalisation of . . . insurance services connected with the movements of capital shall be effected in step with the progressive liberalisation of capital" (Art 61 (2)). And that the " . . . movement of capital between Member States shall be freed from all restrictions by the end of the first stage at latest" (Art 67 (2)). If this is to be the case then a number of areas need to be taken into consideration regarding Non-Tariff Barriers (NTBs). Through its concentration on the life insurance industry this work indicates the technical barriers in respect of regulations that need harmonisation, if a SEM in life insurance is to be achieved.

In Chapter Four, an insurance regulation matrix is constructed through the information supplied by Financial Times (1992), Munich Re (1988), Sigma (1988-94) BIIC and CEA working papers, Pool (1991) and a survey of the EU insurance industry undertaken by the author. Carter and Greenway (1991), Dickinson (1990, 1994), Carter and Diacon (1991), and Ellis (1990; 1994; 1995) provide a general understanding of the insurance industry in Europe. Vipond (1995) outlined a view of insurance representation at the EU level and indicated how national positions are compromised in the main European interest group, the CEA. Cecchini (1988) undertook an analysis of the benefits to be gained from the single market and the extent to which insurance was an important aspect of this. A political emphasis is illustrated in the Commission White Paper (1985), the Treaties (1988), the Maastricht Treaty (1991) and the Commission Report (1992). Randone (1990) and Canzano (1994) indicated that the way forward was in planning and creating a strategy for Europe and along with Jur *et al* (1989) acknowledged the need for legislation that facilitated cross-border trade.

Pool (1992) illustrated the link between the evolution of the European Union, its growing membership, its institutions and the progression of its legal framework. He described how the Commission and the treaties are part of the decision-making process. However, he did not indicate whether or not the insurance industry had a part to play in this process; the CEA contended that it did and that as an interest group, it was central to the process.

sion and co-operation between supervisors was be the way forward. Loheac (1992) argued that the third generation of insurance directives constituted a "cultural revolution" which affected all European financial sectors and that the operation of insurance would not be left unaffected by legal developments in the EU. Indeed, all Member State industries would be affected in some way by the changes in legislation and, as integration grew, differing legislative norms would become more apparent and the more difficult it would become to meet minimum conditions to overcome this diversity (Loheac 1991). Loheac (1992) identified regional grouping through integration and a convergence of regulation that he hoped would create further trading between Member States.

Corley (1992) considered that the Third Life Assurance Directive would allow a SEM in life insurance, at least as far as supervision was concerned[8]. However, he argued that there were differences in the attitude to risk between Member States, which were not a result of regulation or economic development. Heseltine (1992) looked toward greater harmonisation in the SEM and proposed further consultation with business and welcomed constructive dialogue between the insurance industry and government. Indeed, he stated that this was " . . . an absolutely essential foundation" (p 5) as were the close relations between the insurance industry and the Department of Trade and Industry (DTI). Heseltine (1992) argued that " . . . less legislation is the UK way" (ibid) and contended that he wished to persuade the rest of the EU of this. However, he did take into account the special nature of insurance and the need for a modicum of regulation.

---

[8] The Third Life Assurance Directive is the latest legislation regarding cross-border trade for life insurance in the SEM. It allows home supervision and a licence to trade anywhere in the EU. It it defined further below.

Palliser (1992) considered that the insurance industry had been shaped by legislation and " . . . that in time the harmonisation of regulatory frameworks should introduce open competition in the life insurance market across the Community" (p 4). Additionally, Majone (1990; 1996) Mayer (1995), McGowan and Seabright (1995) and Ogus (1993) provide an overview of regulation in general and how it has evolved especially in respect of the EU.

Ket was discussed by Fitchew (1990), who indicated that change would not be immediate and realised as early as 1990 that the completion of an internal market in insurance would only be in its infancy by 1993. Frangoulis (1988) considered that there would be little change especially over the first four or five years. He thought that the industry would need time to acclimatise to the changes. O'Leary (1988) reinforced this but he argued that eventually the single market would be realised and the UK should ready itself for this. Russell (1988) admitted that harmonisation was likely to happen and that two areas should be prioritised regarding regulation: protection and market opportunities.

This work illustrates how the SEM is evolving and indicates how this may be part of integration processes that are creating further European union. It argues that the Treaties force European integration and through *self-interest* and *mutual assistance* industries and sectors are proactive in the formation of the SEM and this necessitates extensions of the Treaties and further integration. European information can primarily be found in the Official Journals Commission and Parliamentary publications. The interest group negotiations and compromises can be detected and understood through CEA, BIIC and ABI briefing papers.

Included in the process of European integration is the free movement of services and this is where the need to harmonise the insurance industry springs from. The Commission White Paper (1985) and Cecchini (1988) identified the losses that Europe incurs because of the NTBs that Member States create; this gave an economic impetus to European Union whereas the treaties exemplified the political will. Life insurance was an important area of harmonisation in the completion of the SEM. However, agreement in this industry is invariably difficult to attain. This study provides an empirical account of the decision-making processes regarding the Third Life Assurance Directive and the attempt to create a single market in life insurance.

CONCLUSION

It has been necessary to break the literature review down into three parts: Methodology, Post-War European Integration Theory and Life Insurance and European Union. This has been done to illustrate the extent of the literature used in the work and how each part relates to the others. Functionalism, neo-functionalism and interest groups are related because the theories rely heavily on interest group usage; this is especially so of neo-functionalism. Each part of the theoretical literature concludes that there is a necessity for empirical studies and considers that European integration theory should be reassessed through these empirical studies. This may allow us to discover the limits of European integration.

This work revisits and reassesses European integration from both theoretical and empirical perspectives. The methodology attempts to understand European integration from a grounded theory perspective. Grounded theory considers that theories are not proved or disproved but added to or detracted from. Theory is on-going and an interaction between inductive and deductive processes. Through grounded theory methodology, some of the criticisms levelled at neo-functionalism may be overcome, especially with respect to the absence of a dependent variable. On an empirical level an analysis of the decision-making processes regarding the European life industry attempts to generate further understanding of European integration processes. The literature indicates the debates and channels of influence that were at work in the creation of the single market in life insurance and signaled the direction that the empirical study should take in the creation of a substantive theory. Basically, the three areas provide the means by which a better understanding of the European integration process may be achieved and indicate levels of understanding that have been managed to date. The next chapter introduces the methodology of grounded theory and illustrates the data collection processes and interpretations that are the bases of the substantive theory.

Chapter Two

APPLYING GROUNDED THEORY

Induction introduces us to first principles and universals, while deduction starts from universals. Therefore there are principles from which deduction starts which are not deducible; therefore they are reached by induction (Aristotle, 1983; p 207).

INTRODUCTION

The main aim of this chapter is to illustrate how this study has applied grounded theory to European integration. To do this, the research, initially undertook a comparative analysis and open coded Member State life insurance legislation. Through induction, deduction and verification the analysis has formulated tables, matrices and model to illustrate European decision-making processes. Grounded theory aims to construct substantive theory through coding data. Substantive theory necessitates four central criteria. *Fit, comprehension, generality and control*: the theory should be induced from diverse data and be faithful to reality (it should *fit*). Secondly, the *fit* should be *comprehensible*; thirdly, the data should be comprehensive and interpretations conceptually wide (there should be *generality*); and fourthly, in relation to generality, it should be made clear when conditions apply to specific situations and phenomena (there should be *control*) (Corbin and Strauss, 1990). Indeed, hypothesis-proposing relationships among concepts should be ground from the data. This chapter explains how the study constructs a substantive theory and illustrates the extent to which it (the substantive theory) relates to pre-existing formal theories.

Substantive theory emerges from the analysis of a " . . . particular situational context", whereas formal theory " . . . emerges from a study of phenomenon under many different types of situations" (Corbin and Strauss, 1990; p 174). However, it is argued that theories are never complete but always in the process of construction.

THE PHILOSOPHICAL ROOTS OF GROUNDED THEORY

The Discovery of Grounded Theory (1967) " . . . provided a strong intellectual rationale for using qualitative research to develop theoretical analysis" (Charmaz, 1983; p 109). The approach provides the qualitative research area with a defined structure to enhance its credibility. Effectively, it was a demonstration against the predominance of quantitative research. Glaser and Strauss (1967) draw on Dewey (1950) Mead (1962) Blumer (1969) and the pragmatist tradition. Dewey (1950) provided the basis of this when he argued that " . . . flowers can be enjoyed without knowing about the interactions of soil, air, moisture and seeds of which they are the result. But they cannot be understood without taking just these interactions into account and theory is a matter of understanding" (p 12). Theory cannot answer questions " . . . unless we are willing to find the germs and roots in matters of experience" (ibid). In the acquisition of knowledge, an essential element " . . . is the perception of relations, especially the relations between our actions and their empirical consequences." (Scheffler, 1974; p 197). In such a way the world around us and we as individuals take on deeper meaning; in this context, humans need experience and the means of storing that experience. However, experience is more than " . . . a passive registering or beholding of phenomena; it involves deliberate interaction with environmental conditions, the consequences of which are critically noted and fed back into the control of future conduct" (ibid). Pragmatists considered that from " . . . the child's exploration of its environment to the scientist's theorising about nature the pattern of intelligent thought is the same: a problem provides the initial occasion of inquiry. Action is blocked, conflicts or difficulties create an unsettled situation. Deliberation is blocked; action turned inward; the resultant elaboration and competition of hypothetical ideas sparks action once more.

Such action tests the idea that initiated it, for if the action settles the initial difficulty, the idea has worked in reorganising conduct in a more effective pattern. . . . Experiment for Dewey is, experience rendered educative" (ibid, p 196).

Grounded theory can be understood in terms of *symbolic interaction* (Mead, 1962) where the " . . . individual enters as such into his own experience only as an object not as a subject; and he can enter as an object only on the basis of social relations and interactions" (p 225). Through the language and structure of roles we become a generalised other; we attain a consciousness of self as a generalised other. This may allow the individual to take an impartial and general standpoint in observing and evaluating one's own conduct when one becomes a generalised other or the object of one's own reflection. At this point one has become self. "One now regularly takes an impartial and general standpoint in observing and evaluating one's own conduct (however). . . . The organised community or social group which gives to the individual his unity of self may be called the generalised other and is the attitude of the whole community" (Blau, 1952; pp 162-163 author's brackets).

Blumer (1962; 1969) built on the work of the pragmatist tradition and considered that, " . . . ordinarily human beings respond to one another, as in carrying on a conversation, by interpreting one anothers' actions or remarks and then reacting on the basis of interpretation" (Blumer, 1969; p 71). Grounded theory builds on this understanding and considers that research should be grounded out of reality and that the researcher should get out into the field and discover/comprehend what is going on. People have an active role in shaping the world and through interrelationships in terms of meaning, action and conditions the nature of experience continually evolves (this creates changes in understanding phenomenon) (Corbin and Strauss, 1990). Indeed, grounded theory is primarily inductive and pursues the interpretations of those involved in the situation that is being researched and the interpretations of the researcher in relation to the data. Through this process grounded theory is enacted and substantive theory constructed.

Grounded Theory as Methodology

Grounded theory generates substantive theory through comparative analysis and coding. It does not attempt to undermine theory but improve it " . . . a theory's only replacement is a better theory" (Glaser and Strauss, 1967; p 28). "Grounded theory is based on the systematic generation of theory from data, and itself is systematically obtained from social research. Thus, the grounded theory method offers a rigorous orderly guide to theory development that at each stage is closely integrated with a methodology of social research" (Glaser, 1978; p 2). Through the general method of comparative analysis, grounded theory wishes to create a theory made up of general categories. It is not necessary to know the concrete situation better than those involved in it. The analyst simply wishes to develop theory that applies to relevant behaviour. Theory is never a finished product, but always in the process of development. Generating a theory from data means that most of the ideas or hypotheses are not only derived from the data but are worked out in relation to the data as the research progresses.

While logico-deductive theory seeks to verify deduced hypotheses, grounded theory suggests that there should be a change of emphasis in respect of research methods and aims to emphasise the prior step of discovering what concepts and hypotheses are relevant to the area under research. Ultimately, the relationship between categories and sub-categories which are discovered during the research should be as a result of information contained within the data only, or from deductive reasoning which has been verified within the data, but not from previous assumptions which have not been supported (Cottingham and Hussey, 1996).

Research should be approached with an open mind and as much objectivity and distance as possible. However, it is acknowledged that such objectivity is difficult, as everyone is instilled with subjective tendencies; yet recognising subjectivity is part way to overcoming it. This may be considered to encompass theoretical sensitivity which is initially gained by entering the research " . . . with as few predetermined ideas as possible especially logically deduced, a priori hypotheses" (Glaser, 1978; p 3). Such enables the researcher to remain sensitive and " . . . record events and detect happenings without first having them filtered through and squared with pre-existing hypotheses and biases" (ibid). Each of us has predetermined ideas as each of us has different levels of sensitivity which depend on " . . . previous reading and experience with or relevant to the area. . . . Theoretical sensitivity refers to the attribute of having insight, the ability to give meaning to data, the capacity to understand, and the capability to separate the pertinent from that which isn't. . . . It is theoretical sensitivity that allows one to develop a theory that is grounded conceptually dense" (Strauss and Corbin, 1990; pp 41-40).

In a later publication, Glaser expanded on his earlier definition. "Theoretical sensitivity refers to the researcher's knowledge, understanding, and skill which foster his generation of categories and properties and increase his ability to relate them into hypotheses, and to further integrate the hypotheses, according to emergent theoretical codes. Accomplishing this result in relevance, fit and work are the criteria of grounded theory" (Glaser, 1992; p 27).

Grounded theory suggests that there is an over-emphasis on verification theory and wishes to demote the idea that the discovery of relevant concepts and hypotheses are *a priori* to research. For further see (Glaser and Strauss, 1967; Glaser, 1978; Charmaz, 1983; Strauss, 1987; Strauss and Corbin, 1990; Corbin and Strauss, 1990; Glaser, 1992; Strauss and Corbin, 1994). Grounded theory posits that theory is derived from data and consequentially illustrated through characteristic examples of data. Theory cannot be divorced from the process by which it is developed. Subsequently, most hypotheses and concepts are generated through the data and worked out in relation to the data during the course of the research (Glaser and Strauss, 1967).

Initially, grounded theory is inductively derived from the study of the phenomena it represents. Data collection, analysis and theory are reciprocal with each other; one does not start with a theory, which is then tested but an area of study from which what is relevant to the area becomes apparent. Induction needs to be grounded in social phenomena or observations and experience; hence the link between induction and grounded theory (ibid).

Charmaz (1983) reiterated Glaser and Strauss (1967) when she proposed that data collection and analysis are undertaken simultaneously and that interpretations are formed through data discovery and vice-versa. The approach allows for emerging ideas because it provides for further data collection. It accepts that one of the main strengths of the grounded theory approach is one where data and ideas are derived through the research rather than through *a priorism.* Verification is secondary to understanding processes, not simply the processes of the phenomenon, but the understanding that social life itself is a process. "As such, theoretical analyses may be transcended by further work either by the original or later theorists. In keeping with their foundations in pragmatism, then, grounded theorists aim to develop fresh theoretical interpretations of the data rather than explicitly aim for any final or complete interpretation of it. . . Although every researcher brings to his or her research general preconceptions founded in expertise, theory, method, and experience, using the grounded theory method necessitates that the researcher look at the data from as many vantage points as possible" (Charmaz, 1983; pp 111-114). Data should be analysed as it emerges and through coding, "order created" (ibid).

This study acknowledges that it is easy to find a problem with a theoretical concept by identifying that certain data is missing. This could be the charge against most analyses. However, as Glaser and Strauss (1967) put it: "If each debunker thought about the potential value of comparative analysis . . . he would realise that he has merely posed another comparative datum for generating another theoretical property or category" (p 22). Despite what those concerned with evidence may say, nothing has been disproved, only another comparison created (ibid).

An Application of Grounded Theory

In general terms " . . . analysis makes use of constant comparisons. As incidents are noted, they should be continually compared against other incidents for dissimilarities and likenesses" (Corbin and Strauss, 1990; p 9). In this study the author initially undertook a comparison of EU Member State life insurance legislation and the extent to which this legislation allowed trading freedom in the national life insurance market identified (Oyen, 1990). A study of the European life insurance industry was undertaken and a convergence of Member State legislation asserted. The initial research relies on a comparative study of legislation and links this to national differences. This is a standard means of generating theory and is usually accomplished early in the study to put the "story straight" (Glaser and Strauss, 1967; Strauss and Corbin, 1990; pp 116-142). "Making comparisons assists the researcher in guarding against bias . . . comparisons also help to achieve greater precision (the grouping of like and only like phenomenon)" (Corbin and Strauss, 1990; p 9). Fundamentally, one is seeking regularities and this also creates order and helps with data integration.

THEORETICAL CODING

Theoretical coding is the basis of grounded theory. The essential relationship between data and theory is a conceptual code. The code conceptualises the underlying patterns of the data. "Thus, in generating a theory by developing the hypothetical relationships between conceptual codes (categories and their properties) which have been generated from the data as indicators, we discover a grounded theory" (Glaser, 1978; p 55).

Coding illustrates " . . . the fundamental analytical process used by the researcher" (Corbin and Strauss, 1990; p 9). Charmaz (1983) considers that coding incorporates " . . . the initial phase of the analytical method (and) is simply the process of categorising and sorting data. Codes then serve as shorthand devices to label, separate, compile and organise data. Codes range from simple concrete, and topical categories to more general, abstract conceptual categories for an emerging theory" (Charmaz, 1983; p 111). However, " . . . in grounded theory research there are three basic types of coding; open, axial and selective" (Corbin and Strauss, 1990; p 9).

Open coding examines phenomena through comparing and categorising data, whereas axial coding is the re-structuring of the whole process by finding connections between the data. Selective coding illustrates how the phenomenon fits around a core category (in this context, European integration). Such leads on to 'process' whereby changes in the data are monitored and made explicit. As noted above, grounded theory is both inductive and deductive, the deductive nature coming into play primarily in the pursuit of process. "As you have probably noticed while coding we are constantly moving between inductive and deductive thinking" (Strauss and Corbin, 1990; p 111). When process is difficult to identify, the researcher may turn to deductive analysis so as to identify, possible situations of change, " . . . then go back to the data or field situation and look for evidence to support refute or modify that hypothesis" (Strauss and Corbin, 1990; p 148).

OPEN CODING

"The goal of the analyst is to generate an emergent set of categories and their properties which fit, work and are relevant for integrating theory. To achieve this goal the analyst begins with open coding" (Glaser, 1978; p 56). Attention should be fixed on a category and the properties that emerge continually coded and analysed, these are the initial basic steps. Ultimately, one constantly compares and continually categorises.

In practical terms, the open coding process was used to create a scale of one to twelve on which a totally liberal regulatory environment is valued at one and a completely state-controlled or nationalised regulatory environment is valued at twelve. A prescribed regulatory environment is not one of primarily self-regulation, nor is it state-controlled: it is a market with tight government regulations (see the Regulatory/Legislative Environment Table 4.1 and the Data Collection Scheme, Table 2.1).

The higher the number on the table, the greater the regulation and state control indicated in the Member State's legislative system. Through further comparative analysis and open coding each Member State was understood to be at some point on a matrix scale (see Life Insurance Regulation Matrix One, Fig 4.1).

Once this had been accomplished, it was felt that some further investigation was necessary and a survey of the European life insurance sector was undertaken (see Data Collection Scheme, Table 2.1, and survey A). The matrix was subsequently revised taking into consideration the survey results, which also raised further questions (Life Insurance Regulation Matrix Two, Fig 4.2). Ultimately, a secondary analysis was made of the data and further coding generated. In summary, through the coding and categorisation of each national market's legislation, a regulation table and matrix were created which could be further analysed and verified through a survey. The survey then added data to the regulation matrix and a greater understanding of the European life insurance industry regulatory structure was generated.

AXIAL CODING

Axial coding involves bringing the analysis together and provides unity. It indicates the overall system, which the categories created through open coding are part. In this work, axial coding is illustrated through the:

(a) Causal conditions.
(b) Phenomenon.
(c) Context.
(d) Intervening conditions.
(e) Action/Interaction.
(f) Consequences.
(Corbin and Strauss, 1990; pp 96-97).

An application of axial coding in this work is identified through:

(a) Membership of the EU.
(b) The creation of the SEM and legislation to create regulatory environments.
(c) The European decision-making process.
(d) The harmonisation of different Member State concepts of market conditions (life insurance industries).
(e) Interaction between Member States and decision-making bodies.
  (i) Goal orientation (purposeful) regulation as similar to one's own as possible. Interaction between Member States at the European interest group level.
  (ii) Evolutionary changes (processional) compromised issues. Interaction between interest groups and the EU decision-making institutions.
(f) Outcomes or the creation of a harmonised SEM in the life insurance sector; a move towards further European integration.

In more specific terms, the *causal conditions* and *phenomenon* are membership of the EU and the on going evolution of the SEM. The *context* is the possible shift in sovereignty in terms of the decision-making process and market control. The *intervening conditions* are the necessities of harmonisation and the implications this has for integration; such is illustrated through the compromises made by Member States in respect of regulatory environments. It portrays the need for *action/interaction* between Member States and the European decision-making institutions in terms of the evolutionary changes taking place i.e. the need to harmonise and create a SEM and the goal oriented interaction of creating legislation as close to one's own as possible. Finally, the *consequences* are the creation of the SEM through harmonisation and further European integration.

Glaser (1992) considered that axial coding " . . . undermines and confuses the very method that he (Strauss) is trying to build" (p 61). This process forces the data and negates theoretical coding. The grounded theorist should code categories and properties and allow theoretical codes to emerge where they will. Strauss and Corbin consider that axial coding allows a more focused means of discovering and relating categories. "That is, we develop each category (phenomenon) in terms of causal conditions that give rise to it, the specific dimensional location of this phenomenon in terms of its properties, the context, the action/interaction strategies used to handle, manage, respond to this phenomenon in light of that context, and the consequences of any action/interaction that is taken. Furthermore, in axial coding we continue to look for additional properties of each category, and to note the dimensional location of each incident, happening or event" (Strauss and Corbin, 1990; pp 114-115).

The study used Corbin and Strauss' axial coding as a framework and it allowed the emergence of sub-categories (compromise, negotiation, interaction, difference and understanding) which provided insight into the core category of European integration and the process of interaction between self and common interest.

SELECTIVE CODING

"Selective coding is the process by which all categories are unified around a core category" (Corbin and Strauss, 1990; p 15). The core category in this study is European integration. Regulatory environments, the creation of the SEM and specifically a SEM in life insurance are " . . . other categories and stand in relationship to the core category as conditions, action/interactional strategies, or consequences" (ibid). The selection of data and the creation of other categories have been processed with the core category in mind. "The core category represents the central phenomenon of the study, it is identified by asking questions such as; what is the main analytical idea presented in this research? What does all the action/interaction seem to be about?" (ibid). The answers to which are: the integration processes at work in the EU, how Member States' action/interaction create the SEM and how this adds impetus to European integration. These areas are identified and unified through axial coding (compromise, negotiation, interaction, difference and understanding).

PROCESS: SELF-INTEREST & SOCIAL MUTUALITY

Process is also built into the theory. "Process analysis can mean breaking a phenomenon down into stages, phases, or steps. Process may also denote purposeful action/interaction that is not necessarily progressive, but changes in response to prevailing conditions" (Corbin and Strauss, 1990; p 10). Consequently, when the life insurance industry and EU decision-making institutions are analysed, processes and action/interaction are identified through interest groups. The changes and compromises made by interest groups and sectors are interpreted in relation to the changes the SEM has brought and is bringing about. Indeed, the rationale in relation to interest group membership is investigated and analysed through a survey of UK interest group membership (see survey C).

The analysis identified process in the Member State regulatory structures because of their membership of the EU, membership of interest groups and the creation of a piece of legislation that would harmonise the different regulation environments. This would create the need for compromise; and the research sought to identify why and how compromise and change would take place. Consequently, a model was constructed through semi-formal interviews, participatory observation and survey C (see Data Collection Scheme, Table 2.1). Each survey assisted in theory generation; the results of survey A (see Data Collection Scheme, Table 2.1) describe the processes at work which lead to theory generation and are used as secondary analysis with regard to the comparative analysis of Member State insurance industries. "Comparative analysis requires secondary analysis when populations from several different studies are compared, such as different nations or factories" (Glaser and Strauss, 1967; p 188). Surveys B and C are used in the same way with regard to the decision-making model (see Data Collection Scheme, Table 2.1).

From an assumption of the maximisation of *self-interest*, the convergence of legislation is examined. However, the research does recognise the difficulties with indicating *self-interest* alone as a motivator and considers that an ethical/welfare standpoint is a factor, that common interest is also part of the process (Sen 1992).

Through a compromise being reached at the European level, *self-interest* is sacrificed for the common interest even though this is initially in a limited area[1]. However, ultimately welfare is realised throughout Europe in terms of peaceful co-existence and economic expansion. As Scheingold indicated " . . . integration was good by definition since it was directed at economic reconstruction and permanent reconciliation between nations whose conflicts had led to bloody wars. . . . A 'United States of Europe' seemed almost by definition likely to serve the cause of a peaceful and prosperous future" (Scheingold, 1971; p 30). Furthermore, self-interest is both enhanced and detracted from through interest group membership. When companies joins an interest group they do so to ensure their interests. However, these interests need to be compromised if they are to remain a member of the interest group (see Olson, 1971; Grant and Marsh, 1977; Marsh, 1978; Moe 1980; Coleman and Grant, 1988). Each of these interactions indicate process.

The Data Collection Scheme

Data collection incorporates interviews, participatory observation and surveys. Sampling was based on the grounded theory technique of *theoretical sampling. Theoretical sampling* is undertaken on the basis that " . . . concepts have *proven theoretical relevance* to the evolving theory" (Strauss and Corbin, 1990; p 176). *Proven theoretical relevance* identifies concepts that are significant enough to be considered *categories* " . . . they are deemed significant because (1) they are repeatedly present or notably absent when comparing incident after incident (2) through coding procedures they earn the

[1] Welfare in this work is based on the concept of the social contract, as in, the need for people to work and exist together so they are able to pursue their self interest. It is based on Kant's civic constitution, Durkheim's organic society and Rawl's veil of ignorance. It is giving up one's individual freedom in certain areas for the welfare or general good of all.

status of categories. . . . The aim of theoretical sampling is to sample events, incidents, and so forth, that are indicative of categories, their properties and dimensions, so that you can develop and conceptually relate them" (ibid, p 177).

Table. 2.1.
Data Collection Scheme

Survey A: Survey of European Union life insurance companies. Allows an understanding of market environment perceptions from separate Member States. *Open sampling* and *relational and variational sampling*

Survey B: Survey of European Parliament, Permanent Representatives, Member State insurance interest groups, Lobbyists and the Commission. This provides a picture of the parts played by organisations in the decision-making process. *Relational and variational sampling*

Survey C: Survey of UK insurance companies to ascertain interest group utilisation. *Discriminate coding*

Interviews: The interviews are supplemented by survey C and provide an in-depth understanding of the EU decision-making process with regard to the Third Life Assurance Directive. *Relational and variational sampling* and *discriminate coding*

Observations and preliminary discussions: This incorporated three months in Brussels working with a European political consultant (GJW), a period with the European section of a UK company (Commercial Union) open discussions and close contact with the Association of British Insurers (ABI). *Open sampling*

Theoretical sampling involves three processes: *open sampling* which relates to *open coding*; *relational and variational sampling* which is associated with *axial coding*; and *discriminate coding* which is linked to *selective coding.*

Following an inductive analysis of the different Member States' life insurance legislation and a survey (survey A, see Table 2.1) of the European life insurance industry, a regulatory environment matrix was created. This part of the analysis illustrates *open sampling* where the aim is " . . . to uncover as many potentially relevant categories as possible along with their properties and dimensions" (ibid, p 181) and the beginnings of *relational and variational sampling*. Indeed, the survey validates the relationships between the categories and identifies processes. From this some propositions were formed and the sampling gradually became specifically *relational and variational.*

The sampling was undertaken purposefully. This encompassed choosing individuals and documentation that demonstrated variations in the categories and what happened when change occurred. Fundamentally, as with the coding process the distinction between relational and variational sampling and discriminate sampling became unclear. *Discriminate sampling* is direct and deliberate and is indicated in the choice of interviewees and survey C. "In discriminate sampling, a researcher chooses the sites, persons and documents that will maximise opportunities for verifying the story line, relationships between categories" (ibid, p 187). Sampling in grounded theory studies is concerned with the " . . . representativeness of concepts in their varying forms. In each instance of data collection, we look for evidence of its significant presence or absence, and ask why?" (ibid, p 190). Grounded theory studies look " . . . for incidents and events that are indicative of phenomena" (ibid). Indeed, they pursue density and " . . . the more interviews, observations and documents obtained, then the more evidence will accumulate, the more variations will be found, and the greater the density will be achieved. Thus there will be wider applicability of the theory, because more and different sets of conditions affecting phenomena are uncovered" (ibid pp 190-91). This process subsequently set up a number of questions, which were investigated through semi-formal interviews with key individuals involved in the creation of the Third Life Assurance Directive, and through participatory observations of the European decision-making process. These gave an understanding of the political process and enabled further construction of a theoretical model. Table 2.1 summarises the data collection process in terms of three surveys, the interviews and participatory observations. In survey A, three hundred questionnaires were sent to insurance companies in eight of twelve Member States, (the UK, Germany, France, Italy, Belgium, Netherlands, Spain and Eire). Four Member States were omitted mainly because of problems with translation and difficulties in terms of acquiring addresses. The response rate was 35-40%, which are listed and analysed below in Chapter Four. The survey wished to illustrate the perceptions of the Member States life insurance industries regarding national life insurance regulation and the creation of a single market. It also aimed to determine the extent of freedom allowed by the amount of regulation within a particular Member State and to illustrate what the respondents considered to be the optimum regulation for trading and the amount of legislation necessary to enable this.

A survey of the European life insurance industry was used instead of interviews, because a broad sample was required. The results, which incorporated the industry's understanding of the SEM and the EU were added to the initial regulatory environment matrix. Indeed, the survey provided an understanding of the differences in Member State normative thinking in respect of life insurance regulation and raised the question of where and how compromise takes place in the creation of the SEM. The questionnaire follows *self-interest rationality* in terms of competitive advantage in the evolving EU: however, at the same time it attempts to recognise other motivational aspects in the process.

One may consider that an environment free of regulation is impossible and in a post cold war world, total state control untenable. This may be indicated by competition policy at the SEM level. It may be argued that no trading structure can exist without some form of regulation, which invariably indicates legislation. The survey wished to ascertain the extent legislation had an effect on Member State regulatory environments and what type of regulatory environment would be most amenable to all Member States at the EU level.

In a second survey (survey B, see Table 2.1), questionnaires were sent to interest groups, lobbyists and Permanent Representatives (Finance Committees). This survey was of a qualitative nature and gave information on which the interviews were based. Finally, a third survey (survey C see Table 2.1) of the UK insurance sector attempted to ascertain how companies approached the European and national legislatures. Respondents were asked to indicate the extent to which they agreed or disagreed with a series of statements using a Likert scale. This survey was used to identify the extent to which interest groups were used in the process of legislation creation and looked to verify or question the idea that European interest groups are used in the process of EU decision-making.

THE ROLE OF SURVEYS IN GROUNDED THEORY

Within the grounded theory methodology, surveys and quantitative data play an ambiguous role. "The sociologist whose purpose is to generate theory may of course collect his own survey data, but, for several reasons, he is more likely to analyse previously collected data-called secondary analysis" (Glaser and Strauss, 1987; p 187). However, the researcher should give him/herself the " . . . freedom in the flexible use of quantitative data or he or she will not be able to generate theory that is adequate . . . (and) in taking this freedom he must be clear about the rules he is relaxing (ibid, p 186). Such flexibility will allow the richness of qualitative data to become apparent " . . . and lead to new styles and strategies of quantitative analysis, with their own rules yet to be discovered. . . . For example, in verification studies cross-tabulations of quantitative variables continually and inadvertently lead to discoveries of new social patterns and new hypotheses that are often ignored as not being the purpose of the research" (ibid).

Basically, grounded theory wishes to relax the rules of verification and accuracy of evidence to enable further theory generation " . . . the way they are relaxed for purposes of generating theory could apply to many styles of analysis" (ibid, p 187). "One might use qualitative data to illustrate or clarify quantitatively derived findings; or, one could quantify demographic findings. Or, one could use some form of quantitative data to partially validate one's qualitative analysis" (Strauss and Corbin, 1990; pp 18-19). Such may be realised through triangulation. Indeed, as grounded theory itself is a theory it may never be completed (this would contradict grounded theory). Consequently, although surveys are not purely grounded theory techniques, used in certain ways they may benefit theory generation. In this context, they may be utilised in a grounded theory study and eventually they may be considered as part of the technique. This, one may speculate, is the direction in which Glaser and Strauss pointed in 1967. In 1992 Glaser makes this clear. "To repeat, qualitative analysis may be done with data arrived at quantitatively or qualitatively or in some combination" (Glaser, 1992; p 11). And how they may be used " . . . together effectively . . . depends on the research" (ibid, p 12).

THE INTERVIEWS

Interviews were used to investigate decision-making processes at the European level. Over an eight-week period working for a political lobbying company (GJW Political Consultants) in Brussels, the author was able to gain access to decision-makers. Interviews were undertaken with the Commission; insurance interest groups; the UK Permanent Representative (Finance Committee), and lobbyists. Further interviews were undertaken in Paris and the UK (see p 128 for a list of Interviewees). The interviews were 'moderately structured' (Carlson, 1984) and were based on a number of informal discussions with individuals from the UK insurance industry. In carrying out the interviews, the interviewer gave a brief outline of what was thought to be the process. Direct questions were then asked which allowed for further questions, further elaboration was pursued until little more could be ascertained. The direct questions asked were in the forms outlined below.

Each interview attempted to look at the same phenomenon from a different perspective and enable data saturation and triangulation. The interviews were conducted between surveys B and C and indicated the need for survey C. Open coding, the surveys and consequent matrix indicates the need for legislative convergence. Additionally, the interviews and survey C allow the construction of a model of EU decision making processes. Indeed, they illustrate, verification and the outcome of selective and axial coding. Subsequently, through the use of both the matrix and the model, a substantive theory is constructed that illustrates convergence and harmonisation procedures in the EU. As note above, through the interviews a number of sub-categories emerged.

SUBSTANTIVE THEORY

The substantive theory is built through coding, categorisation and process. The matrices provide the basis of the substantive theory in that they acknowledge that separate Member States pursue different market regimes. This sets up the problem of understanding how compromise is reached. The interviews, participatory observations and survey C further construct the substantive theory with regard to the EU decision-making process. This substantive theory has implications for the formal theories in terms of spillover, supranationality, sub-national utilisation and sovereignty.

"A substantive theory generated from the data must be formulated, in order to see which of diverse formal theories are, perhaps, applicable for furthering additional substantive formulations" (Glaser and Strauss, 1967; p 34). This illustrates that theories are never complete but processes in themselves. In this context, one may question the extent to which neo-functionalism, intergovernmentalism etc may be labelled formal theories. Indeed, one could argue that they are substantive theories of functionalism and realism in that they have not really emerged from studies under different types of situations i.e. integration processes external to western Europe.

FORMAL THEORY

"A formal theory is composed of a model plus an indefinite number of interpretations, and there is a sharp distinction between model and interpretation. A model is not affected by any of its interpretations, but can be understood and studied in abstraction from all of them. . . . A substantive theory . . . is . . . about something in the real world" (Diesing, 1972; p 31).

Consequently, substantive theory needs to be verified and if changes to the theory are to be made there must be references to empiricism. The formal theory " . . .can be understood and studied in abstraction . . . one can . . . make deductions, search for inconsistencies, study the effects of changes in those postulated, and add new terms without referring to anything empirical" (ibid).

In the context of this work, the formal theory is broadly integration theories based on Kantian and Hegelian thought and specifically theories relating to European integration. The substantive theory is generated through an analysis of the EU life insurance industry and decision-making processes and the quantitative and qualitative data. Indeed the substantive theory aims to understand or dispute the formal theories (specifically neo-functionalism and intergovernmentalism) and eventually discover the limits of European integration. Theory is open-ended because as new categories or properties are generated, there is a place for them in the scheme. However, this does not incorporate total re-design. This research wished to investigate, verify, question and ideally, further understand European integration through an analysis of European decision-making processes in relation to European integration theories.

Conclusions

This work illustrates grounded theory processes in the following ways. Firstly, a comparative analysis through the open coding of individual Member States' life insurance legislation and regulatory regimes; with the subsequent creation of a legislation/regulation table and a regulation matrix; further coding through a survey of Member State insurance industries verified and refined the matrix. This investigation raised questions with regard to how legislative differences between Member States may be resolved. Secondly, through an interview programme, process is identified and illustrated through a European Decision-Making Model. The model and the matrix provide the building blocks of the substantive theory.

Thirdly, axial and selective coding processes are illustrated by the matrix and the model fitting together around the core category of European integration through the creation of the SEM. Axial coding draws all parts of the analysis together: it is the pivot or the axis of theory building. Fourthly, substantive theory is formulated through the grounded theory in relation to the formal theories of intergovernmentalism and neo-functionalism. These are illustrated as substantive theories in relation to realism, functionalism and integration theory which in themselves could be understood as substantive theories of Kant's 'Civic Constitution' in *Idea for a Universal History with a Cosmopolitan Purpose* and Perpetual *Peace: A Philosophical Sketch* (Kant, 1995) and Hegel's concept of recognition.

In empirical terms this work investigates the process of European integration through supranationality, spillover and interest groups by analysing the shifts in decision-making in terms of the European life insurance industry and the creation of the Third Life Assurance Directive. Furthermore, in this analysis: (a) Neo-functionalism and Intergovernmentalism = formal integration theories; (b) The author's theory building through the work = substantive theory. Finally the work generalises the situation regarding the life insurance industry (the substantive theory) and posits elements of both intergovernmental and neo-functional spillover in the process of European integration.

With regard to the UK insurance industry certain legislation has to be effected to ensure its ability to compete in the SEM. Consequently, the need for advantageous legislation is fundamental. In this context the survey attempted to identify the industry's subjective interests on a European level and investigate how they were agreed upon. One would consider that subjective interests would be voiced by organisations that speak for their membership e.g. interest groups or large companies.

Through grounded theory techniques a substantive theory is built to enable, an understanding of integration theory and allow a greater comprehension of the SEM, European Union and European integration. Open coding and comparative analysis initiated a survey and provides a deduction (to create an SEM Member States need to compromise their normative regulatory environments). Axial and selective coding of the phenomenon suggests further induction through interviews and participatory observation. Finally, the induction procedures illustrate the need for a further survey, which allows for data saturation and an in depth understanding of the phenomenon. Throughout the analysis induction and deduction go hand-in-hand. One is continually analysing the data in the process of building theory. One is continually challenging theory through collecting and analysing data. Ultimately, " . . . methodology is the theory of methods" and the " . . . grounded theory methodology is in itself a theory which is generated alongside the substantive theory it is generating" (Glaser, 1992; p 7).

This work recognises the difficulty in giving precise definitions of induction and deduction and the point where the former begins and the latter ends (and *vice-versa*) and acknowledges the grey area between the two. Such is considered by Alfred Marshall argued that " . . . (y)ou make all your contrasts rather too sharply for me. You talk of the inductive & deductive methods: whereas I contend that each involves the other & that historians are always deducing, & that even the most deductive writers are always implicitly at least basing themselves on observed facts" (Marshall, cited in Coase, 1995; p 169). Ultimately, Marshall wished to emphasise the mutual dependency of induction and deduction. Strauss and Glaser aimed to do the same but each with different weightings. This study accepts the interdependency of induction and deduction because an interaction between the two is at work in this research.

As with the problems of delineation between induction and deduction the same may be said in respect of emergence and forcing[2]. Ultimately, one may

---

[2] There is a dispute between Glaser and Strauss that revolves around the issue of the emergence and forcing of data. Glaser considers that Strauss' and Corbin's " . . . pet theoretical code violates relevance and forces data" (Glaser, 1992; p 28). He contends that such a structured outlook undermines the emergent, empirical and endless ways of relating substantive codes. "The researcher must be aware of the vast array of theoretical codes to increase his sensitivity to their emergence in the data" (ibid). However, in their work Strauss and Corbin address their book to those " . . . who are about to embark on their first qualitative analysis research project and who want to build theory at the substantive level" (Strauss and Corbin, 1990; p 8). In other words, it is a simplification, which may lead the researcher into the more difficult nuances of grounded theory.

Verification also seems to be a sticking point between the scholars. However, on closer examination neither is pursuing pure verification; each wishes for it to add to theory generation not to negate or disprove " . but add variation and depth of understanding" (ibid p 109). Glaser argued that the " . . . two types of methodologies should be seen in sequential relation. First we discover the relevances and write hypotheses about them, then the most relevant may be tested for whatever use may require it" (Glaser, 1992; p 30). Whereas, Corbin and Strauss saw it as an aspect of the grounded theory method; they considered that statements should be verified against data, not to " . . . necessarily negate our questions or statements, or disprove them, rather . . . add variation and depth of understanding" (Corbin and Strauss pp 108-109). It is just as important to " . . . find differences and variation as it is to find evidence that supports our original questions and statements. The negative or alternative cases tell us that something about them is different so we must move in and take a closer look" (ibid p 109). However, each considers that it is possible to utilise verification as part of theory generation, the latter as part of grounded theory and the former as a methodology in its own right (see Strauss and Corbin, 1990; pp 107-109, Strauss, 1987; pp 11-15 and Glaser, 1992; pp 27-30).

Strauss (1987) makes his position clear where he contends that induction, deduction and verification are the very basis of grounded theory. "Because of our earlier writing in *Discovery* (1967) where we attacked speculative theory - quite ungrounded in bodies of data - many people mistakenly refer to grounded theory as 'inductive theory' (however), as we have indicated all three aspects of inquiry . . . are absolutely essential" (Strauss, 1987; p 12 author's brackets). "Grounded theory is of course inductive; a theory is induced or emerged after data collection starts. *Deductive work in grounded theory is used to derive from induced codes conceptual* consider, that grounded theory should be interpreted as it was by Glaser. "By its very nature grounded theory produces ever opening and evolving theory on

---

guides as to where to go next for which comparative group or sub-group, in order to sample for more data to generate the theory" (Glaser, 1978; pp 37-38).

Glaser and Strauss' disagreements are based around their emphasis on deductive and inductive processes; Strauss considers that induction, deduction and verification are essential elements of grounded theory. Induction is primarily based on experience with the same kind of phenomena at some point in the past. It may be apparent because of personal experiences, exploratory research into phenomenon, previous research or because of theoretical sensitivity (knowledge of technical literature). "As for deduction: Success at it rests not merely on the ability to think logically but with the experience in thinking about the particular kind of data under scrutiny" (Strauss, 1987; p 12). This means drawing on experience as well as thinking about the phenomenon and may include comparative analysis to further the deductive powers (ibid). He also indicates that experience and learned skills are very important for verification. "If . . . experience and associated learned skills at verification, deduction and induction are central to successful enquiry, do not talent-gifts-genius contribute to that success?" (ibid, p 13).

The extent of the difficulties emerge in the two latest works. Strauss and Corbin propose that in grounded theory there is a continual movement between inductive and deductive thinking and that their statements are deductively proposed and verified (Strauss and Corbin, 1990). There is a continual comparison of incidents " . . . there is a constant interplay between proposing and checking. This back and forth movement is what makes our theory grounded" (ibid). Glaser posits that it is at this point that Strauss and Corbin indulge in " . . . full conceptual description by forcing the data and leaving the emergence of grounded theory out completely" (Glaser, 1992; p 71). The sticking point is the confusion between induction and deduction. Glaser charges that he (Strauss) " . . . confuses induction with testing deductive hypotheses which are forced on the data (and) that it is not inductive to say the data disproves an hypothesis, it is simply a verification" (ibid). However, Strauss and Corbin contend that it is necessary to continually verify " . . . concepts and relationships arrived at through deductive thinking must be verified over and over again against actual data . . . we are building grounded theory and it is the grounding or verification process that makes this mode of theory building different" (Strauss and Corbin, 1990; pp 111-112). In response to this Glaser argues that Strauss and Corbin are developing a verificational method. "It simply tests forced conceptual hypotheses" (Glaser, 1992; p 92). It is not a method that generates theory but one that verifies; it is a theory that forces the data rather than allowing it to emerge. For Glaser it was crystal clear that Strauss and Corbin had created a verification method.

a subject as more data and new ideas discovered. This nature also applies to the method itself and its methodology" (Glaser, 1978; p ix).

Glaser (1979) argued that the " . . . analyst must remember it is the idea he is using not the person it was borrowed from . . . it is only a slight easy step for the analyst to get lost in referring to the man and his work and to forget the theory being generated and the work it took to establish an emergent fit" (p 8). Strauss considered he took the idea further Glaser disagreed. Interpretation is everything.

"Interpretation is grounded in something we have in advance . . . understanding operates in . . . an involvement whole that is already understood". Effectively the environment or background determines possible ways of questioning. However, interpretation is also " . . . grounded in something we see in advance - in foresight" (Heidegger, 1962; p 191). Additionally, interpretation is made on the basis of those around you through symbolic interaction. The individual is both subjective and objective in this context. Interpreted by self in relation to society and interpreted by society in relation to self through self-indication[3]. "Self-indication is a moving communicative process in which the individual notes things, assesses them, gives them a meaning, and decides to act on the basis of meaning" (Blumer, 1962; p 183). However, to accomplish this some foresight is necessary, even if it is only a comprehension of language or culture. This is how this study approached the data, with the acknowledgement of social interaction and foresight. This foresight takes into consideration the theories that already exist regarding integration and European integration. These are perceived as formal theories. Additionally, the researcher brings to the analysis expertise, knowledge and theoretical sensitivity. However, also bringing minimal preconceptions especially in the form of deduced *a priori* hypotheses. Effectively, objectivity is continually pursued through the recognition of subjective influences throughout the research process.

The main aim of the work is to develop a substantive theory and use it to discover the limits of European integration. Indeed, the " . . . research findings constitute a theoretical formulation of the reality under investigation rather than consisting of a set of numbers or a group of loosely related themes"

[3] There is a great deal of scope for research to identify the links between phenomenological and the pragmatic approaches of symbolic interaction in relation to different methodologies. However I am afraid it is beyond the scope of this study.

(Corbin and Strauss, 1990; p 24). To accomplish this the study analyses the harmonisation and integration processes in the in the insurance industry and relates the findings to a number of formal theories; specifically intergovernmentalism and neo-functionalism. The author's understanding of theory is explained further in the following chapter.

Chapter Three

IDENTIFYING INTEGRATION THEORY

Theory is always for some one and for some purpose. All theories have perspective. Perspectives derive from a position in time and space. . . . Of course, sophisticated theory is never just the expression of perspective. The more sophisticated a theory is, the more it reflects upon and transcends its own perspective; but the initial perspective is always contained within a theory and is relevant to it's explication (Cox, 1981; p 128).

INTRODUCTION

This chapter provides an analysis of theory and illustrates the differences between formal and substantive theories through an overview of integration theory. It indicates how a grounded theory understanding of theory building will be used in this analysis.

What historians have discussed relating to distinction between moralism and cynicism " . . . political scientists have talked in terms of idealism and realism. While the idealists have regarded law as the foundation of world peace . . . the realists have pointed out that it is power . . . that governs the world" (Ringmar, 1994; p 90). Indeed, in understanding the world as it ought to be in relation to how it is there is minimal room for nuance and usually one is forced to come down on one side or the other (ibid). "Virtually every major international relations theory has been criticised because it does not successfully predict outcomes" (Luchner, 1992; p 34). The subject area is saturated with ideological stances, which continually slant the debate.

"Depending on who is arguing, it is either power theory, integration theory or interdependence theory that is not precise enough" (ibid, p 43). Haas criticises power theory and questions its use as either a guide for understanding the state or international relations. Keohane and Nye, whose theory of interdependence owes much to integration theory, argue there is no such thing as integration theory but only integration studies. (Luchner 1992). However, is this not the difficulty of all analysis within the social sciences? Luchner (1992) inquires whether " . . . international relations scholars (are) . . . continually reinventing the wheel, and if so why do we keep repeating ourselves" (ibid p 36 author's brackets). Is it not to develop better theory? If we are to build theory, do we not have to build on what is already there? Without past theory and the continual reassessment and re-analysis of it we ignore the development of human thought and a means by which our understanding may be enhanced. Of course, this raises questions of how theory may be defined. In the strictest sense, theory should have shared assumptions and predict outcomes. However, the extent of prediction and the methods that should be applied are serious bones of contention not only in integration theory but also in most social sciences. All that can be said of most prediction in the social sciences is that they are generalisations or trends: to expect more would be to crave omnipotence. This illustrates a shift from the naive realism of *positivism* to the critical realism of *postpositivism*[1].

The more information one has regarding the likelihood of an event, the greater the generalisation may be. In the late 1990s EMU was far more likely to take place in the EU than political union. However, with the actuality of EMU, political union became more likely and generalisation in this direction more feasible i.e. the chance that it may be realised in one form or another becomes more realistic. Additionally, to have contended that political union would definitely happen 12 months following EMU would have been

[1] Positivism and postpositivism are paradigms of inquiry. Positivism considers that an apprehendable reality exists through which immutable and natural laws may be derived. Postpositivism also considers that reality exists but it considers that because of the human condition (the flawed human intellect) it cannot be apprehended perfectly. Consequently, reality must be subjected to wide critical examination so it can be understood as near as possible (but never perfectly). Of course, definitions of theory are different when understood from a critical theory or constructivist perspective. This analysis remains in the postpositivist paradigm in its use of grounded theory.(see Guba and Lincoln, 1994 for further).

unacceptable but to consider political union as a future probability is more realistic (which in itself is a generalisation). Consequently, the methodology used in this work posits that theory is not simply about predicting it also deals with understanding and generalisation. Theory is never completed but continually added to. Ultimately, this work builds a substantive theory in relation to formal theories through grounded theory techniques.

To fully comprehend different ideas of European integration, it is worth noting the philosophical issues and theories that both generated and juxtapose it. These are the Kantian ideas of *Civil Constitution, Perpetual Peace* and functionalism as well as the realist school based on the Hegelian idea that any integration must be brought about by the nation-state. Indeed, this interpretation of international relations underpins intergovernmentalism. However, there is another interpretation of Hegelian thought which considers that in the quest for recognition nation-states adhere to international law and it's legal requirements. Hence, integration is not underpinned by the nation-state alone.

Firstly, this chapter discusses Kantian and Hegelian political thought to identify the underpinnings of realism and functionalism. Secondly, it indicates how intergovernmentalism draws on realism. And finally, the chapter illustrates how neo-functionalism is linked to aspects of functionalism. Overall, this chapter will give an overview of the particular theories in relation to Kantian political thought and integration theories (functionalism, realism, intergovernmentalism and neo-functionalism) and provide some general principles. In addition, the chapter overviews a number of theories based on intergovernmentalism and neo-functionalism, these include state-centricism, multilevel governance and historical institutionalism. Each of these theories could be seen as different level of formal theory. For instance, neo-functionalsim could be perceived as a substantive theory in relation to functionalism; likewise with functionalism in relation to Kantian political thought. The more abstract and general the more the theory is of a formal nature.

Kantian Political Thought; Universal History and Perpetual Peace

In his categorical imperative Kant argued that duty and obligation should bind humanity. His philosophy is deontological in which the basis of good is a Goodwill. Indeed, the only thing that " . . . can possibly be conceived in the world . . . which can be called good without qualification (is) a Goodwill" (Kant, 1987; p 17). Fundamentally, goodness is not dependent on results but by virtue of it being good. Goodwill is fostered by human beings through acting rationally in accordance with the principles laid down by the categorical imperative. Kant identified the difference between hypothetical and categorical imperatives. Hypothetical imperatives are based on 'if' (if you want to do a do b) such imperatives define what we should do to reach some end. Categorical imperatives do not depend on a particular end, they are ends in themselves they are moral duties. Indeed, moral duties are categorical because they should be followed because they are duties and for no other reason. The only answer to the question why should one do their duty? Is because it is one's duty. If another answer existed the imperative would become hypothetical.

A categorical imperative is one that a fully rational agent would follow. In this context Kant sets up three formulas. First, act only on a maxim or principle that through your will you would have as a universal law of nature. Secondly, act in such a way as to treat people as means and not ends. Finally, only do something if you are prepared for everyone else to be able to do it as well. According to Kant the highest aspiration of human beings is the development of Goodwill which is developed by acting rationally in accordance with the principles of the categorical imperative.

In his work *Perpetual Peace a Philosophical Sketch,* Kant considered that no " . . . conclusion of peace shall be considered valid as such if it was made with a secret reservation of the material for a future war" (Kant, 1995; p 93). Indeed, a suspension of hostilities does not guarantee a lasting peace. Kant considered that to achieve perpetual peace, it is necessary for it to be formally instituted and this needed to be concretised in a legal civil state. Such a legal state should be based on a constitution which is founded on three principles " . . . firstly, the principle of *freedom* for all members of society (as men); secondly, the principle of the *dependence* of everyone upon a single common legislation (as subjects); and thirdly, the principle of legal quality for everyone (as citizens) . . . a constitution based on cosmopolitan right, in so far as individuals and states, co-existing in an external relationship of mutual influences, may be regarded as citizens of a universal state of mankind (*ius cosmopoliticum*)" (ibid, pp 98-99). This idea was first illustrated eleven years earlier in *Idea for a Universal History with a Cosmopolitan Purpose.* In this, Kant purports nine propositions that indicate a guiding purpose for history.

In *Universal History,* Kant argued that " . . . all natural capacities of a creature are destined to evolve completely to their natural end . . . (and) . . . the unsociable sociability of man" moving toward the " . . . achievement of universal civil society which administers laws among men" is the highest problem nature assigns to humanity (ibid, p 16 author's brackets). Only once a civil society has been attained can nature's other problems be solved. Humans need to exist within society because this creates a feeling of being more than human (as more than the developed form of their natural capacities). At the same time humans are unsociable because they feel hostility to those around them and expect hostility in return. It is this process that forces humans to protect themselves by aspiring to hold rank among their peers. Need forces humanity into curbing its natural aspirations to ensure a peaceful existence, unsociability initiates the "just civil constitution" and this incorporates laws to which all are answerable and no one is above. However, Kant recognised that one nation may attain a "just civil constitution" but unfortunately antagonisms would still exist between states (ibid). "The problem of establishing a perfect civil constitution is dependent on the problem of a lawful external relation among states and cannot be solved without a solution to the latter problem" (ibid, p 18). Each state will expect the same antagonisms, which forced it into seeking its own civil constitution. Through war and the threat of war, the full potential of humanity cannot be realised: consequently humanity is forced to seek the means of ensuring equilibrium. Through self-interest humanity is forced to accept mutual existence. This work considers that this is the basis of process in terms of European integration: mutuality and peace created through self-interest. Through self-interest acceptance and fostering a common interest.

The theories in this work investigate past attempts at equilibrium, and those being pursued in the present, with an emphasis on peaceful co-existence in the future. The concept of the League of Nations and a united Europe was initiated through such an attitude i.e. the pursuit of a civil constitution to ensure perpetual peace. The premise of the European Coal and Steel

Community (ECSC) was peace: its objective was to alleviate the prospect of war in Europe by controlling the products necessary to conduct a war. Through the pursuit of peace, Kant perceives a world civil constitution and as indicated above, this work contends that Europe fits into such an understanding in that it is an evolutionary or dialectical movement away from the nation-state toward such an entity.

HEGELIAN RECOGNITION & THE EU

Through the categorical imperative Kant attached morality to an abstract self, which was divorced from cultural experience and historical circumstance. Hegel contended that there was no such self because to will was to will something. Self had to be a self in relation to some other thing. Hegel labelled the Kantian abstraction *Moralität* and his own *Sittlichkeit*. "While *Moralität* referred to abstract principles and ought-to-be's *Sittlichkeit* referred to the existing moral obligations of actual communities. To act in accordance with *Sittlicheit* was thus necessarily to follow the given social and to perpetuate the already existing" (Ringmar, 1994; p 93).

Hegel (1977) argued that conventionally philosophy concerned itself with acceptance or rejection. That there was a failure to understand how the diversity of philosophical systems illustrate " . . . the progressive unfolding of truth, but rather sees in it simple disagreements" (ibid, p 2). Indeed, Hegel outlined his understanding of dialectics through his philosophy. "The bud disappears in the bursting forth of the blossom, and one might say that the former is refuted by the latter; similarly, when the fruit appears, the blossom in its turn is shown up as a false manifestation of the plant, and the fruit now emerges as the truth of it instead" (ibid.). This process indicates that each part is on the one hand distinct but on the other fluid and unified. Each part of the process is necessary and each part is mutually dependent on the other. Such is similar in the world of ideas " . . . he who rejects a philosophical system . . . does not usually comprehend what he is doing in this way: and he who grasps the contradiction between them . . . does not, as a general rule, know how to free it from its one-sidedness, or maintain it in its freedom by recognising the reciprocally necessary moments that take shape as conflict and seeming incompatibility" (ibid.). In Hegel's philosophy we can observe such a process in our understanding of international relations. Indeed, there is a means by which we can move from a purely realist interpretation of Hegel to one that incorporates an acceptance of international law and the international community.

For Hegel phenomenology was the science that described the development of "natural phenomenal consciousness . . . by way of science and philosophy toward the absolute knowledge of the absolute" (ibid). He considers that truth may be found through history and philosophy; philosophy because it tells us what should be in the world and history because it identifies this as it unfolds over time. Phenomenology deals with the way things seem for consciousness or with forms of consciousness. Fundamentally, the starting point is the naïve mind's emergent comprehension of reality that is external to it. Furthermore, he goes on to discuss how mind becomes aware of itself. Self-consciousness is neither exclusively subjective nor objective. Subjective awareness of self is not enough to enable self-consciousness. It cannot tell us what we are like in the world. We need a complimentary objective stance. This means that the self needs an objective recognition of its own consciousness which will provide an understanding of it's own reality. Only another being can do this, through reflecting for that consciousness a sense of its own external being. Objective truth lies in mutuality of recognition. Indeed such an understanding may be discerned in pragmatism and symbolic interaction. Others define self and self defines self in relation to the definition of others. Community defines the self and self defines community. This transition is however, not that straightforward because initially the existence of the other will be perceived as a threat to being and a negation of self. Through Hegelian recognition the methodology based on symbolic interaction and the EU based on mutual recognition of rules regulations and cultural differences are synthesised. Indeed, mutual recognition is an important legal mechanism in the process of European integration (see below).

Prior to being confronted by other the subject has existed in a world of things. In this way the subject deals with the other by treating it as a thing and validates its own image as an entity in control of a sea of things. Because it does not yet see itself in an objective form (it only knows itself a subjective entity) it initially treats other consciousness as things to be controlled. This is exemplified in terms of the Hobbesian state of nature and the world prior to the Kantian civil constitution. Further it may be identified in the way that some men treat women and the way young children treat others as things.

Finally, the rationale behind war may be perceived in this equation the other encompassing the tribe or nation.

The need to subdue the other leads to conflict and enslavement, which denies an opportunity for full understanding and self-consciousness through mutual recognition and consensus by the means of Kantian civil constitution. Recognition is needed. However, the only form of recognition understood is subordination and in the attempt to reduce the other. Encapsulated in the life-death struggle is the emergence of social life and political union. In the struggle for recognition and humanity's unsocial sociability embryonic social relations are founded.

Death does not solve the problem of recognition and realisation of consciousness that initiated the problem. Victory must be recognised before death is reached. Indeed, a master-slave relationship arises, which underpins the emergence of recognition, self-consciousness and social life. Hegel doesn't mean that all relationships are enslaving but that this is the dialectical basis for political, economic, social relationships etc. The struggle for recognition is an ongoing process it is a continuing feature of social life. For Hegel the master-slave relationship is not simply an early social structure. "The development of social relationships . . . is not . . . simply . . . one leading from one to another, but self inclusive, each earlier stage incorporating in a higher form the earlier ones, the master-slave relationship is a protean source of the various relationships, political, economic, social and sexual" (Hampsher-Monk, 1992; p 426).

Initially, the master seems to have won the day. Consciousness and recognition has been won and self-validated. However, when one looks a little closer this is not so clear. For full self-awareness consciousness needs the recognition of another consciousness. The master has only won by reducing the other consciousness to slavery in the victor's eyes the status of thing. For the master there is no other self in the world. In this context, the master exists in a world of things there has been no progression of consciousness and because the slave mediates this independence the mind is now passive. "His consciousness has progressed no further than its existence in a world of unconscious objects" (ibid p 427). The master wanted recognition from someone of equal status someone that he/she also respected. The slave however, is conscious of another independent mind in the world. Although forced to recognise this other the slave does so and consequently progresses from an individual alone in the world of things (as a subjective self) to an objective awareness of self (through the master). In putting these two perspectives together (a) consciousness experienced subjectively, in self and (b) consciousness experienced objectively, in another, the slave is able to have an objective awareness of the self's subjectivity. The positive in enslavement relates to an understanding of the futility of ego, which clears the consciousness and the importance of labour. "Objective truth lies in their mutual and consequently developed recognition of the other as a personality" (Hampsher-Monk, 1992, p 425). The master's perception of reality is defined by consumption alone whereas through labour " . . . the slave . . . increases his awareness of himself and his relationship to an initially intractable Nature in the course of transforming it for his master" (ibid p 427). As noted above this transition is not easy as the individual primarily perceives others as a threat to self (ibid). However, Hegel continually indicates that humans cannot organise a total concept of self unless this is in relation to others. The difference between master and slave is gradually overcome by the slave's ability to progress through labour the slave is able to educate self and become someone through his/her labours on both personal capacities and the surrounding world. "In this way recognition and personal identity came to be seen as achievements. . . . Hegel envisioned social relations as becoming increasingly equal as more and more individuals freed themselves from both from the determination of nature and the . . . subjugation . . . imposed by others" (Ringmar, 1994; p 94). "Consequently, individuals can attain their ends only in so far as they themselves determine their knowing, willing and acting in a universal way and make themselves links in this chain of social connexions. In these circumstances, the interest of the Idea-an interest of which these members of civil society are as such un-conscious-lies in the process whereby their singularity and their natural condition are raised, as a result of the necessities imposed by nature as well as of arbitrary needs, to formal freedom and formal universality of knowing and willing the-process whereby their particularity is educated up to subjectivity" (Hegel, 1967, p124).

This can be related to nation-states and their quest for recognition on the international stage. In the ethical community the individual has a right to recognition and the law guarantees that a people are given the opportunity to develop. Indeed, the law is a structure that provides meaning for our lives " . . . we submit ourselves to a certain way of life, and as a result we come to see ourselves as persons of a certain kind. . . . By following the rules . . . a person is making demands on the people around her to recognise her as a legitimate member of their group" (Ringmar, 1995; p 95).

The debate at the international level revolves around the realist argument and the functionalist argument. Realism is based on a Hegelian interpretation of the state and international relations. Hegel (1967) argued that "(i)nternational law springs from the relations between autonomous states. . . . The nation-state is mind in its substantive rationality and immediate actuality and is therefore the absolute power on earth" (p 212).

In this context Hegel denies international law and provides the basis for a realist interpretation of international relations, which considers that nation-states are sovereign. However, Hegel provided a defence of international law when he argued that law was more than a construct for telling right from wrong. It was also a means of " . . . determining the class of subjects to whom the law itself applies" and provides for the " . . . constitution of individual identities" (Ringmar, 1995; p 92). Indeed, Ringmar (1995) has undertaken a historical analysis, which identifies a number of problems with the realist interpretation of Hegel. He considers that in a period of state creation as state identities are formed legal requirements are crucial. Indeed, features of law contribute to this: first, law gives substantive context to actions that political entities perform; and second it provides a standard by which political entities may be recognised as things of a certain kind. As noted identity formation is Hegelian and through transferring this formation toward the state Hegel can shed new light on international law, the EU and it's membership. Through identity formation, the EU is constructing another political community that is beyond the nation-state but not international. There is a transferal of sovereignty to a supranational institution, which is not international.

Following two world wars the EU does not pursue subordination it is about integration. Democratic states voluntarily transfer sovereignty to a supranational entity. There is a need for both subjective and objective recognition in their interpretations of self. European imperialism and subjugation of other cultures did not provide the colonists with a full understanding of self. Following this failure a new strategy is developing, one that provides recognition for the European states followed the imperialist route. In Joseph Conrad's 'Heart of Darkness' this was 'the horror the horror'. Indeed, through this interpretation of Hegel we may find the dialectical step from the nation-state to the Kantian civil constitution and functionalism. Through recognition the EU and neo-functionalism we may observe the bridge between conflict and peace. We may identify the link between realist and functionalist comprehensions of integration theory and indicate the progressive unfolding of truth and the consequent limitlessness of European integration.

REALISM AND INTERGOVERNMENTALISM

The intergovernmental critique emphasises the importance of the nation-state in the process of European integration and is based on a realist model and one interpretation of Hegelian ideas in terms of international relations. "For realism, theory consists in ascertaining facts and giving them meaning through reason. It assumes that the character of a foreign policy can be ascertained only through the examination of political acts performed and of the foreseeable consequences of these acts. Thus we can find out what statesmen have actually done, and from the foreseeable consequences of their acts we can surmise what their objectives might have been" (Morganthau, 1973; p 4).

Based on the concept of power, realism is encapsulated by the motives of nation-states. Effectively, international relations, in the form of foreign policy, are pursued by nation-states alone. Consequently, these are the motors of change. However, " . . . political realism does not assume that the contemporary conditions under which foreign policy operates, with their extreme instability and the ever present threat of large scale violence cannot be changed. . . . Nothing in the realist position militates against the assumption that the present division of the political world into nation states will be replaced by larger units of a quite different character, more in keeping with the technical potentialities and the moral requirements of the contemporary world" (ibid, p 9-10).

But this may only be achieved through the forces at a territory's disposal and these forces are encapsulated by the nation-state. "The realist cannot be persuaded that we can bring about . . . transformation by confronting a political reality that has its own laws with an abstract ideal that refuses to take those laws into account" (ibid, p 10). The questions are: will the nation-state make itself obsolete? And do such laws or such a reality actually exist? Indeed, Keohane and Nye (1997) argued that " . . . integration among states is slight and lasts only as long as it serves the national interests of the most powerful states. Transnational actors either do not exist or are unimportant" (p 24).

The realist model identifies international politics as continually in a state of conflict, as dominated by struggle. Four assumptions underlie a realist understanding of international relations:

(a) States are the dominant protagonists in international politics.
(b) States act as coherent units.
(c) Force is an effective instrument of international policy.
(d) High politics such as foreign policy and military security will always out weigh low politics e.g. economic policy.
(ibid).

Based on the realist critique, intergovernmentalism considers a number of points. Firstly, it considers that regional integration should take global criteria into account. Secondly, it contends that the real power-houses in the process of European integration are the nation-states and that these would remain committed to national interest. Finally, intergovernmentalists think that the transference between low and high politics will never take place; integration would be condoned in technical fields to ensure mutual benefit but would never move into areas like defence, monetary policy and national security (George, 1994).

There is no need to dispute the first of these points because international variations and historical change effect most entities. The second of these assumptions denies the neo-functional idea: that through sector bargaining the political process would shift from the national to the supranational and overcome the dichotomy that the realists create for themselves. Indeed, the realists consider that things will change, but only through the perpetuation of what already exist's (the nation-state). However, if the EU encompassed a larger nation-state, then in this context it would fit into the intergovernmental and neo-realist perspectives. Neo-realists argue that nation-states have their own interests and are sovereign structures that are capable of acting in a unitary manner. However, even though nation-states regard each other with hostility they " . . . can engage in co-operative activities through the formation of regimes, but only to enhance or protect their respective power in the interstate system. Any action which either diminishes that capability deliberately or assigns it irrevocably to another polity is (theoretically) incomprehensible" (Schmitter, 1996; p 3). The third assumption may be disputed through citing the creation of the euro and the decision-making powers that the European institutions have incrementally accrued. Richardson (1996) argued that it was necessary to take low politics as seriously as high politics. Indeed ninety per cent of European integration is about low politics and to fully comprehend this process it is necessary to understand how a range of non-governmental actors interact and how low decisions and policies evolve into legislation. European integration is " . . . not simply the outcome of inter-state bargaining" (p 5) but a complex process involving numerous actors. However, modern government is not ad-hoc but a procedural means of dealing with different preferences. Thus, such procedures may involve neo-functional as well as intergovernmental processes.

FUNCTIONALISM

Mitrany (1943, 1944, 1965, 1970, 1975a, 1975b, 1975c) concentrated on international institutions and perceived their existence as means by which international divisions may be overlaid by inter-state agencies through which the interests of countries would gradually be integrated. The premise of the process was benefit: international welfare would overcome emotional attachment to the state and provide international institutions, which would enable both prosperity and peace. Mitrany identifies the international organisation of communications as a functional heading e.g. railway communications would be administered at the "logical limit of co-ordination" obviously at the level of the continent. "Shipping, on the other hand, would be administered in inter-continental terms but not universally. Land bound states would have little to offer the function of the organisation. Telecommunications, broadcasting and air travel would be organised on an international scale" (Mitrany, 1975a; p 116). Effectively, administration should be undertaken at the most logical level to enable efficient functional decisions.

Mitrany (1975a) considered that the two main objectives of government were stability and the management of change. "As regards the first it would not be difficult constitutionally if the political will was there, to translate the instruments and experience of national life into the needs of the international order; but with regard to peaceful change the problem in the two spheres is utterly different" (ibid, pp 131-132). The task was perceived as the building up of a common interest in peace. However, universal organisations in the context of the League of Nations and the United Nations were not yet achievable, and this was born out by their failure. Mitrany acknowledges the federal system on the one hand but sees it of limited scope, and in logical terms ". . . at the expense of general unity" (Mitrany, 1975b; pp 121-122). For Mitrany, functional organisation would create integration and peace.

As it became more apparent that the nation-state was able to adequately assume a wide range of welfare functions to ensure the well being of its people. This led to a rethink of the state's position in the functionalist process. Indeed, it was concluded that rather than by-pass the state, it would need to be an element in the integration process. The welfare aspects of the state could be integrated on, if not world, then a regional basis; this was a shift from functionalism to functional integration (Mitrany, 1944).

It may be argued that functionalism allows for the changes and adaptations that social evolution creates: that it is pointless to work towards some specific end as is attempted in a federalist model because humanity is incapable of delineating the end point. All one may achieve is a concept of community that indicates organisational networks each designed to meet a specific social, economic or technical need. Functionalism provides change through " . . . linking authority to a specific activity and seeks to break away from the traditional link between an authority and a definite territory" (Mitrany, 1975a, p 125).

Mitrany (1943) argued that the " . . . new approach toward the goal of international collaboration is free from dogma . . . and offers a line of action that might overcome the deep-seated division between the needs of material unity and stubborn national loyalties" (p 126). Mitrany provides a broad test for moves toward an international order, the means by which change is brought about and aptness of the change to the given time. This is also illustrated in the organisations necessary to administer the process. Each organisation would be designated a specific task that would be fluid and evolve as the functional need changed. A political dimension would exist to direct the network i.e. in terms of planning and interaction. Through this process it was hoped that a system of peaceful co-existence would emerge. Through interdependence and the multi-involvement in solving socio-economic problems, the psychological and material bases of war may be alleviated.

At the very least, the structure could be a pluralist international community where national control is marginalised through functional linkages; or one of greater extremity where the nation-state disappeared and was replaced by an international administrative body where organisational patterns were determined by functional rationality.

As far as functionalism is concerned, the process of integration may be initiated at the intergovernmental level or at the transnational. Governments that cannot deal with international problems single-handedly or groups that have similar interests may create functional organisations. In either scenario, the main impetus of organisational growth is 'technical self-determination'. This incorporates the increasing autonomy of technical organisations in that " . . . administrative convenience and efficiency demand that an expert body be not unduly hampered in its investigations by the necessity of constantly new instructions and authorisations" or as Mitrany put it " . . . certain agencies are born with or achieve 'functional autonomy' by virtue of the desirability of such an autonomous status" (cited in Sewell, 1966; pp 250-51).

Functional 'needs' in the expression of 'demands' by social groups indicate social and structural goals that incorporate a means by which these structures may be met. These directions are adhered to by governments and experts, which illustrate common needs rather than individual power. Functionalism is about building communities through collective education and technocratic management: it is based on the understanding that nation-states exemplify political tension and pressure and if they are not to lead to a catastrophe international political integration must take place. The beneficiaries of this process would exemplify greater support for the integration process and further co-operate as the process intensified.

Functional theory constitutes, " . . . a body of propositions (still interconnected) which serve to map out the problem area and thus prepare the ground for its empirical investigation by appropriate methods. More precisely, the propositions serve to classify phenomena, to analyse them into relevant units, or indicate their interconnections and to define rules of procedure and schemes of interpretation. Theory here equals conceptual scheme or logical framework" (Haas, 1964; p 7). In this context, functionalism is a scheme of procedure, a scheme of interpretation and a theory: a conceptual scheme or a logical framework.

Haas (1964) argued that disharmony prevails where politicians rather than interest groups exercise authority: that things can only improve when the government of humans is replaced by the administration of things. He points out that there is little hope of achieving a general state of welfare when human loyalties are bound to the nation-state. Once freed from a position of national insecurities, humanity would be able to strive toward the good of all. Functionalism is interested in bringing states together to engender peaceful co-existence to actively encourage a state of peace. Efforts are initially directed toward economic and social reform in a bid to remove the causes of conflict. Welfare, rather than power, incorporates the functionalist ideal and technocrats concentrating on specific areas rather than polity would take centre stage. Technical interests would eventually become fused and this would engender change. Indeed, a number of these ideas echo the thoughts of Kant.

Functionalism accepts that the concept of the nation-state will be difficult to overcome especially in respect of a move towards some form of world community. Most concede that the concept of a world community will be unrealistic until the idea of a world citizen is apparent. Likewise, with the EU: until the idea of the EU citizen becomes a reality true union will be difficult to achieve. On the one hand, Europe may be understood as a dialectical step in the functional process, whereas, on the other, it could be perceived as dysfunctional in that it creates no more than another super-state which would add to rather than detract from the world's problems. Both contexts illustrate different interpretations of Hegelian thought. However, functionalism and neo-functionalism are similar in that they stress:

(a) Economic welfare.
(b) Technical co-operation.
(c) Utilitarian factors of integration.
(d) Prerequisite of a pluralistic social setting.
(e) The role of technocrats.

The two theories differ over the dynamics of integration rather than the result; functionalism adheres to a community model, whereas neo-functionalism primarily subscribes to supranationalism.

NEO-FUNCTIONALISM

Neo-functionalism understands the integration process as one where political actors are persuaded to allocate their loyalties and political activities towards another setting. Political actors are persuaded to do this through pressures from organised groups that express demands for further integration. The neo-functional model does not need overall consent: it is driven by self-seeking interest groups who are restrained only by the acceptance of the rules of the game and ultimately common interests. It has been posited that integration results through the process of institutionalised patterns of interest group politics undertaken in existing organisations. (Haas, 1964). In this context, separate Member State life insurance industries and companies.

Haas (1958) argued that European integration was " . . . the process whereby political actors in several distinct national settings are persuaded to shift their loyalties, expectations and political activities toward a new centre, whose institutions possess or demand jurisdiction over the pre-existing national states. The end result of a process of political integration is a new political community, superimposed over the pre-existing ones" (p 16).

This stance identified the concept of supranationalism and condoned the pursuit of a united Europe through functionalist means. However, not all neo-functionalists agree with the Haas' model because it seemed to deny other outcomes; following the stagnation in European integration over the 1960s theorists have described integration in different terms. The functional model lies at the heart of the neo-functional view of European integration. Through observing the European Coal and Steel Community (ECSC) Haas (1958) argued that the process of integration could not simply be explained in terms of technical self-determination and the learning of co-operation. Out of the acceptance of such came the set of ideas that underpin neo-functionalism.

Haas (1958) provides an outline of neo-functionalism. Political parties and interest groups accept that action should be taken at the supranational level. Interest groups and political parties organise and function beyond the nation-state and define their interests in the new environment. Interest groups and political parties through their interaction sow the seeds of ideological agreement, which overtake those based at the national level. There is an adherence to the rule of law by the parties involved which include governments and interest groups, and when decisions are opposed dissatisfactions are channelled through legal avenues rather than issuing threats or ignoring the situation (Haas, 1958).

Recently, neo-functional thinking has found " . . . its way back into our theorising after almost twenty years of neglect (which) indicates that judgements on integration theory were at times a bit too general" (George, 1994; pp 40-41 author's brackets). Additionally, Keohane and Hoffman (1991) have argued that many of Haas's ideas in respect of neo-functional processes have been open to distortions in the contemporary literature. Hence, in attempting to discover the limits of European integration it is necessary to revisit neo-functionalism and assess it in relation to other European integration theories.

SUPRANATIONALITY

Haas (1958) argued that supranationality was central neo-functionalism and that it constituted a means by which a political community may be realised. He defined it as, " . . . neither federalism nor intimate intergovernmental co-operation, even though the institutions it employs resemble those of a federation more than the United Nations or NATO. Supranationality is a unique style of making international decisions, unique because of the nature of the participants, the context in which decisions are made and the quality of decisions produced" (Haas, 1964a; p 64).

Heathcote (1966) identified supranationality as " . . . an academic notion-predicted rather than experienced, and to be arrived at after a process of evolution (that) supranationality may never be realised, but the ideal has already enriched international affairs" (p 162 author's brackets). Because of De Gaulle some considered that European institutions were incapable of supplanting their national counterparts. "The supranational organ of the Community, a Commission, 'proposing' to a 'disposing' Council, was in the event unable to introduce a 'new method' or style to international politics, let alone to erode the sovereignty of the surprisingly recalcitrant nation-state" (ibid, p 168). The Gaullist boycott wished to weaken the position of the Commission: this it achieved and thereby obstructed the process of closer union. However, as today's position exemplifies, this only delayed the process of supranationality. As Haas (1964a) pointed out; "(in) supranational systems . . . the compromise pattern involves splitting the difference between the final bargaining positions of the participants. More significantly still, supranational systems feature a bargaining process which I call upgrading common interests" (p 65).

Haas (1964) considered that De Gaulle's vision of changes in Europe were neither supranational nor federal but confederal. As indicated by the " . . . former Prime Minister Debre. In Europe, legitimate power is the power, which comes from national sovereignty, and against this power arbitrary outside tyrannies like the so-called supranational institutions can do nothing. European unity is becoming, and will continue to become, a reality through the will of those who legitimately wield power in each of the countries which together make up Europe" (Press Conference Paris 1960, cited in Haas, 1964; pp 66-67).

It was in response to such an understanding that Heathcote (1966) may have considered that: "Supranational structures may not survive into 1966 . . . but . . . the Common Market need not entirely dissolve" (ibid, p 168). Nation-states join international organisations for increased protection, and then use them to enhance their national power and prestige. However, eventually she concedes that the model may succeed, providing that the leading powers desire it. Is this the situation with Germany today? Does the *Self-interest* of Member States with the support of the leading power create spillover and increase supranationality? The leading power in this context (Germany) is tied closely to further integration because of its political position (or lack of power at an international level).

Both Haas and Lindberg " . . . drew attention to the distinction between power issues (high politics) and welfare issues (low politics) and argued that the latter . . . bore the potential for the collective pursuit of common interests. Over time, progress in 'low politics' would produce fundamental political consequences" (Gehring, 1996; p 228). This is exactly what the realists and intergovernmentalists deny; that there could ever be a shift from low politics to high politics. Indeed, through the incremental creation of the SEM toward EMU low politics have produced fundamental political consequences.

Haas (1958) outlined the concept of supranationality and the pursuit of an integrated Europe through functionalist means. He did not determine a constitution or federal end. However, his language did indicate that loyalties would be transferred to a supranational government whose rules were legally binding. In this context Haas' political community is less of a prediction than it may first appear. Furthermore, it is difficult to define dependent and independent variables in this context[2].

Lindberg, like Haas, does not prescribe an end or a dependent variable. His definition of integration is as follows: "(1) The process whereby nations forgo the desire and ability to conduct foreign and key domestic policies independently of each other, seeking instead to make joint decisions or to delegate the decision-making process to new central organs; and (2) the process whereby political actors in several distinct settings are persuaded to shift their expectations and political activities to a new centre" (Lindberg, 1963; p 6).

The difference between the theorists lay in the premises of their theoretical propositions. Haas (1958) based his analysis on the ECSC or sector-specific integration, whereas Lindberg (1963) concentrated on the general aspect of the EEC. Indeed, the latter approach indicated that political as well as administrative mechanisms enable decision-making to take place. "Lindberg's modification disentangled political integration from the fate of the participating nation-states and opened neo-functionalism to a more intergovernmental perspective. While it did not rule out that political integration might lead to a 'new political community', it emphasised the possibility that it could remain in a state dominated by collective decision-making (supplemented with some delegation of power)" (Gehring, 1996; p 230).

This understanding has implications for later theories that consider the EU to be a confederal entity with intergovernmentalism, transnationalism and supranationalism working in tandem (Wallace, 1983; pp 403-436). However, both Haas and Lindberg argued that integration was a peaceful process. Indeed, they both consider the necessity of central decision-making institutions and both leave their scale and scope open. Furthermore, they each indicate changes in the expectations and activities of the political actors. These considerations are illustrated through the dynamics of supranationality and spillover (spillover will be investigated below).

---

[2] A dependent variable is an identifiable outcome and neo-functionalism is unable to illustrate this for the EU. Independent variables, in the context of European integration may include, the Treaties, direct elections, the SEM, EMU etc. However, these could be defined as dependent variables themselves i.e. they are or once were identifiable outcomes.

This work considers that the EU may be identified as a supranational entity in evolution and that this in itself is a process of decision-making. Supranationality is greater in some areas of the EU than others. Under the first pillar (e.g. single market, agriculture fisheries and transport) supranationality is at its most formidable. Under the second pillar (common foreign and security policy) supranationality is a little more tenuous. However, there are instances of supranationality in terms of common foreign policy e.g. the GATT negotiations. Furthermore, the Treaty of Amsterdam incorporates the Shengen Agreement (the removal of internal frontier checks and enhances co-operation between police forces and legal systems. The latter of these has implications for the third pillar (co-operation in terms of home affairs and issues of justice. Indeed, this pillar will be greatly affected by the European Convention on Human Rights. Other areas that the Amsterdam Treaty deals with include, how European foreign policy will develop and will a European army evolve? Finally, the concept of supranationality is bound up with the different stages of integration the EC was set up under the SEA and it is in this Treaty that the renewed pace of supranationality may be observed. However, supranationalty has been taken further in the EU, which was set up by the Maastricht Treaty as it will be taken further yet again by the Treaty of Amsterdam.

Supranationality is not the antithesis of intergovernmentalism, but as Haas argued " . . . a cumulative pattern of accommodation in which the participants refrain from unconditionally vetoing and instead seek to attain agreement by means of compromises upgrading common interests". Indeed, structurally it encompassed " . . . the existence of governmental authorities closer to the archetype of federation than any past international organisation but not *yet* identical with it" (Haas, 1964a; pp 64-66 and 1958; p 59). What it will become is unclear, supranationality is a process rather than an end. The on going accumulation of European treaties and their integrative affects may identify this process. This indicates the difficulty of the dependent variable and the problem of teleology; neo-functionalism fails to posit a clear end toward which a regional system should move. Haas (1970) argued that the " . . . verbally defined single terminal conditions which we worked in the past - political community, security community, political union, federal union - are inadequate because they foreclose real-life possibilities" (p 633). Others considered the European programme as " . . . a pluralistic system in evolution from nationalism to regionalism using economic integration as a means of promoting political unity" (Mally, 1973; pp 239-240). This study believes that supranationality has two levels of epistemology; on the one hand, it is material in that it is the decision-making institutions in existence at a given time; while on the other, it is part of the abstract process of integration. As Mitrany noted, we have no knowledge of what the end may encompass so why invent one?

SPILLOVER

A second central theme in the concept of neo-functionalism is spillover. This is where integration in an industry or sector creates its own impetus and necessitates further integration both in the same, and in other sectors. "Specifically, the term spillover describes the accretion of new powers and tasks to a central institutional structure, based on changing demands and the expectation on the part of such political actors as interest groups, political parties and bureaucracies" (Haas, cited in Kirchner, 1976; p 3). Effectively, there is an interplay between spillover and supranationality in that the " . . . establishment of supranational institutions designed to deal with functionally specific tasks will set in motion economic, social and political processes which generate pressures towards further integration" (Tranholm-Mikkelsen, 1991; p 4). Haas asserts that perceptions of *self-interest* are the driving force in the process and that this will only be generalised " . . . if the actors, on the basis of their interest-inspired perceptions desire to adapt integrative lessons learned in one context to a new situation" (Haas, 1964; p 48). "Neo-functionalism stresses the instrumental motives of actors; it looks for the adaptability of elites in line with specialisation of roles; neo-functionalism takes self-interest for granted and relies on it for delineating actor perceptions" (Haas, 1971; p 60). Haas considers that a new central decision-making body may evolve through earlier incremental steps; he also questions whether the formation of such an institution may have been foreseen by certain individuals and used to presage their designs.

This work undertakes an analysis of the life insurance industry and its place within the European integration process. The SEA indicates that services are an important aspect of the harmonisation process. Much had been done in the area of goods, but little in the service area and even less in financial services. Furthermore, life insurance is a product that needs to be regulated and the extent of regulation reveals nuances in Member State interpretations of the SEM. The three generations of insurance legislation provided the impetus for pensions' legislation and banking legislation, which in turn created the need for further capital market legislation. This indicated a shift from services to capital. It can be argued that once a state becomes part of the EU the spillover effect comes into operation. If a Member State is to be part of the SEM, then it must adhere to European regulations, which in themselves will necessitate further legislation.

The extent to which pressures from industries/sectors provide a positive impetus for integration (all of which are attempting to exploit the situation to their own ends) is determined by the benefit to the industry/sector of being involved in the integration process. It may be that the spillover process then draws another industry/sector into the integration process if the payoff is agreeable to the industry/sector involved. If another industry/sector does become involved in the integration process this extends the authority of the supranational entity. Fundamentally, the supranational authority is looking for consensus and a means of upgrading the common interest (Haas 1964).

With the intensification of the integration process in Europe, the spillover process and the supranational composition of the EU are, one may posit, more identifiable than ever. Helen Wallace considers that due to the internal market programme, " . . . (it) could . . . be argued that the neo-functionalist concept of spillover is now being vindicated" (H. Wallace, 1990; p 219 author's brackets).

For neo-functionalism, spillover is the means by which the integration process is achieved and co-operation in one-area spills into another. Spillover " . . . refers to the specific process which originates in one functional context initially separated from other political concerns, and then expands into related activities or it becomes clear to the chief political actors that the achievement of the initial aims cannot take place without such expansion" (Haas, 1958; p 523).

Legislation in one industry/sector creates the need for legislation in other industries/sectors and/or further legislation in different areas of the same sector if a true SEM is to be achieved. January 1 1993 was not the end but a part of the spillover process. This is what Haas labelled the " . . . expansive logic of sector integration". Indeed, the " . . . swapping concessions from a variety of sectors. . . . No statesman, even if he deeply dislikes the process, can permanently isolate his nation from a commitment to unity which is only partially implemented, unless he is willing to pay the price in diminished welfare" (Haas, 1958; p 243 and pp 283-317). However, the extent to which changing incentives created by spillover allowed an explanation for task expansion has been a point of contention for neo-functionalists. Nye (1971) argued that the functional linkage of tasks has been a less powerful mechanism than was originally believed to be the case. Whereas, Lindberg and Scheingold (1970) denied that spillover led to the Common Market. Indeed, this analysis attempts to ascertain the extent to which, in Helen Wallace's words, spillover " . . . has been vindicated" (H. Wallace, 1990; p 219).

There are two main understandings of spillover outlined in this study. First there is Spillover 1 (S1), which considers that spillover occurs because of the impact it has on differentiated actors, including multinationals, interest groupings, the Commission and national organisations. These actors form coalitions to increase EU decision-making in new industries/sectors and enhance integration in industries/sectors where agreements have already been reached. Second there is Spillover 2 (S2), which argues that spillover is a result of past policies created by Member States. They remain central to the integration process and continue to make crucial policy decisions in the EU. (Member States remain central actors but they are dictated to by past actions). "Neo-functionalists, such as Haas, purport to describe the mechanism of the linkage between integration in economic and political sectors through the concept of spillover. They use the concept to describe a dynamic and more or less automatic integrative process, gradually encompassing ever more functional sectors until, the final stage, a political union is reached" (Kirchner, 1976; p 2).

This study considers that one may identify links in one industry, the insurance industry (vertical neo-functional spillover); between the legislation in the financial services sector i.e. between insurance, banking pensions etc (horizontal neo-functional spillover). It is also recognised that an intergovernmental process of spillover is at work within European integration i.e. in the guise of the SEA, the Maastricht Treaty and the Treaty of Amsterdam, and that " . . . spillover requires prior programmatic agreement among governments, expressed in an intergovernmental bargain. Such a bargain is clearly important in accounting for the Single European Act" (Keohane and Hoffman, 1991; p 17). This type of spillover (spillover from treaty to treaty) may be labelled intergovernmental spillover (this is indicated by definition S2 above). However, it is apparent that wider transnational processes are also providing an impetus to harmonisation and European integration. In this context, the work contends that intergovernmental spillover is usually confined to providing the environment for further neo-functional spillover (vertical or horizontal) to take place e.g. through the SEA and the Maastricht Treaty (this is illustrated by definition S1 above). Fundamentally, one may posit that there is an interaction between neo-functional and intergovernmental spillover, which widens and deepens European integration.

As it becomes more difficult to pass further directives/regulations in an area, further amendments to the treaties become necessary. This was apparent with regard to the SEA, the Maastricht Treaty and the Treaty of Amsterdam and, one may argue, will become even more obvious as the ramifications of EMU intensify. "The current ascendancy of a qualified supranational style of decision-making is shown by the way in which, thanks to the Single Act, the Council now functions. . . . The revival of a supranational style of decision-making and the strengthening of European institutions in the Single Act resulted most immediately from decisions by governments to press in their own interests, for a removal of internal economic barriers and for institutional change that would permit such a policy to be carried out" (Keohane and Hoffman, 1991; pp 16-17).

At the moment, an impasse is apparent regarding pensions, taxation and capital markets because they come under the unanimity rule. Such was made clear late in 1999 when the UK government vetoed universal EU saving tax levels. However, these one may assume, will be overcome following monetary union. This analysis attempts to illustrate European integration in respect of one sector and argues that supranationality, sub-national interests and spillover may be discerned in this process. This is examined through an analysis of the decision-making processes in the European Union; an understanding of the life insurance sector in Europe and where and how it designated its emphasis in the creation of the Third Life Assurance Directive.

SUB-NATIONAL INTERESTS

Pool (1992) argued that ". . . insurers are certainly much better organised as a pressure group than the other players in the insurance markets. Even they, however, have not always found it easy to arrive at a common perception of what a common market should mean for them" (p 11). The Commité

Européen des Assurances (CEA) was established in 1953 and for many years has acted on behalf of its membership regarding to European issues. The main objectives of European interest groups are two-fold. Firstly, they should ". . . promote the exchange of information and try to find common denominators" (Kirchner, 1980; p 109). And secondly, ". . . co-ordinate and exert pressure for adopted policies through the European organisations and the national affiliations on both the EC and the national government" (ibid).

Camerra-Rowe (1996) pointed out that different sectors undertake different strategies when it comes to lobbying European institutions. Indeed, firms often have an incentive to lobby directly. . . . However, it is rare for a firm, even a large one, to rely on one channel of representation" (ibid, p 6). As data presented by Coen (1997; 1998) verified, large companies do lobby the Commission directly. There is a high degree of lobbying strategies and activities undertaken by large companies in the EU. Indeed, there is evidence that ". . . this new lobbying activity is a function of the changing regulatory competencies of the European Commission" (Coen, 1998; p 76). This provides the basis for a number of difficulties. Companies that lobby directly undermine the role of interest groups because the message they carry may not represent the whole sector. Also, they may have limited incentives to compromise their positions in the collective because they are able to lobby themselves. Finally, they may force the association to reach consensus, which may lead to the acceptance of the lowest common denominator and undermine the effectiveness of the interest group. However, it is evident that sub-national activity exists through large companies lobbying the EU institutions directly. Yet even though ". . . single firm representation is heard, the firm concerned is usually told that the Commission would wish to explore the issue further by talking to the interest group concerned in order to ensure that it gets a more representative opinion" (Greenwood, 1997; p 4). Furthermore, even though there are a number of interest groups from separate Member States, competition gives way to co-operation through resolving issues at the EU level (Browne, 1990). This is achieved by moving the ". . . analysis from the domain level to the issue level in order to provide a common substantive context for elite/pluralist interpretations" (ibid, p 477). This is echoed by Coen (1998) who considers that through issue based politics the Commission has ". . . institutionalised its bargaining position with business and has created a form of 'elite pluralism' . . . (which) requires that firms develop . . . pan-

European political alliances in exchange for access to restricted entry forums" (p 77, author's brackets).

The European insurance industry is mainly made up of medium-size enterprises, which in general lack the political weight and resources to undertake direct action in Brussels (although the nature of the EU insurance industry is gradually changing through mergers and acquisitions). However, these companies are still small in relation to the larger multinationals. As a result, both national and European interest groups have a greater influence on the Commission and their membership. Companies need to accept the interest group's ". . . policy position even if it does not take account of their particular interests because they cannot effectively represent their own views. As a result, and paradoxically, the more fragmented insurance sector was better able to undertake collective activity in pursuing Community policy" (Camerra-Rowe, 1996; p 21). However, even though the likes of Allianz could lobby directly, it only does so intermittently. This is because ". . . Allianz dominates the insurance sector. Because of its size, the national and the European trade associations have generally taken the views of the firm into account in drawing up policy positions" (ibid, p 19). Indeed, in some instances, Allianz's position on certain issues became the national association's position. This was verified by SMEs who took care not to contradict Allianz in the formulation of policy (ibid). Furthermore, a change in the position of a Member State interest group can also have an effect on EU policy. For instance during the early nineties the French interest group started to change its stance on regulation. It " . . gradually swung to join the liberalising elements of the CEA . . . a position which has supported the European Commission . . ." (Vipond, 1995; p 107) regarding the Third Life Assurance Directive.

Browne (1990) questions whether organisations exist that integrate policy domains and issues within a domain. The provision of three generations of life assurance directives indicates a policy domain integrated in the domain of financial services and the Third Life Assurance Directive is an issue within this policy domain (p 484). The Third Life Assurance Directive is a narrow issue and this brought about success. Indeed, the CEA is concerned with other issues relating to the policy domain of insurance. However, other interest groups deal with other policy domains relating to banking, capital markets and pensions, which belong to the domain of financial services. In this way issues can remain narrow and successes more frequent (p 490). Furthermore, Browne

(1990) considers that interest groups and other lobbying organisations create coalitions in terms of the goals they pursue. It is considered that the CEA is more integrated than those organisations identified by Browne because it has a policy domain that becomes more integrated as European integration intensifies. Indeed, the CEA has become an interest group with a developed issue identity.

"In order to be effective Euro-lobbyists, groups must be able to co-ordinate their national and EC level strategies, construct alliances with their European counterparts, and monitor changing national and EC policy agendas" (Mazey and Richardson, 1993; p 191). However, regarding their different cultures and understandings about what would be best for a SEM, how may this be accomplished? How are policy-domains and focused issues constructed? How do separate Member State industries overcome self-interest and work toward a collective good? The rest of the study will explore these questions.

STATE-CENTRIC AND MULTILEVEL GOVERNANCE

Hooghie and Marks (1997) link neo-functionalism (through supranational actors and interest groups) to multilevel governance and intergovernmentalism to state-centric governance. They conclude that the state-centric approach is not capable of fully explaining European policy making processes; that EU decision-making and policy-making are of a multilevel nature. Indeed, Marks *et al* (1996) supply an interesting interpretation of the present situation. "Multilevel governance does not confront the sovereignty of states directly. Instead of being explicitly challenged states in the European Union are being melded gently into multilevel polity by their leaders and the actions of numerous sub national and supranational actors. State-centric theorists are right when they argue that states are extremely powerful institutions that are capable of crushing direct threats to their existence" (p 371). However, it is not necessary " . . . to argue that states are on the verge of political extinction to believe that their control of those living in their territories has significantly weakened" (ibid).

The intergovernmental approach adheres to the state-centric model. This considers that the " . . . overall direction of policy making is consistent with state control" (Hooghe and Marks, 1997; p 22). Furthermore, " . . . the core presumption underlying the state-centric governance model is that European integration does not challenge the autonomy of nation-states. "State-centrists contend that EU membership preserves or even strengthens state sovereignty and that European integration is driven by bargains among member-state governments" (ibid, p 21).

If the state-centric model is to be considered the dominant means of decision-making in the EU, three conditions would need to hold. Member State representatives in the Council of Ministers should be able to impose their understandings and preferences on other European institutions. Generally, Member States should be sovereign in relation to other Member States; Member States should be able to control sub national interests (ibid).

The multilevel governance model is based on certain aspects of neo-functionalism. It considers " . . . that European integration is a polity-creating process in which authority and policy making influence is shared across multiple levels of government sub-national, national and supranational" (ibid, p 22). The model accepts the central role played by Member States in the decision-making process and considers that elements of control have been passed on to supranational institutions. Consequently, in certain areas Member States have lost aspects of their sovereignty. "In Short, the multilevel governance model claims that the locus of political control has changed. Individual state sovereignty is diluted in the EU by collective decision-making among national governments and by the autonomous roles of the European parliament, the European Commission, and the European Court of Justice (ECJ)" (ibid, p 22).

If the multilevel governance model is to be accepted a number of premises must hold. Initially the supranational institutions (European Parliament and Commission) should share authority with the Council of Ministers. Secondly, that the individual Member State executives should be unable to continually stamp their authority on collective decision-making. And finally (especially in respect of this paper) we would require that ". . . that sub-national interests mobilise directly in the European arena" (ibid, p 24).

Historical Institutionalism

Historical institutionalism attempts to identify how institutional settings mediate political differences, it includes both formal organisations and informal rules that structure organisational conduct. Indeed, a widely accepted definition of historical institutionalism identifies " . . . the formal rules, compliance procedures, and standard operating practices that structure the relationship between individuals in various units of the polity and economy" (Hall, 1996; p 19). Blumer (1994) provided a historical institutionalist account of governance in the EU. He argued that it is possible to hypothesise " . . . that strategies and goals will be influenced by the institutional arrangements which political forces are confronted with" (p 369). However, even though he omits a detailed analysis of the role of interest groups he does indicate that there has been a proliferation of them in Brussels since the SEA and that this illustrates a response to the institutional dynamics. Such was reiterated by Greenwood (1997) who noted that the " . . . variety of interests with a stake in European public affairs is vast. It includes firms, professions, employers, and labour groups. . . . The Commission has estimated that there are some 3000 interest groups attempting to exert influence on European public affairs" (pp 2-3). Pierson (1996) provides a three-step model based on historical institutionalism in which institutional changes and policy choices create unintended consequences. Consequently, decisions taken at a certain time e.g. the SEA locks the integration process onto a particular path and into certain preferences that are difficult to predict. However historical institutionalism goes beyond institutions and institutional devices it deals with the values, beliefs and cultures of the structure. In this context, European Union has come to resemble a multi-tiered state, which may be identified in terms of institutions of government and instruments of government (see Bulmer, 1994: p. 358).

Conclusions

This chapter has outlined four major theoretical schools and their underlying philosophies, each of which encapsulates different values and goals. This investigation incorporates different elements of each theory, but relies heavily on an analysis of neo-functional and intergovernmental processes of change. Furthermore, in relation to these theoretical schools later understandings of European integration have been examined in terms of state-centric multilevel governance and historical institutionalist approaches. Indeed, these theories may be seen as formal theories in relation to the authors attempt to construct a substantive theory. It is apparent that functionalism and neo-functionalism have their roots in Kantian political theory. Where, realism and intergovernmentalism are more closely bound to Hegelian thought. However, as noted above certain interpretations of Hegel can be seen as a stepping stone between the two attempts at understanding integration and the generation of a democratic international society.

Functionalism argues that there is a general trend of areas of common interest creating reliance on each other in the international sphere. Neo-functionalism provides the basis for the general functionalist theory to be used on a regional basis (in this case the EU). In so doing, it identifies a supranationality and spillover and emphasises sub-national interference in the decision-making process. This does not mean that the international perspective has to be discarded: the supranational body could be perceived as a means of transition from the national toward a larger entity. Indeed, this could be the dependent variable that intergovernmentalism might pursue. A larger nation-state, it is only the process that would be disputed. Indeed, this may be overcome through Hegelian recognition.

As an integration theory, neo-functionalism utilises aspects of functionalism and allows an analysis of a specific creation, the EU. Of course in this context one may argue that neo-functionalism is a substantive theory because it only deals with the EU. However, neo-functionalism allows an adaptation of functionalism in that it provides a means by which the construction of propositions about regional integration may be understood. It allows for a dialectical shift away from the nation-state toward a supranational unit. the dimensions of which are uncertain.

FUNCTIONALISM

Coincidence of common goals through international institutions.

NEO-FUNCTIONALISM

Coincidence of common goals at regional level in federal/constitutional and plural terms through a functional/institutional spillover/supranational process. Closely tied to multi-level governance.

REALISM

Power politics initiate the motives of nation-states. Larger units may be brought about but these will only be created by and become larger nation-states.

INTERGOVERNMENTALISM

The major propellant in the shift toward European Union is the nation-state. Similar to realism (at the EU level) and has a state-centric perspective.

HISTORICAL INSTITUTIONALISM

Institutions afford an extensive role in shaping politics and is closely linked with multi-tiered or multilevel governance. Today's decisions define the routes and outcomes of tomorrow.

In realist and intergovernmental terms, international society is divided by conflict, nationalism and high politics (defence, foreign policy, etc). In functional and neo-functional terms, international society should be described in terms of education, or the perceived advantages that are learnt through experience there is a shift away from national governments. Through integration processes there is a gradual move away from a concentration on the national level through the realisation of the advantages of co-operating at the international or, in the case of neo-functionalism, the regional level (Taylor, 1968). Functionalism is peace-orientated and through an emphasis on co-operation and integration pursues a world system. As outlined above, the author considers that the process is built on the Kantian concept of "a just civil constitution" (Kant, 1995).

Neo-functionalism is an integartion theory of international relations, which affects our understanding of the international environment. Haas (1975) considered that the " . . . search for world order is nothing but an attempt to conquer turbulence. Theories of regional integration have a lot to teach us still about non-violent methods for collectively solving international problems, for coping. They can find a place in the intellectual armoury of studying alternative world orders. But this armoury must be stocked with new concepts as well. I shall suggest that this process has begun in the European Community at the level of policy, and that these policies and the institutions devised to implement them *illustrate the attempt to deal with turbulence rather than deal with political integration*" (p 180). Indeed one may argue that through the attempt to deal with turbulence integration is brought about. Functionalism identifies aspects of human interest's needs and desires. Haas (1964) identifies function as the needs and purposes, which relate the organisation to its environment. Out of this arises the concept of system: " . . . do we look for the impulse generating organisational action in the organisation itself or in the environment?" (Haas, 1964; p 7).

This work concentrates on the operation of the changing life insurance industry. This is examined, on the one hand, as a social organisation in transition and on the other as an entity that through integration is involved in changing its own social environment. The analysis has identified a changing process through the Third Life Assurance Directive, how this was agreed upon and the compromises that each Member State industry needed to make to achieve the new environment. This, it is argued, is a process of integration. The analysis concentrates on European integration and the extent to which different theories may be considered as the best means of explaining the process. To do this it constructs a substantive theory in juxtaposition with the existing formal theories. Indeed, this leads on to the main aims of the analysis, which are:

(a) To ascertain the extent formal theories are in operation in the process of European integration.
(b) To create a matrix and model that illustrate certain assumptions that may be used to demonstrate the extent of neo-functionalism/intergovernmentalism processes. These incorporate the building blocks of a substantive theory.
(c) To illustrate how far the EU is a supranational construct/process and the extent to which it is being created through spillover or task expansion.
(d) To provide a substantive theory that may allow further understanding of the limits of European integration.
(e) To illustrate how the substantive theory is juxtaposed and linked to formal theories.
(f) To provide further understanding of state-centricism, multilevel governance and historical institutionalism

The rest of the study intends to use grounded theory techniques to explore these objectives. In the next chapter, the object is to indicate how the different legislative structures of the individual Member States provide differing regulatory environments. It is argued that regulatory environments are identifiable through individual Member State legislation. And may be differentiated between themselves and in relation to the evolving SEM. Additionally, a survey of the EU insurance industry adds to the codification of Member State legislation and a regulation matrix of the Member States and EU legislation is created. This provides the basis of the substantive theory.

Chapter Four

DEVELOPING SUBSTANTIVE THEORY[1]

You Greeks oh isn't it great to be rid of plots and battles?
Before another pestle dishes us, come let us wrestle
And pull peace out of her pit, who is so beloved by all.
You farmers, merchants, labourers,
Craftsmen, aliens, visitors. . . . Come one and all to a man.
(Aristophanes, 1970; pp 233-234).

INTRODUCTION

Ellis (1994) inquired whether " . . . the Single European Market is a cohesive unit subject to a unified set of laws, or whether it is in fact, really made up of twelve separate national markets with distinct legal systems?" (p 41). The purpose of this chapter is to examine the different legislative environments and consequent regulatory regimes with regard to life insurance in the EU. However, prior to this we must classify the regulation that underpins the insurance law of the EU into three parts: Insurance company

[1] In this chapter there is a comparative analysis of Member State regulations pre-Third Life Assurance Directive. It is recognised that since this analysis there have been many changes to individual Member States legislation and subsequent regulation. Indeed, this factor substantiates the author's understanding of the harmonisation processes. Each Member State has needed to bring it's regulatory environment into line with that indicated by European legislation.

law; insurance intermediary law; and insurance contract law. "The aim underlying insurance company law is to protect the policyholder . . . by ensuring the financial stability of insurance companies. . . . In the case of insurance intermediaries . . . protection may extend to the supervision of insurance selling practices" (Ellis, 1995; pp 46-47). Indeed these two areas were dealt with by the Third Life Assurance Directive whereas the area of contracts was not. A contracts directive was proposed but agreement could not be reached (the implications of this are discussed below). Consequently, this chapter primarily deals with the implications of the first two forms of insurance regulation.

Legislation underpins regulation because interpretation of the legislation creates the regulatory environments and the subsequent trading structure. In general, policy-makers find ways of overcoming conflict through negotiation and compromise. Indeed, because societies cannot be based on conflict alone, as Jordan and Richardson put it " . . .the logic of negotiation appears inevitable" (cited in Mazey and Richardson, 1996; p 201). "This may be *especially* true in a policy-making system such as the EU where European-level officials face unique problems in formulating laws which can be made to work (and are acceptable) in . . . very different Member States. Each of these states has different regulatory styles and traditions and it is an exceptionally difficult task to produce proposals which can mobilise the necessary winning coalition. . . . One way of doing this it to integrate interest groups directly into the various stages of the policy process from problem identification through to policy implementation" (ibid).

Through a comparative analysis of Member State legislation in respect of the life insurance industry, theoretical coding (see Chapter Two) and a survey of European life insurance companies, a regulation matrix is constructed. Through grounded theory techniques the study pursues greater understanding of the European integration process and the extent of interference by Member States in the formulation European life insurance regulations. Such will establish the underpinnings of a substantive theory which will be developed further in the following two chapters.

The initial questions that were asked when one broached the subject of regulation in the EU were; what are regulations? How would one define them? And how do regulations and the EU fit together? Additionally, the concepts need to be understood in their historical context, with regard to their theoretical underpinnings and more practical applications.

Firstly, the chapter gives a brief definition of regulation. Secondly, it provides an example of the coding categorisation and dimensionalisation processes in relation to the initial parts of the research. Thirdly, the coding process is further identified through a technical explanation of how the categories and dimensions were arrived at. Indeed, it outlines how each Member State's life insurance industry underwent a comparative analysis and was coded in a regulation type category. The 12 (pre-enlargement) Member State life insurance industries are then pin-pointed on a regulatory environment table and matrix (see the Regulatory/Legislative Environment Table and Life Insurance Regulation Matrix One). These display the amount of regulation on a scale of 1-12. Each unit of the table and matrix illustrates the regulatory regime of the given Member State and displays the type of legislation that indicates the regulatory environment.

Fourthly, a survey (via a postal questionnaire) of European life insurance companies in eight Member States is added to the existing coding and creates a more precise understanding of the area under analysis. This is illustrated through the augmented matrix (see the Life Insurance Regulation Matrix Two, fig 4.2). Indeed, the survey takes into consideration the legislative positions of the Member States and in the case of eight Member States allows individuals from separate life insurance sectors to contribute their own perceptions of the legislation that underpins their regulatory environments. The regulation matrix is intended to reflect Member States' regulatory positions during 1993-94 i.e. prior to enlargement and the enactment of the Third Life Assurance Directive.

In the questionnaire, respondents were also asked to indicate which type of life insurance regulatory environment prevailed in their own Member State and what type would be most advantageous (a) for their own company, (b) for the European Union (c) to allow greatest consumer protection, and (d) to enable greatest consumer choice. The results added to the coding and categorisation process, assisted in identifying a compromise convergence point and allowed some verification of the pre-suppositions accrued through the comparative analysis of the Member State regulatory environments. (The methods and methodology were illustrated in greater depth in Chapter Two)

REGULATION: A DEFINITION

Regulation has a multitude of definitions. However, for the purposes of this work it shall be considered as " . . . a politico-economic concept and, as such, can best be understood by reference to different systems of economic organisation and the legal forms which maintain them" (Majone, 1990; pp 1-2). Regulation is an attempt to correct market failure in the form of " . . . monopoly power, negative externalities, failures of information, or insufficient provision of public goods such as law and order or environmental protection" (Majone, 1996; p 263). Furthermore " . . . market activities can be regulated only in societies that consider such activities worthwhile in themselves and hence in need of protection as well as control" (ibid).

It may also be argued that, there is a distinction between social and economic regulation. Social regulation " . . . deals with such matters as health and safety, environmental protection and consumer protection" (Ogus, 1994; p 4). Some regulatory regimes are of a liberal nature whereas others are state-controlled and have been allowed a modicum of monopoly or oligopoly.

Regulation can be traced back to the Tudor and Stuart periods, e.g. through guilds. However, by the late nineteenth century, this tradition had largely disappeared and regulation emerged in coincidence with industrialisation and urbanisation. Dicey (1962) considered that the growth of regulation illustrated a collective disenchantment with *laissez-faire* that was fuelled by the expansion of suffrage. However, on this there has been disagreement and some consider that there " . . . never was an age of *laissez-faire*, and state intervention did not result from any abrupt shift to collectivist ideology but rather emerged gradually, throughout the nineteenth century, as a pragmatic response to social problems: England stumbled into the modern administrative State without design" (Ogus, 1994; p 7).

Twentieth century Europe saw an immense growth in the use of regulation, which in the UK, resulted from Keynesian ideas and the transferal to post-war planning and nationalised utilities. Such encompassed a shift in economic regulation toward the social in terms of government direction and political accountability. Additionally, over the last fifteen years we have witnessed a process of deregulation or, as some would argue, a process of re-regulation. "Many so called deregulating measures have involved not the removal of external constraints but rather a change to less interventionist methods and forms. . . . Some areas of social regulation have continued to grow, notably those pertaining to the environment and financial services" (ibid, p 10).

Finally, the evolutionary process toward the SEM and its impact on regulatory frameworks needs to be taken into account. Different regimes create barriers to trade. Consequently, harmonisation of regulations was posited. However, harmonisation proved a lengthy business and through the SEA, which initiated Qualified Majority Voting (QMV), and mutual recognition European integration was intensified[2].

Industrial societies generally accentuate a tension between two systems of economic organisation: the market system and the collectivist system. The former is where individuals and sectors are allowed to function with minimal interference in the pursuit of their own goals whereas the latter controls and directs behaviour through intervention. Of course, there are gradients of these perspectives in the EU, each Member State illustrating its own cultural tradition in the legislation and regulation they adhere to.

---

[2] *Mutual recognition* is a ruling by the ECJ which states that if a product meets the stipulated standards in their home Member State then it may be sold anywhere in the Union. Indeed one could interpret mutual recognition from a Hegelian perspective and consider it as a mechanism for identifying subjective and objective concepts of self. Mutual recognition encapsulates an important mechanism in the pursuit of the SEM as it gives a framework for the facilitation of compromise. However, where diversity is so great, there will be a need for greater rather than less harmonisation of Member State legislation. The principle of mutual recognition " . . . pre-supposes agreement on a number of basic rules . . . these minimum harmonisation requirements . . . are only possible because common interest, mutual confidence and a high degree of economic convergence exist between EEC member states" (Loheac, 1991; p 409). One has to question if "minimum harmonisation requirements" have been met in respect of the life insurance market. The achievement of such requirements is extremely rare and even if there is a "high degree of economic convergence" in the life insurance market, the practical realities of achieving an SEM through mutual recognition alone are apparent. A convergence process must be undertaken prior to the actions of *mutual recognition* coming into play (ibid). The idea behind *mutual recognition* suggests spontaneous legislative adaptation; however, it does not deal with all regulation and as a convergence point is necessary for it to be effective it could be conceived as an impetus that encourages legislative change and compromise. This convergence point is indicated in Figure 4.1 and 4.2; the regulation matrices.

As noted above this work takes into consideration the special nature of life insurance and other financial services products. Indeed, the work posits that products such as life insurance and pensions are closely linked to individual cultures. "Differences in the way distinct countries subjectively value insurance products have not come into being by chance. They have evolved out of historical developed differences in values between one national society and another" (Hofstede, 1995; p 423). This situation exists between separate Member States and relates to other financial services products. It is from this starting point that it is assumed that through a study of the life insurance industry generalisations may take place. Furthermore, the work uses a qualitative methodology and generalises from one similar situation to others (this is discussed in Chapter Two and illustrated through the Spillover Model see Figs 6.1 & 6.2). In this chapter there is a comparative analysis of Member State regulation regarding life insurance and it is posited that the conclusions may be used to understand regulation convergence to financial services in general.

Coding and Categorisation: Member State Life Insurance Industries

"The grounded theory approach is a qualitative research method that uses a set of procedures to develop an inductively derived theory about a given phenomenon" (Corbin and Strauss, 1990; p 24). These procedures are coding techniques, which, for this study, initially encompass a comparative analysis of the EU life insurance industry and the different regulatory systems of the separate Member States. The qualitative data on each regulatory environment is broken down in terms of open coding and restructured initially on a table and later refined in a matrix. The *category* of 'Regulatory Environment' emerged following an analysis of Member State legislation and regulations. Through further research *conceptual labels* emerged in terms of liberal, prescribed and state-controlled regulatory environments and each of these was made up of the *properties* outlined in The Regulatory/Legislative Environment Table (Table 4.2) A *category* is a " . . . classification of concepts. This classification is discovered when concepts are compared one against another and appear to pertain to a similar phenomenon (Corbin and Strauss, 1990; p 61). Furthermore, *conceptual labels* are placed " . . . on discrete happenings, events, and other instances of phenomena" (ibid). Indeed, these concepts are made-up of *properties* and *characteristics* that are indicated by the overall category. Finally, the Member States are given *dimensions* through the " . . . location of properties along a continuum" (ibid), in this work a regulation matrix (see Life Insurance Regulation Matrix One, Fig 4.1). This process was pursued through the use of *code, theoretical* and *operational notes* and *diagrams. Code notes* illustrate separate types of legislation in the different Member States and how aspects of the legislation link together and fluctuate under *conceptual labels*; *theoretical notes* link different types of cultural existence to the conceptual labels and questions how compromise takes place. Through the *operational notes* the need for further research is illustrated. The *operational notes* guided the research in respect of: who to survey; the questions to be asked; and further into the research, who should be interviewed and the structure the interviews should take. Overall, the research was visually represented through *diagrams*, which illustrated the relationship between concepts. Indeed, the *diagrams* illustrate a " . . . visual sorting process that helps you identify how the categories are related to one another" (ibid p 197).

"Numerous alternative economic rules could have been used as the basis for EC trade liberalisation, from pure *laissez-faire* to the creation of an encompassing set of EC regulations and standards" (Garret and Weingast, 1993; p 177). This chapter defines these alternatives and indicates their existence through theoretical coding, a comparative analysis, a survey and the creation of a regulation matrix.

Table. 4.1
Regulation Scale

1-2 = self-minimal regulation
3-4 = minimal regulation; independent regulatory bodies
5-6 = moderately regulated without state ownership
7-8 = highly regulated without state ownership
9-10 = highly regulated with minimal state ownership
11-12 = highly regulated with a profusion of state control.

Table 4.2: Regulatory/ Legislative Environment Table

(Category) *Regulatory Environments* Liberal (Conceptual Label)	*Legislative/Regulatory Stipulations* (Properties)	*Member States* (Dimensionalisation)
1	Completely free market	
	Approval of Company	
2 - 3	Solvency Margins	Luxembourg
	Policyholder protection	
	Evaluation of Liability	Netherlands
	& Rates	UK
3 - 4	Open Access to Insurance	
	Information	Eire
Prescribed		
5 - 6	Price Controls	Belgium
	Marketing Controls	Denmark
	Solvency Deposit	Spain
7 - 8	Policy Approval	
	Regulation of Contract	Germany
State-Controlled		
9 - 10	State Controlled	France
	Companies	
	Contractual Obligation to	Italy
10 - 11	State	
	Intense Monitoring of	Portugal
	Companies	Greece
12	Proof of Ability	
	Total State Control	

Following the initial comparative analysis of the Member States life insurance legislative environments and regulatory structures, they were coded into three categories, which designated the preferred type of legislation, which indicated their regulatory regimes. These were: (a) liberal, (b) prescribed and (c) nationalised (state-controlled) (the initial coding is illustrated in Table 4.1 and 4.2).

Through the open coding, each Member State was allocated a position between one and twelve on the matrix. A totally free market would be at point one on the scale, while a state controlled market would be at point twelve. This is not to say that there are no differentiation's within each market type, as

Table 4.1 and 4.2 display, but it does allow a means of defining different regulatory environments. Initial open coding allowed a comparative analysis of the regulatory environments of the individual Member States and to illustrate the process involved in the pursuit of a single market in relation to the normative perceptions of legislation and market norms. Each state has a different cultural tradition in relation to financial institutions and investment. These are illustrated through historical attitudes and economic ideologies, which in turn are exemplified through legislation and the subsequent regulation relating to life insurance (Hofstede, 1995; 1995). Basically, through coding the research is identifying particular phenomena in the data and grouping concepts around them. This reduces the number of units with which the research needs to work. "The process of grouping concepts that seem to pertain to the same phenomenon is called categorising" (Strauss and Corbin, 1990; p 65) (see Table 4.2). "Once our attention is fixed on a category, we begin to examine and discover emergent properties about the category by constantly coding and analysing. Such categories and properties only conceptualise what we see, but with the theoretical codes we form the connections between them which yield hypotheses-which in turn suggests how the incidents and categories thereof may be related to each other" (Glaser, 1992; p 39).

Liberal Regulatory Environments

A liberal regulatory environment lies between one and four on the twelve-point scale and is characterised by the basic premise of self-regulation with minimal legislation. Four EU life insurance industries were identified as having relatively liberal environments in respect of their legislation and subsequent regulations. They were Eire, Luxembourg, the Netherlands and the UK. These life insurance regulatory structures were perceived as relatively liberal in comparison with other EU Member States. However, one may consider that the Irish system, although until 1936 extremely free, was close to the prescribed regulatory environment. Neither the UK, Luxembourg, nor the Netherlands were disposed to regulations which demand governmental approval with regard to policy design or premium rates, and traditionally the Irish regulation was left in the hands of an actuary, though in 1984 financial tests were implemented in Eire.

Fundamentally, prior to 1936, " . . . the general character and operation of the Irish market resembled that of the UK. . . . In 1936, however, the Irish insurance market became protected so far as entry was concerned . . . an insurance company would not be granted a licence. In Ireland there are technical reserves, minimum solvency and guarantee funds for life insurers. However, the regulatory authority has the power to take action if the solvency level of a life company is endangered" (ibid, p 153).

The Irish regulatory environment is not as free as the other liberal environments. This is due to the process of Europeanisation that has been apparent in this market. The Irish market has brought in, to a far greater extent than the UK, the European Union's (Life Insurance) regulations on top of the EU Minimum Solvency Margin Directive (1979) and therefore one may argue that it borders the prescribed regulatory environment. "Traditionally the minister left detailed financial control of authorised life insurers in the hands of the company actuary. Here again, the European influence has brought about change through the introduction of three financial tests: technical and mathematical reserves, minimum solvency margin and certification of returns for all life insurers" (ibid, p 156).

However, ultimately it was judged that the Irish life market was not prescribed because life insurance company returns are completed and submitted to the ministry, which as with the UK and Dutch regulatory environments, ensured solvency margin requirements.

Luxembourg also adhered to EU legislation and its legislation of 1984 incorporated two Directives; the Co-insurance Directive (1978) and Life Assurance Directive (1979). However, it is primarily concerned with the separation of life and non-life insurance with only a passing interest in solvency margins.

One may consider that Luxembourg regulation was the most liberal in Europe as neither policy wording nor rates were open to supervision. Luxembourg mainly relies on the industry itself to undertake supervision and where problems arise, the Officer of the Commissioner for Insurance (OCI) is consulted. However, the OCI does have some power and can force insurance companies to comply with Article 18 of Insurance legislation (24 Feb 1984) and may ultimately withdraw approval. This legislation " . . .modified existing legislation in order to bring it into line with existing EU directives" (ibid p 202) (Co-insurance Directive 78/473 and the First Life Assurance Directive 79/267). It was considered that the first of these enabled EU risks to be covered through a lead insurer by a number of Member States. "Since it is the lead insurer who agrees the premium rate and conditions, the State (Member State) of the risk would have been able to use the mechanisms applied to insurers established in its territory to ensure that the insurance product contained in the co-insurance contract matched in every way what locally established insurers provided. The participation of insurers from other states would thus have no effect, from the customer's point of view, apart from making it easier to find direct cover (without recourse to reinsurance) for large risks" (Pool, 1990; p 39 author's brackets).

Fundamentally, companies in Luxembourg were closely monitored and adhered to Article 4.1 of the 1984 legislation which states that " . . . undertakings shall not be granted approval unless they assume one of the following forms: limited company, company limited by shares, mutual insurance association, or co-operative society" (Financial Times, 1992; p 204). Even the liberal markets have some form of regulation. However, in the case of Luxembourg it was minimal in respect of life insurance and external companies were taking advantage of this factor. "The market . . . is liberally regulated with little involvement in the supervision of policy wordings or rates. . . . Supervision is based on firm principles but exercised in a flexible way, minimising unnecessary bureaucracy" (ibid).

The Dutch industry was supervised by an independent agency called the Verzekeringskamer (VK), and companies report to this agency which enables governmental control over investment regulations and solvency margins. Each of the Member States' regulatory systems rely on some reporting to a regulatory body.

Supervision in all four liberal regulatory environments was based on the concepts of self-regulation and self-determination in respect of both products and premiums. This is interposed by a regulatory structure of minimal prescription, which mainly determines insolvency regulations and supervisory bodies. With regard to the Netherlands the main legislation over the last 70 years has been 'Wet op Levensverzekering-bedrijf' (WOL) established in 1922 in the wake of two company insolvency's. This legislation was superseded in 1987 by the 'Wet Toezicht Verzekerings-bedrijf' (WTV) which monitored company insolvency margins through VK supervision and brought Dutch legislation into line with that of the EU. This indicated that European legislation affected the national and consequently impinged on the normative experience of the Member State. Such is also clear within the Irish market where its most recent legislation attempted to bring it in line with that of the EU.

In the Netherlands, supervision " . . . is of a predominantly liberal character, with the emphasis on retro-active financial supervision. The insurance company can therefore in principle determine its own company strategy (such as premiums and conditions) in accordance with its own opinion within the limits and rules laid down in the law. . . . The liberal supervision appears to protect the insured public adequately, and is efficient from an economic point of view, in that most Dutch insurance products are generally priced lower than in other European countries which operate stricter supervision" (ibid, p 213).

The UK industry was supervised primarily through the Department of Trade and Industry (DTI) with regard to solvency control, which relied on the principle of 'freedom with disclosure'. In general, " . . . insurers are free to compete as they choose in the marketplace, provided that they meet certain requirements designed to ensure the continuing solvency of all entities underwriting policies of insurance" (Financial Times, 1992; p 291). However, following membership of the EU and a number of company failures, the regulatory framework was intensified " . . . partly through the perceived need to protect policy-holders . . . and partly as a result of changes arising from the implementation of European Community directives" (ibid). Minimum valuations of liabilities were identified by a supervisor and the life office 'freedom with disclosure' allowed the actuary liberty to initiate: reserve calculations; premium calculations; product design; investment choice with regard to reserves. The actuary was however, statutorily bound to ensure office solvency and meet minimum reserve levels and asset cover.

In the UK, the Insurance Companies Act (1982) and the Insurance Companies Accounts and Statements Regulations (1983), ensured publications of balance sheets, a life fund account and annual valuations. The Policyholders Protection Act (1975) as amended by the Policyholders Protection Act (1997), determined that in the event of insolvency's a fund is available, paid into by the industry as a whole, which covers 90% of policy-holder losses.

The Financial Services Act (1986) initiated trading supervision through the Life Assurance and Unit Trusts Regulatory Organisation (LAUTRO) and the Financial Intermediaries Managers and Brokers Association (FIMBRA). The Financial Services Act polarised agents into two categories; independent brokers were tied to FIMBRA; and company representatives who sell only the products of a certain company to LAUTRO. The Act (1986) ensured that independents follow certain regulations which include detailed record keeping, disclosure of commission and best advice (this may be described as an undertaking by the broker to ensure that the proposed investment meets the customer's needs at least to the extent that any other product may). However although these bodies are independent in name, they are tied to the insurance business. This has been illustrated by the shift toward a body with greater independence, the PIA. Of course, this has recently been surpassed by the Labour party's plan for a regulatory body which will oversee the whole of the sector; the Financial Services Authority (FSA) Indeed, through these provisions, one could argue that the UK was moving toward the Belgian model.

Adherence to such regulations proved to be expensive and to cut costs, many small and medium independents tied themselves to insurance companies. Many banks and building societies have also given up their independent status, although many banks have moved further into the life and pensions market by initiating their own subsidiary life offices. Consequently, there was an element of co-operation between banks and insurance companies in the UK market, although this was tainted with a growing propensity towards competition.

Although there are similarities between these four Member States in that they each fall into the liberal category, there are also differences between them. As it is generally agreed that a totally free market is an abstract notion (as some form of regulation is always necessary), none of the Member States can be given a number one on the matrix scale (see Life Insurance Regulation Matrix One, Fig 4.1). Consequently, the most liberal market (Luxembourg) is at point two. Luxembourg is self-regulated. However, when problems do arise, the Officer of the Commissioner for Insurance (OCI) is consulted under its general insurance legislation. In considering the Luxembourg situation, one must be aware of the small size of the market and the ease with which it may be monitored.

The UK and the Netherlands had very similar regulatory environments and both may be positioned at point three within the matrix (see Life Insurance Regulation Matrix One, Fig 4.1). As indicated above, the UK predominantly relied on 'freedom with disclosure' which allowed an actuary the discretion to initiate reserve calculations; premium calculations; and investment choices regarding reserves. The actuary was, however, obliged to report this information to the Department of Trade and Industry (DTI) and is statutorily bound to ensure solvency levels, minimum reserve levels and asset cover. Of course, as indicated above, this has and in 2000 was still in the process of change.

The Dutch life insurance industry was also supervised through a regulatory institution which, although independent, was still sympathetic toward the industry and is mainly concerned with minimal supervision of insolvency regulations. Legislation is minimal, however the most recent brings it into line with general European legislation.

The Irish environment was the most closely regulated in the liberal category and borders the prescribed. Traditionally, Irish supervision (which corresponds with the number four on the matrix) was left in the hands of an actuary (see Life Insurance Regulation Matrix One, Fig 4.1). However, it had tighter regulations and was more closer to EU legislation than any of the liberal markets. In Eire, there were technical reserves, minimum solvency delineation's and guarantee funds are required. Ultimately, the authorities could take action if solvency levels were threatened.

Therefore, liberal regulatory environments are similar in respect of ideology in that they have liberal legislation ethos and limited regulation. However, despite these similarities each market has distinct differences. It could be argued that the reason for this lies in the regulation which has been defined by Member State legislation. One may consider that the differences relate to a cultural existence that is manifest in the economic sphere through definite legislation, regulation and institutional norms. The differences between the Member States in this area do, however, seem to be diminishing, as the European legal system becomes more apparent. All four above Member States have had to bring themselves into line with EU legislation, which for them, means moving towards more rather than less regulation.

PRESCRIBED REGULATORY ENVIRONMENTS

This section provides an explanation of what may be described as prescribed regulatory environments. Germany is the Member State with the most prescriptive regulation whereas Spain and Denmark have a little less; Belgium leans furthest in the direction of the liberal. Indeed, one may consider

Belgium as a compromise between the liberal and prescribed regulatory environment types and one, which could typify European regulations.

A prescribed regulatory environment lies between five and eight on the scale and within this range one is looking at moderate to tight legislation but without or with limited state interference in the companies themselves. The comparative analysis and open coding has identified four Member States with lesser or greater degrees of prescription and identified their position on the matrix. Belgium, point five on the scale, Spain and Denmark, point six, and Germany, point eight. One may argue, that through its legislative programme the French regulatory environment falls into this category. However, at the time of the study, it still had a preponderance of state ownership and will be treated as a nationalised regulatory environment.

In the past the Belgian environment has had liberal life insurance regulation and until 1930 supervision of the system was not contemplated. However, in general, the regulatory environment has been indicative of the state of play at the European level because in the post-war period the Belgian structure evolved in line with EU directives.

Belgian supervision was extended in 1975 and all insurance was brought under the auspices of the Office De Controle des Assurance (OCA). The OCA was monitored by the Minister for Economic Affairs. However, the process was undertaken through a committee, which interacted with the ministry and indicated necessary changes in respect of legislation and how it should be administered. The committee consisted of six members who were drawn not only from insurance but other areas: the legal profession, other financial institutions and academia. As many areas as possible were taken into consideration; consequently, profitability is not the only benchmark, but it is an important consideration. Indeed, the OCA undertook close supervision of existing regulations. It did not determine policy rates, it simply ensured that legislation was activated and adhered to through three main areas:

(1) Technical Supervision.
(2) Legal supervision of compliance with regulations.
(3) Financial supervision.

One may contend that the Belgian method displayed a consultative (and more democratic) dimension and one that gives an indication of how legislative decisions and supervision may be conducted in the future. Indeed, as noted above, the Belgian approach may display the traits of the evolving SEM in life insurance and illustrate an attainable compromise between the different life insurance regulatory environments.

The Spanish regulatory environment was similar to the Belgian, although it did have its own distinct historical route. Until the death of Franco in the mid-seventies and the implementation of the new Spanish constitution in 1978, insurance was supervised by legislation passed in 1912. Indeed, it was not until the Socialist party attempted a reformation of the regulatory system in the early 1980s that any real legislation was formalised. The Insurance Control and Supervision Act, (Ley de Ordenación del Seguro Privado) was implemented in 1984 and with a royal decree in 1985 formed the basis of control and supervision in the Spanish market. This legislation looked towards a number of changes in Spanish regulations; these included solvency fields, policyholder protection, professional standards and the re-grouping of companies through mergers. Supervision in Spain was straightforward: companies applied to operate in the market then looked to register. Once registered, companies were monitored in respect of solvency, advertising and products, etc by the Dirección General de Seguro, which reports directly to the ministry.

In Germany, life insurance is tightly controlled and companies have to seek approval with regard to product design and policy terms. There are two main pieces of legislation, which relate to insurance. These are Versicherungsvertragsgesetz (VVG), which relates to regulated the relationship between insurance companies, the insured, policy-holders and beneficiaries; and the Versicherungsaufssichtsgesetz (VAG) which was responsible for the regulations relating to the supervisory body Bundesaufsichtsamt fur das Versicherungswesen (BAV). "The underlying principle of the insurance supervisory law is the system of 'substantive state supervision' (materielle Staatsaufsicht)" (Financial Times, 1992; p 103). Within this framework " . . . the operations of an insurance company are controlled legally, economically and financially from the beginning of its activities to the end of its winding up procedure" (ibid).

BAV designated premium rates, a specified mortality table for each product, and maximum interest rates and expenses. Such a situation induced a small differentiation in the prices of products and led to limited competition regarding product range. Because most companies had a complete product range, competition emanated from bonus distribution. Between 95% and 98%

of profit was distributed to the policyholders. A general regulation indicated that 90% of total profit should be distributed, but competition forced bonuses up.

Denmark was supervised through a legislative framework, which established a number of acts. These included the Insurance Companies Act (1981) which prescribes public supervision and company format. The Business Competition Act (1989), which supervised monopoly and price control, the Insurance Contracts Act (1930), which concerned relationships between insurance parties, i.e. each other and customers; and the Marketing Act (1975) under which the ombudsman adjudicated whether insurance company marketing activities were in line with accepted practices. To ensure adherence to legislation and compliance with law 127 (3) a division of the Danish Ministry of Finances supervised the industry.

As mentioned above, the Dirección General de Seguros, an insurance board directly responsible to the Ministry of Finances, supervised the Spanish life insurance industry. Spain developed the fastest growing life insurance industry in premium income terms in recent years indicating the largest growth rate in the EU. In the latter part of the 1980s, this was as high as 70% (Sigma, Swiss Re; 4/90 - 1/92). The reason for this growth was the social security crisis, which has prompted individuals to arrange their own pensions, which had subsequently improved sales.

In Belgium, formal approval regarding conditions and rates was abandoned and the principles in relation to insurance governance reformed. Belgian legislation was specific in content but it allowed general applications in respect of product by product profitability and the process of contractual obligations in individual cases. Effectively, supervision was non-systematic and allowed for both prudence as well as profitability. Consequently, both company and consumer needs were dealt with through the existing legislation. The Danish regulatory environment was a little more prescribed in respect of this and Danish companies submitted detailed financial statements, which included annual accounts and group reports. However, in respect of solvency margins, technical reserves and capital adequacy, EU directives provided the legislation.

The Danish life insurance market was not as liberal as its non-life insurance market and this illustrated the limited onus the Danes put on EU legislation to indicate their regulatory structure. There are more comprehensive directives in respect of non-life insurance, which the Danish have subsequently implemented.

The German environment was highly regulated. This ensured high consumer protection and safe but low-yielding products. Historically, Germany has undergone two periods of hyper-inflation. This may have much to do with a risk-averse attitude and the factor of limited product innovation. Once again, the prevailing legislation and consequent regulatory structure was indicated by cultural and socio-historical circumstances.

As with the liberal regulatory environments, the prescribed environments illustrate the changes that EU legislation is bringing about with extreme clarity. The lesser-prescribed markets have the fewest changes to make and this is apparent in their adroitness at bringing in European directives. This was particularly so of Belgium. However, in this respect Belgium was followed closely by both Spain and Denmark. Until 1990 a life insurance company in the Danish Market was state controlled. As EU legislation changed, so too did the Danish market. Consequently, an interaction is apparent between national legislation, European legislation and regulation formulation.

The Danish market was marginally tighter than the Belgian with respect to regulation (see Life Insurance Regulation, Matrix One Fig 4.1). In Belgium supervision was non-systematic and negotiation was apparent, whereas, the Danish system called for detailed financial statements i.e. annual accounts and group reports. However, in respect of solvency margins, technical reserves and capital adequacy legislation, Denmark and Belgium were very similar.

Spain has undergone a legislative transformation since the late 1970s and this brought about many changes in life insurance regulations. Changes have included the introduction of solvency fields, policyholder protection, and professional standards. Effectively, the Spanish regulatory environment was very similar to the Danish and was consequently, also given a six on the scale (see Life Insurance Regulation Matrix One, Fig 4.1).

Within the prescribed market environments there are differing amounts of prescription in that some border on the liberal and others on the state-controlled. Germany is the most prescribed (point eight on the scale), whereas in Spain and Denmark, (point six on the scale) although regulation is tight, more flexibility is allowed. Belgian regulation (point five on the scale) indicated most succinctly the impending single market environment in respect of its existing legislation. What was apparent was the consultative nature of Belgian supervision and how this did not negate but was indicative of EU guidelines. As with the liberal environments, a convergence procedure can be detected with regard to EU legislation and consequent regulatory requirements.

State-Controlled Regulatory Environments

The state-controlled regulatory environments were placed between nine and twelve on the scale; and the open coding process placed four Member States in this category. These are France, Italy, Portugal and Greece. At the time of the study, each had a state-controlled element to its life insurance market in that there was a preponderance of state ownership in respect of life insurance companies.

In France, state-control was a post-war phenomenon, while in Portugal nationalisation did not occur until 1974. The Greek market had not been formally nationalised, but the market was state controlled. Within the matrix the Member State markets are determined in respect of legislation on the one hand and the percentage of the market controlled by state run companies on the other. Thus, France was point nine, Italy point ten and Greece and Portugal point eleven (see Life Insurance Regulation Matrix One, Fig 4.1).

In France, regulation was extensive. However, this was changing continually. "French insurers used to be seen as . . . hidebound by regulatory red tape of the former all powerful Direction des Assurances . . . this over simplified view is now dating rapidly" (Financial Times, 1992; p 81). The principles of state control were laid down by statute in the 1930s and pertain (ed) both to contractual obligations and to the financial structure of the companies. As regards the legal status of insurance contracts, the controlling authority (until July 1991 the Direction des Assurances) had wide prerogatives, from the drafting of the legislation to the enforcement of compliance by the companies. . . An important aspect of this control was the obligation of insurers to obtain official approval for all new products or types of contract. The controlling authority also regulates and watches over the financial and prudential requirements (equity, computation of reserves and investment strategy) prescribed by the Code des Assurances" (ibid, p 87 author's brackets).

The Greek and Italian life insurance industries were state-controlled in that state-owned companies exist in the market and enjoy certain benefits because of this. In Greece, 45% of the market was controlled by eight state-controlled insurance companies (Financial Times 1992). "The Greek market has traditionally been highly regulated . . . this situation is in large part a legacy of heavy government control . . . [which has] led to administrative rigidity and as a consequence high operating costs" (ibid, p 143).

In Italy, insurance companies surrendered a percentage of their business to the state controlled Instituto Nazionale delle Assicurazioni (INA). Following 1 April 1987, life companies writing life business for less than 6 years give 30% of new business, for 6-10 years, 20% and for over 10 years, 10%. This led to unfair competition in the market and allowed the evolution and maintenance of a dominant position (Munich Re, 1988). The Instituto per la Vigilanza sull Assicurazioni Private de Interesse Collectivo (ISVAP) supervised the Italian market. This was set up by the Ministry of Industry and Commerce and gives approval to insurance matters on its findings. There was no legislation in respect of this but the market accepted the situation.

Each Member State was highly regulated (even though Italian regulation is not legislated, it was universally accepted). However, each Member State was becoming less regulated as EU legislation dictated. In Portugal, the position was that 51% of the sector remained in the hands of the state and 33% in France (Munich Re, 1988). In all cases, the state-controlled institutions were the largest in the Member State life insurance markets.

Regulation in France was supervised by the 'Direction des Assurance' which the Ministry of Economy set up. Rules were strict with regard to individual life insurance business. Approval was needed for product design, premiums and policy conditions. However, changes were underway to alleviate these restrictions. There was also much consultation with regard to regulation changes, and prior to any changes the 'Conseil National des Assurance' (made up of representatives of the insurance industry and authorities) was referred to. There was also a powerful consumer lobby in France. which was also consulted.

Figure 4.1: Life Insurance Regulation Matrix One

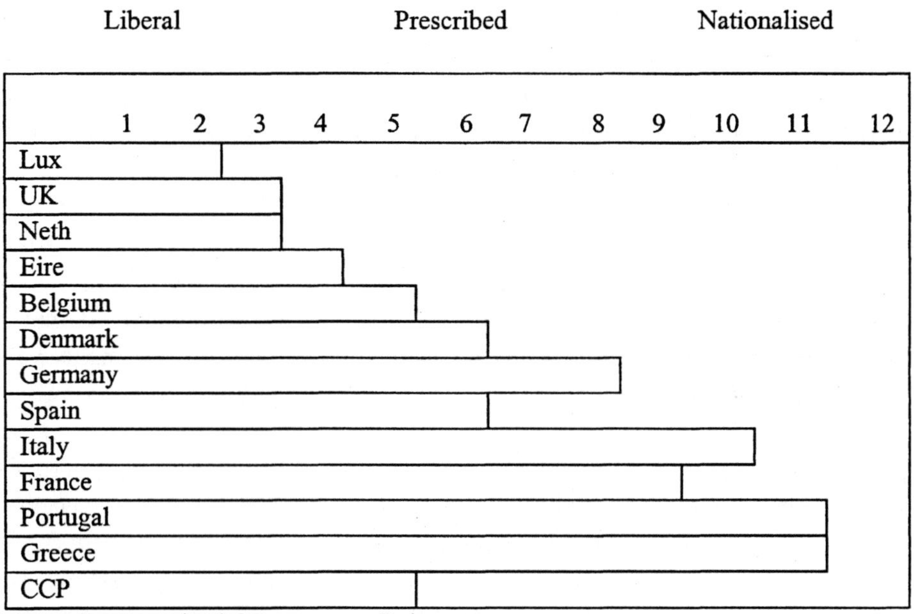

CCP = Compromised Convergence Point

Matrix compiled from an analysis of Munich Re. (1988), Financial Times (1992), Sigma

Re. (1988-93), Pool (1991), BIIC and CEA Working Papers.

The Portuguese environment was supervised by the 'Instituto de Seguros de Portugal' (ISP). This was founded in 1982 and consequently initiated the 'Plano da Explarocao' in 1985 this outlined a standard basis for life offices. The ISP exercised complete control over the life insurance market; approval for product design, premium rates, and policy wording had to be applied for and quarterly returns inclusive of profit projections had to be submitted to it by all life insurance offices. This, one may argue, was a market in which a company was open to total scrutiny.

From June 1988 there had been greater liberty regarding expenses although the ISP still determined the mortality base, and the technical interest rate. However, it was expected that because of extended freedoms with regard to non-life tariffs these would follow in the life insurance market. "The insurance market is tightly controlled by government regulation. All insurance businesses must be approved by the Portugese Ministry of Finance" (Financial

Times, 1992; p 232). The Ministry of Finance consulted with the ISP prior to any approval. In both France and Portugal, the banking sector had recognised its potential with regard to distribution. This was especially so in France where the market was more developed. These distribution channels have mainly been used in rural areas and as Portugal was primarily a peasant-based society they were used to penetrate this market. In Greece, the insurance sector was dominated by the banks, which were in turn controlled by the state.

All four state-controlled life insurance regulatory environments were moving toward more liberal trading structures (even though for some Member States this needed to be forced). Each recognised the changes needed to facilitate competition in the single market while EU directives attempt to harmonise supervision in the direction of free market environments. The French environment could be described as the weakest state-controlled regulatory structure. This may be illustrated by the failure of the French government's attempt to force a merger between two insurance companies where the companies involved did not discern market benefit. But it succeeded in relation to a bank and insurance company merger where market benefit was recognised. Greek life insurance, as with the financial sector as a whole, was highly regulated. One may consider that this is the legacy of heavy control in the immediate post-war period. However, usually following European Commission insistence, regulation is slowly being liberalised to comply with EU legislation.

In both France and Portugal, the banking sector had recognised its potential with regard to distribution. This was especially so in France where the market was more developed. These distribution channels have mainly been used in rural areas and as Portugal was primarily a peasant-based society they were used to penetrate this market. In Greece, the insurance sector was dominated by the banks, which were in turn controlled by the state.

Regulation was tight in all four, state-controlled life insurance regulatory environments and is typical of a nationalised ethos. Yet in each Member State changes were underway to allow greater freedom and enable competitive markets in line with the single market environment. Each of the state-controlled structures had a different nationalised tradition and on the regulation matrix, they range between nine and eleven (see Life Insurance Regulation Matrix One, Fig 4.1 above). However, each Member State within this category was changing its legislation, which would allow greater freedom and was in line with the impending SEM.

REGULATORY ENVIRONMENT SURVEY AND ANALYSIS

To supplement the categorisation and provide further coding of the EU regulatory environments, a survey (survey A) was conducted to investigate the perceptions of life insurance companies throughout the EU. The main purpose of the questionnaire was to gain an understanding of how the Member State industries viewed their own regulatory environments and what they considered would be most advantageous for them at the EU level. The questions were formulated in relation to the above regulation categories dimensions and properties and emphasised basic questions such as **When? Where? What?** and **How Much?** The questions allowed the research to move beyond the " . . . technical literature and personal experience" (Strauss and Corbin, 1990; p 76). Indeed, the survey assisted and enhanced the inductive process (ibid).

Survey A
A Survey of the European Life Insurance Industry

(1) How liberal or state controlled is your national life insurance market?
(2) Where would you place the Single European Market (SEM) life insurance sector in respect of regulatory freedom?
(3) What type of regulatory environment do you consider that the SEM should be to allow your company its greatest advantage?
(4) What type of regulatory environment do you consider the SEM in life insurance should be to allow the greatest consumer protection?
(5) What type of regulatory environment do you consider the SEM in life insurance should be to allow the greatest consumer choice?
(Respondents were asked to give their answers on the regulation scale of 1-12 which was fully explained to them)

The survey was sent out between Nov 1993 and Jan 1994 and was made up of 300 questionnaires (the sample was constructed on the availability of addresses) and a total of 121 completed questionnaires were received by the author and broken down by Member State as follows;

UK = 36
Germany = 25
Netherlands = 15
Italy = 12
France = 17
Belgium, Spain & Eire (Other) = 16
Total = 121

To provide a more objective analysis of the data, the results of the survey were added to the coding and comparative analysis undertaken above. This enabled a *postpositivist* analysis in that there is the recognition of an abstract reality juxtaposed with the inability of the human intellect to perceive it perfectly. Consequently, the work recognises that a perfectly objective comprehension of reality is always undermined by the subjectivity of the researcher and the researched. The comparative analysis and initial coding indicated both the subjectivity of the author with the objectivity of the data itself, i.e. the legislation and subsequent regulatory environments. The survey results illustrate the subjectivity of the questions with the pursued objectivity of the respondents.

Table 4.3: Perceived Regulatory Environment

	Liberal %	Prescribed %	State Controlled %	Mean (SD)	Categorisation in Figure. 4.1
UK	66.7	33.3	0.0	4 (1.3)	Liberal
Germany	4.0	52.0	44.0	8 (1.9)	Prescribed
Italy	0.0	66.7	33.3	8 (1.0)	S/Controlled
Neth	93.3	6.7	0.0	3 (1.0)	Liberal
France	12.6	18.8	67.8	8 (2.3)	S/Controlled
Other	31.3	62.6	6.3	5 (1.6)	Lib/Prescribed
All	38.1	40.5	21.5	6 (2.4)	N/A

246. 280.6

These two sources compiled together attempt as objective understanding as possible, of the Member States' regulatory environments and what they wished of the embryonic SEM in life insurance.

As noted above, the respondents were asked five questions:

Question One asked how liberal or state-controlled the Member State believed their own national life insurance regulatory environment to be. As with the comparative analysis, the responses were categorised into liberal, prescribed and nationalised markets, for each of the eight responding Member States. The results of question one are summarised in Table 4.3.

The responses summarised in Table 4.3 (Perceived Regulatory Environment) were subsequently used to amend the regulation matrix (Life Insurance Regulation Matrix One, Fig 4.4). The means of the responses illustrated in Table 4.3 were averaged with the assessment indicated in Fig 4.1. This gave equal weight to both the initial coding and categorisation of the regulatory environments and the further open coding regarding the perceptions of the life insurance industry. Indeed, the further coding procedure led to only marginal changes to the categorisation of the markets, indicating a degree of agreement between the two sources of data (see Life Insurance Regulation Matrix Two Fig 4.2).

Figure 4.2 Life Insurance Regulation Matrix Two

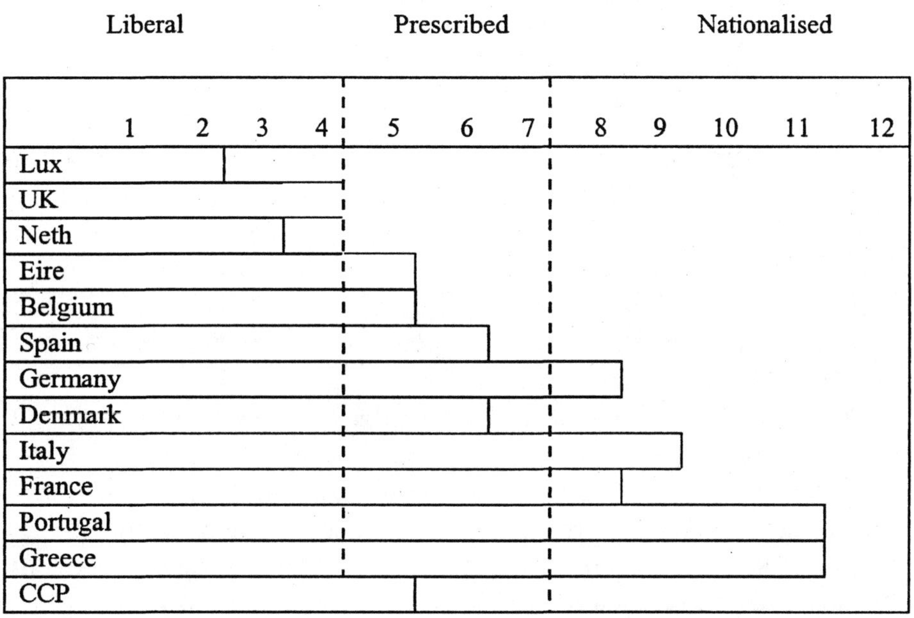

Question Two asked the companies where they would position the SEM at that moment in time in respect of its regulatory environment. This again was on a scale of 1-12 that categorised the regulatory environments as liberal, prescribed and nationalised (the responses are summarised in Table 4.3). In general, there was agreement that the SEM as it stood was located between 7.0 and 5.0 with the mean of the responses of all Member States equal to 6.0, and a 0.standard deviation of 1.5.

Table 4.4 EU Regulatory Environment

	Liberal %	Prescribed %	State Controlled %	Mean (SD)	Categorisation in Figure. 4.1
UK	13.9	69.5	16.7	6 (1.3)	Liberal
Germany	36.0	64.0	0	5 (1.5)	Prescribed
Italy	26.7	73.3	0	5 (1.6)	S/Controlled
Neth	35.7	64.3	0	5 (1.7)	Liberal
France	12.6	62.6	25.0	7 (1.3)	S/Controlled
Other	25.0	68.8	6.3	6 (1.9)	Lib/Prescribed
All	28.3	61.7	10.0	6 (1.5)	N/A

Question Three asked the respondents to indicate which type of regulatory environment would give their company its greatest advantage. The results are summarised in Table 4.5. Generally, the Member States pursue regulatory environments that are less regulated than or similar to their own. However, there are differences between the amount of liberality that each state considers should be allowed. This suggests that a compromise needs to be reached between the prescribed and liberal markets (such a compromise is shown in the Life Insurance Regulation Matrix, Two Fig 4.2).

Question Four asked what type of regulatory structure would allow the greatest consumer protection. Question Five asked which would allow the greatest consumer choice. Each of these enabled an understanding of what the respondents considered a regulatory environment should entail and gave insight into their perceptions in respect of the first three questions. Responses are summarised in Tables 4.6 and 4.7.

Table 4.5 Perceived Most Advantageous EU Regulatory Environment

	Liberal %	Prescribed %	State Controlled %	Mean (SD)	Categorisation in Figure. 4.1
UK	72.2	27.8	0	3 (1.6)	Liberal
Germany	32.0	68.0	0	6 (1.3)	Prescribed
Italy	66.7	33.4	0	4 (1.9)	S/Controlled
Neth	92.9	7.1	0	3 (0.5)	Liberal
France	29.4	70.6	0	6 (1.4)	S/Controlled
Other	50.0	50.0	0	5 (1.2)	Lib/Prescribed
All	58.3	41.7	0	4 (1.5)	N/A

Table 4.6 Best Perceived Environment for Consumer Protection

	Liberal %	Prescribed %	State Controlled %	Mean (SD)	Categorisation in Figure. 4.1
UK	22.2	63.9	13.1	6 (2.3)	Liberal
Germany	20.0	56.0	24.0	7 (2.1)	Prescribed
Italy	50.0	50.0	0	5 (1.2)	S/Controlled
Neth	20.0	80.0	0	5 (0.9)	Liberal
France	11.8	52.9	35.3	7 (2.2)	S/Controlled
Other	25.0	62.5	12.5	6 (1.1)	Lib/Prescribed
All	30.8	53.3	15.8	6 (1.7)	N/A

These responses seem to suggest that the respondents were aware of what was meant by the term regulatory environment. Furthermore, there was a form of hegemony when it came to understanding the survey and the concept of a regulatory environment. However, this is more explicit in terms of the understanding of consumer choice. Indeed, in the construction of the Third Life Assurance Directive, it was around these very issues (the extent of interference regarding choice and protection) that the debates revolved. This is further illustrated in the next chapter.

Table 4.7 Best Perceived Environment for Consumer Choice

	Liberal %	Prescribed %	State Controlled %	Mean (SD)	Categorisation in Figure 4.1
UK	86.1	13.9	0	2 (1.5)	Liberal
Germany	96.0	4.0	0	2 (0.9)	Prescribed
Italy	83.3	16.7	0	4 (0.8)	S/Controlled
Neth	100.0	0	0	3 (1.0)	Liberal
France	70.6	17.7	11.8	4 (2.4)	S/Controlled
Other	88.1	12.5	0	3 (1.4)	Lib/Prescribed
All	87.6	10.5	1.7	3 (1.1)	N/A

Additionally, a series of cross-tabulations were undertaken and a verification of the independence of question one to the other four questions was performed. Two verification methods were utilised. Initially, verification was concerned with whether the respondents' perceptions of their current regulatory systems (question one) was independent of their perceptions of:

(a) the then present perceived EU regulatory system (question two).
(b) the preferred regulatory system (question three).
(c) the best regulation to ensure consumer protection (question four).
(d) the best regulation to ensure consumer choice (question five).

Firstly, the responses to question one were cross-tabulated sequentially with the responses to questions 2-5. Secondly, in each case, a chi-squared test of independence was undertaken. The results are illustrated in Tables 4.8-4.13.

Table 4.8: Q1 - Q2
Perceived Existing SEM Regulatory Environment

Perceived current regulatory environment	Liberal	Prescribed	Totals
Liberal	14	32	46
Prescribed	9	40	49
State Controlled	6	20	26
Totals	29	92	121

$$\chi^2 = 2.07\ (\chi^2_{crit} = 5.99)$$

In this case, the hypothesis of independence at 5% level of significance cannot be rejected.

In general terms, prior to the Third Life Assurance Directive, the Member States did not consider that their regulatory environments were similar to the SEM in general.

Table 4.9 suggests that Member States, when pursuing the SEM, would generally look for a regulatory environment either similar to or a little more liberal than their own. This is supported by the dependency ratio, which suggests that the responses to question one are not independent of the responses to question three. That is, if respondents thought they had a liberal environment, they would like the SEM, to be more liberal or created in their own image. This is also indicative of the prescribed regulatory environments. However, the state-controlled Member States are generally looking for prescribed regulatory environments but some wish for a more liberal environment. Indeed, there is a shift toward more liberal/prescribed regulatory environments, with none wishing to remain state-controlled. Consequently, in the creation of the SEM, the sticking point would be found between the degree of prescription and liberality within the new environment.

Table 4.9: Q1 - Q3
Preferred SEM regulatory environment for company

Perceived current regulatory environment	Liberal	Prescribed	Totals
Liberal	40	6	46
Prescribed	21	28	49
State Controlled	8	18	26
Totals	69	54	121

$$\chi^2 = 28.14\ (\chi^2_{crit} = 5.991)$$

In this case the hypothesis of independence can be rejected at 5% (and 1%) levels.

Tables 4.10 and 4.11 illustrate that there is a general perception that prescribed environments are better for consumer protection with 64% of those in liberal environments agreeing with this. Additionally, there is nearly unanimous agreement that liberal environments allow for the greatest consumer choice. In both instances, the work was able to reject independence at the 5% level between the responses to questions one and questions four and five.

Table 4.10: Q1 - Q4
Regulatory environment best for consumer protection

Perceived current regulatory environment	Liberal	Prescribed/Nat	Totals
Liberal	15	27	42
Prescribed	6	43	49
State Controlled	7	23	30
Totals	28	93	121

$$\chi^2 = 6.86\ (\chi^2_{crit} = 5.99)$$

In this case the hypothesis of independence can just be rejected at the 5% level of significance (but not at the 1% level).

Table 4.11: Q1 - Q5
Regulatory environment best for consumer choice

Perceived current regulatory environment	Liberal	Prescribed	Totals
Liberal	45	1	46
Prescribed	40	9	49
State Controlled	21	5	26
Totals	106	15	121

$$\chi^2 = 8.01\ (\chi^2_{crit} = 5.99)$$

In this case we can reject the hypothesis of independence at the 5% level of significance (but not at 1% level). A final area of verification was concerned with investigating whether the respondents' preferred SEM regulatory system (question three) was independent of questions four and five. In both of these tests, independence is rejected. Thus there appears to be a link between the type of market preferred at the European level and what the industry considers as best for the consumer in terms of protection and choice.

Table 4.12: Q3 - Q4
Regulatory environment best for consumer protection

Preferred SEM regulatory environment for our company	Liberal	Prescribed	Totals
Liberal	25	3	28
Prescribed	33	41	74
State Controlled	8	11	19
Totals	66	92	121

$$\chi^2 = 16.6\ (\chi^2_{crit} = 5.99)$$

The hypothesis of independence can be rejected at the 5% and 1% levels.

Table 4.13: Q3 - Q5
Regulatory environment best for consumer choice

Preferred SEM regulatory environment for our company	Liberal	Prescribed	Totals
Liberal	68	1	69
Prescribed	38	14	52
Totals	106	15	121

$$\chi^2 = 17.7\ (\chi^2_{crit} = 3.84)$$

Again the hypothesis of independence can be rejected at 5% (and 1%) levels

Conclusions

Through a comparative analysis of Member State legislation, open coding and categorisation, the data accumulated through the survey and the study of Member States legislation, we have constructed a regulation matrix. This analysis proposes that through the political impetus of the SEA legislation was reformed to meet the needs of what was becoming the normative perception of the evolving SEM. However, it also proposes that the normative concept of the SEM is tempered by the ideas that the industries had of their own trading structures and that these differ from one Member State to the next. This is because each is used to trading in a distinct regulatory environment. This is explicit to the Third Life Assurance Directive with reference to both the process of formulation and the end result. As a state-controlled environment is out of the question in respect of the basic tenets of the treaties and competition policy, the compromise was taking place between the prescribed and liberal regulatory environments. Indeed, it was between these environments that agreement was being reached and a new regulation formed, through the concepts of harmonisation and mutual recognition.

The state-controlled and greater prescribed environments indicate the convergence process with the greatest clarity as these structures are being forced into bringing their supervision into line with the less regulated markets. However, the more liberal regulatory environments also need to change legislation to bring them into line with European directives. The less prescribed and less liberal markets have the fewest changes to make and this is apparent in their adroitness at bringing in the directives. This is particularly so of Belgium and Eire and to a lesser extent Spain, Denmark, the UK and the Netherlands.

The responses to the survey from the UK and Dutch life insurance industries do reveal a preference for a more liberal environment than is perceived to be the case by much of Europe, and one very similar to what is generally understood to be their home market conditions. In short the liberal life industries preferred the new environment to be as similar to their own as possible this would allow greater certainty and profitability. The prescribed markets preferred greater freedom but not enough to put them at a disadvantage in relation to the liberal markets. Finally, the state-controlled industries preferred less regulation on their trading structure. However, the

Italians preferred to pursue a liberal environment, whereas the French would have remained with one that was highly prescribed.

The matrices and tables attempt to identify a compromise point between the Member States. They also allow a more elucidating comparison between the Member State legislative regimes in relation to a specific market. Indeed, it contends that compromise between the Member States allows a directive to be established between 4.5 and 6.5 and that through mutual recognition these points are integrated at the compromise convergence point (5-6 on the matrix) (see Life Insurance Regulation Matrix, Two Fig 4.2). However, in initial negotiations, Member States and national industries are generally looking for legislation and consequent regulation as similar to their own as possible, i.e.. the UK pursuing three and Germany six. Through compromise and a recognition of what the Commission and Europe perceive as necessary, the parameters of a directive are established (this will be discussed further in the following two chapters). This adds an impetus to integration through the recognition of a European market and calls for harmonisation in further areas. This illustrates spillover to the extent that further legislation will be necessary in life insurance and other financial sectors i.e. banking and capital markets. It also illustrates supranationality because the needs of the Commission and treaties are built into the legislation. No one Member State gets all of its own way: the legislation is both a compromise and one which reflects a European perspective.

In general, the frequency tables and cross-tabulations support the view that each Member State is pursuing its own *self-interest* in the creation of the new market. The work now asks where and how does compromise takes place? To answer this question, we examine the creation of the Third Life Assurance Directive and through a number of interviews undertaken at the European decision-making level. The work considers that through an interaction between Member States, interest groups, supranationality and spillover, elements of European integration may be explored.

Chapter Five

DECISION-MAKING MODELS AND EUROPEAN INTEGRATION

I am European, I am no doubt a European intellectual, and I like to recall this to myself, and why would I deny it? In the name of what? But I am not nor do I feel European in every part that is European through and through (Derrida, 1992; p 82).

INTRODUCTION

In Chapter Four we examined the different preferences of regulatory environments that individual Member States hold. The survey indicates the amount of regulation a Member State would feel most acceptable and the demands it would make to ensure its interests. This chapter builds an understanding of how the different positions (regarding regulatory environments) are compromised by the Member States at the European level. To do this and to indicate how the actions of industries/sectors are influential in the process, the analysis provides:

(a) A European Demand Model, which clarifies this process at the EU and Member State level (see Fig 5.1 p 118).
(b) A decision-making model derived empirically through interviews with representatives of EU and Member State level decision-makers (The European Decision-Making Model Fig 5.2 p 152).

(c) A Survey of UK life insurance companies.

This study argues that there is an interaction between economic sectors and political institutions in the decision-making process and that such an interaction may be located in EU decision-making. This is evident in the life insurance industry because of the amount of differing legislation and the consequent difficulty in establishing a SEM. Overall, through an interaction between interest groups and the EU certainty and clarity are provided. The ground rules are indicated and the parameters of policy formulated. However, in the context of supranationality just " . . . as the European Community is itself still developing its institutions and policies, so the interest group system surrounding the EC has yet to reach a stable state. We are still in the relatively early stages of group adjustment to a shift in the locus of power and it, therefore, is not surprising that the process of interest group intermediation is in a state of flux" (Russell, 1988; p 213).

Building on the understanding outlined in the previous chapter, this chapter, questions the extent of the flux and locates the process in a theoretical framework. Ultimately, one may consider that demands are fed into the system by the companies, either straight to legislatures, or channeled by interest groups.

EASTON'S DEMAND FLOW MODEL

Easton (1965) developed a general model of how institutions may channel conflicts into merged ideological patterns. For Easton there are a number of demands on the political system and he considered that " . . . conflicts over demands constitute the flesh and blood of all political systems from the smallest to the largest, from the simplest to the most complex" (Easton, 1965; p 48).

In his model, Easton illustrates how *expectations, public opinion, motivations, ideologies, interests* and *preferences* transfer into wants which become system inputs. With reference to the life insurance industry and the EU, one may consider that there is an over-riding ideology indicated by socio-historic circumstances out of which the other variables emanate. Thus ideology takes the form of Member State understanding of the amount of regulation that is necessary for their environment, e.g. liberal, prescribed or state-controlled. Interests may be viewed as a Member State's most desired point in relation to the specific environments, the most favoured conditions. This illustrates the need for interest groups at a European and national level because they are the most appropriate vehicles to enable compromise. Preferences are linked closely to both ideology and interests and denote those areas most likely to be accepted (the extent of compromise). Motivations include the need to be involved in the discussion process to ensure legislation as close to one's desired position as possible so as not to undermine trading capabilities (to allow for profit maximisation and certainty). These variables are subsequently transferred into demands.

Demands effectively threaten the system and have to be dealt with. Indeed, any surviving system must have created the means by which demands from different parts of the system can be resolved. Easton (1965) considers that there is a general sequence that deals with the stress that demands create:

Stimulus > System > Response > Outcome.

Demands create a disturbance or stimulus and the system feels the effects; system members respond or fail to respond; the result or outcome reveals how well the system has coped with the stress created by the disturbance. Without demands, the system would not know which decisions to make, as it would be unaware of interests.

Consequently, demands are central to Easton's model because they constitute an expression of opinion that forces the decision-making body to deal with the problem. Easton considers that demands may be:

(a) Specific.
(b) Generalised.
(c) Ideological (a set of demands).

These demands are always directed toward the authoritative body (in this case the EU institutions) to take the desired action (one would consider that this held preferences). Effectively, Easton considers that all demands are the same; only the directions are different i.e. those that push for desired action and those that do not.

Easton defines interests as the means by which a person or group attempts to implement fundamental goals. In such a way a law or policy could be said to be made in a person's or group's interest, the realisation of the interest fulfilling a basic goal. Indeed, ". . . interests might easily be confused with demands. However close a connection there may be between the two, it is important to recognise that conceptually, they are quite separate" (Easton, 1965; p 45). He emphasises this point through delineating interests into categories, i.e. subjective and objective interests.

Subjective and Objective Interests

Easton defines interests as " . . . instrumental values, those means through which a person or group seeks to implement what may be considered to be his or its fundamental goals. In this sense, a person may speak of a law or administrative decree or policy as being in his interest. . . . In this instrumental sense, we may describe interest as either subjective or objective" (ibid).

A subjective interest is one where one's own interpretation of what is necessary is paramount, if broader goals are to be recognised. In this context, the analysis will investigate how fundamentally desirable interests of European Member State life insurance industries are met and compromised to ensure desirable system changes, i.e. the move from a national market to cross-border trade.

"From the subjective point of view, the interest of a person is to be found in his own interpretation of what is necessary if he is to realise his broader goals. . . . More usually, in politics, subjective interests would be attributed to groups, as where they are perceived and voiced by an organisation that presumes to speak for its membership at the very least" (Easton, 1965; p 45).

An objective interest could specify criteria that fail to take the interests of the industry into consideration. "An objective interest may be described as those instrumental needs which others attribute to a person or group according to criteria quite independent of the subjective perceptions of that person or group" (ibid).

Easton (1965) identifies the difference between objective and subjective interests; the interviews in below attempt to identify the insurance industry's subjective interests in relation to the objective interests of the EU. A subjective interest is one, which the industry recognises itself and interprets what is necessary if broader goals are to be achieved.

A subjective interest becomes a demand if it is not met; an objective interest becomes a demand if it is not what the industry requires (some of the difficulties regarding this are illustrated in the previous chapter). In this context interaction between the conflicting areas is necessary.

Chapter Four identified subjective interests and Chapter Five explores how they are agreed. We investigate who voices these interests and how they transform into demands. An objective interest may be described as others interpreting the interests of the group. Such an interest would take into consideration external needs that ensure the goal i.e. the regulatory environment. In respect of the life insurance industry, this would take into consideration cross-border trade and the long-term effects of this on the life insurance industry. At this juncture one would be forced to ask from where an objective interest would obtain the information of what is necessary for the industry's survival? And how happy would the industry be in leaving its fate in Europe to objective interests? However, as Easton (1965) indicated, "... the expression of an interest in a matter is not identical with the input of a demand. To become a demand, there needs to be voiced a proposal that authoritative action be taken with regard to it" (p 47).

This work takes Easton's model into account and uses his understanding of inputs to inform the interviews and EU decision-making. The model provides a framework for the study and a means of bridging the gap between the national and EU decision-making institutions and processes (see Fig 5.1).

Figure 5.1

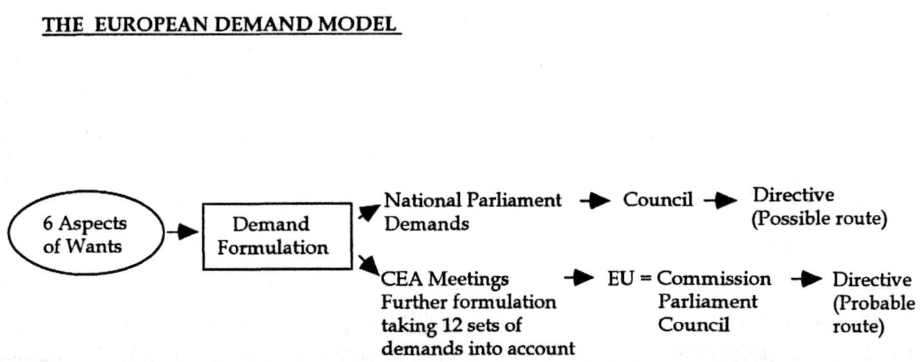

The emphasis on the European dimension intensifies as integration gathers pace and the need to be involved at the European level becomes increasingly apparent. The growth in the number of interest groups and lobbying bodies between direct elections in 1979 and the SEM in 1992 seems to indicate this, as does the growth in the post-SEA era. There are a number of insurance interest groups at the EU level the most important of which is the CEA. At this point both Member State interest groups and insurance companies consider national differences and attempt to reach compromise positions in respect of national ideologies, interests, preferences etc.

Regarding these problems the areas that need investigation are:

(1) How does the national/European life insurance industry recognise its subjective interests with specific reference to the SEM?
(2) Do these interests transfer into demands and how are these demands made of the national or European legislatures?

To enable some answers to these questions, there are five areas that may be investigated and each engenders a certain route that demands may take. These are:

(a) National industries make demands of national legislatures prior to formulation at the European level.
(b) The formulation of demands between national interest groups are compromised between Member State insurance industries at the European level then made of the European and national legislatures.
(c) Companies or national interest groups make demands of their national legislatures which makes decisions and without further consultation transpose these to the European legislature.
(d) The national legislatures formulate the requirements of the industry without consultation.
(e) The European legislature formulates market legislation without consultation.

A number of these questions were investigated by Mazey and Richardson (1996) who interviewed more than forty Commission officials and surveyed fifty officials from a number of DGs. Indeed, " . . . it was clear that officials placed enormous importance on the consultation of interest groups, typical responses were: I see consultation as an important and very useful source of information to ensure that EC legislative measures are efficient and effective in the real world (Dutch Official DG XV). We strongly value open, extensive and continuing consultation, formal and informal - our whole activity is based on this (British official DG XII). Consultation is in general positive as it allows us to broaden the perspective on a given-issue (Spanish official DG XVII)" (p 201).

The above questions were investigated in the interviews that were undertaken with individuals involved in the formulation of the Third Life Assurance Directive. Each of the five strategies necessitates different routes in the decision-making process and these may differ among the Member States. However, a specific model may be posited, different routes illustrated and the most rational strategy indicated.

INTEREST GROUPS AND EUROPEAN INTEGRATION

"Wyn Grant has noted that the relationship between pressure groups and the European Community has, so far, been a relatively neglected subject. In Britain, there are very few general studies of groups trying to influence EC decision-making" (Mazey and Richardson, 1993; p 93). "Direct lobbying of EC institutions constitutes an important part of the decision-making process within the Community and has the effect of increasing EC autonomy over the interests of Member States. There has been a rapid expansion of such activities over the last few years. However, although this phenomenon has attracted a lot of attention, there is surprisingly little systematic research on the topic" (Andersen and Elliassen, 1991; p 173). In addition to a number of recent studies this work is attempting to address this neglect (see Greenwood *et al*, 1992; Greenwood, 1995; 1997; Maloney, 1993; McLaughlin *et al*, 1993; McLaughlin and Greenwood, 1995; McLaughlin, 1995).

This chapter provides an overview of the workings of the EU decision-making processes regarding the negotiations and formulation of the Third Life Assurance Directive. In this context, it identifies embryonic supranationality in EU institutions and the extensive use of interest groups in legislation formulation. Interest groups will be defined as non-governmental organisations that attempt to have an influence on public policy. They are entities that provide an institutional linkage between sectors and government.

More precisely they are "... those types of organisations whose political task it is to reflect the interests of the economic or occupational sections they represent" (Lieber, 1974; p 29). Indeed, interest groups are described as "... those organisations which are occupied ... in trying to influence the policy of public bodies in their own chosen direction ... European interest groups ... are centrally organised associations of interest groups ... each of which represents either a number of similar groupings or both national groupings and European industry committee groupings" (Kirchner, 1980; p 96).

Interest groups apply pressure. Consequently, the terms pressure group and interest group will be used inter-changeably. Interest groups can either be of a sectional or of a promotional nature. We concentrate here on the sectional interest group category which usually represents the interests of professions, producer groups, occupations or trade unions. In particular, we concentrate on the sectional interests of the life insurance industry.

In the 1990s, following the SEA and the Maastricht Treaty, a number of research projects on European business interest groups were undertaken. Mazey and Richardson (1993) conducted a number of empirical studies but according to Grant (1995) overall the research picture was still opaque. "There is little consensus about the importance of different types of interest groups, about the influence they can exert on the politics and policies of the EC and the effect their activities have on the development of the integration process" (Kohler-Koch, 1994; p 166, cited in Grant, 1995; p 99).

However, the importance of interest groups in the European decision-making process had been recognised, hence the time and effort that is now being spent on them. "Since the early 1980s ... growing numbers of organised interests ... have come to recognise the increasing importance of European Community legislation. ... It is no longer possible to understand the policy process ... without taking account of the shift in power to Brussels" (Mazey and Richardson, 1993; p 191).

Indeed, the SEA created an impetus for the use of interest groups. With Qualified Majority Voting (QMV) and the SEM programme, lobbying in Brussels became imperative. "However, as several groups discovered to their cost, lobbying in the European Community is far from a simple matter" (ibid). In Europe, the process of lobbying is far from a 'cloak and dagger' scenario, it is quite the opposite. In Brussels, lobbying is open, uncertain and unpredictable. "Thus, in order to be effective Euro-lobbyists, groups must be able to co-ordinate their national and EC level strategies, construct alliances with their European counterparts, and monitor changing national and EC policy agendas" (ibid, pp 191-192). Indeed, the European institutions (especially the Commission and the Parliament) have been ". . . approached directly . . . (and) the two EC institutions have developed a comprehensive network of contacts that cut across, and are independent of, member countries. Increasingly it is necessary for lobbying to be based on broad alliances representing a more European perspective. We might think of this process as Europeanisation" (Andersen and Eliassen, 1991; p 174 author's brackets).

Some commentators consider that sovereignty has increasingly been ceded to the European institutions and that decision-making in the European Union is a balance between intergovernmentalism and the supranational institutions. In the majority of economic areas, it is generally impossible for one Member State to pursue total self-interest. Self-interest has become bonded to the other Member States; " . . national self-interest has partly become a collective European interest . . . forty years of working together has resulted in collective outputs being produced and recognised by the parties involved" (Greenwood, 1995; p 2). The European Commission and Parliament consider that speaking to European organisations allows an understanding of European-wide interests. Indeed, to ensure effective lobbying it is necessary to build coalitions. "Both the European Commission and the European Parliament frequently stress that they want to speak to European organisations. Where possible, therefore, you should seek to build coalitions, and the more representative they are in terms of the sector(s) a proposal will affect, the better. Of course, your interests might be at odds with other companies . . . operating in the same sector as you . . . (and) if they have a good argument and their interests are at stake, companies may be forced simply to lobby on their own behalf" (Club de Bruxelles, 1994; p 96 authors brackets).

Camerra-Rowe (1996) pointed out that different sectors can undertake different strategies when it comes to lobbying European institutions. She considered that on the one hand, the insurance and pharmaceutical sectors have well run interest group representation at the EU level. While on the other, the likes of the biotechnological and automobile sectors companies represent themselves directly at the EU level. Direct lobbying more accurately indicates a company's choices. However, this is expensive and there is no certainty that the Commission or European Parliament will listen to an individual company if its proposals are not similar to the EU's or the sectors objectives. But this does illustrate that on certain matters the concerns of individual companies will be taken into consideration. "While the Commission prefers dealing with associations, its officials have been relatively open to lobbying by individual large firms. Thus, firms often have an incentive to lobby directly. . . . However, it is rare for a firm, even a large one, to rely on one channel of representation" (ibid, p 6). This provides the basis for a number of difficulties. Companies that lobby directly:

(a) Undermine the role of interest groups because the message they carry may not represent the whole sector.
(b) Have limited incentives to compromise their positions in the collective because they are able to lobby themselves.
(c) Force the association to reach consensus; this may lead to the acceptance of the lowest common denominator and undermine the effectiveness of the interest group.

Small and medium-size enterprises or companies that are incapable of lobbying the EU directly intensify the role of the interest group. Members are forced to accept sector compromises and they cannot use the interest group to pursue private advantage. European interest groups " . . . therefore have greater flexibility in the types of positions they take . . . it means that the association has greater political weight because it can claim to speak on behalf of all members" (Camerra-Rowe, 1996; pp 6-8). Of course, the other extreme is where the interest group is so diverse in its membership that agreement can never be reached.

The European insurance sector is mainly made up of small and medium-size enterprises and with the exception of Allianz, lack the political clout and resources to undertake direct action in Brussels. As a result, both national and European interest groups have a greater influence on the Commission and their membership. Companies need to accept the interest group's " . . . policy position even if it does not take account of their particular interests because they cannot effectively represent their own views. As a result, and paradoxically, the more fragmented insurance sector was better able to undertake collective activity in pursuing Community policy" (ibid, p 21)[1]. In

[1] It has been argues that the less concentrated a sector is the less difficulty it has in overcoming the problems of collective action. For instance, the automobile,

this chapter, we examine the initial discussions regarding the legislation and regulatory regimes that should be pursued to create the market most amenable to all Member State life insurance industries. Fundamentally, we consider how effective interest groups were in the creation of legislation and the consequent regulatory environments.

THE COMITÉ EUROPÉEN DES ASSURANCES (CEA)

Insurance interest representation at the EU level is primarily undertaken by the Comité Europeén des Assurances (CEA) which has operated since 1953. Indeed, it is an organisation that existed before the creation of the EEC and this is reflected in its membership (this is not made up solely of Member States). "Nevertheless the single most important function of the organisation is to work through its 'Common Market Committee' which is officially recognised by the EU and through which all insurance directives pass" (Vipond, 1995; p 105). This is reflected by the Commission, which considers

biotechnological and consumer electronics sectors interest groups have been relatively weak, whereas in the pharmaceutical and insurance sectors interest groups have greater influence. (for further see Camerra-Rowe, 1996; Coen, 1998; McLaughlin and Jordan, 1993; Greenwood and Ronit, 1992; Howell, 2000; and Cawson 1992). There is an interesting dilemma with regard to these different ways of lobbying the EU. If one uses interest groups successfully then is the sector adhering to neo-functional processes? Alternatively, others argue that if a company lobby's the EU directly is it adhering to neo-corporatist or meso corporatist processes? This work considers that both understandings are very similar as each includes lobbying a supranational institution and involves the use of interest groups. The EU is evolving, as are its institutions and this is illustrated by the uncertainty of the final (if such occurs) formalisation of relations between interest groups and the EU. Camerra-Rowe (1996) considers that it is unlikely that interest groups will be the prime movers in interest representation in the EU. That the " . . . initiatives the Commission and other EU institutions undertake to regulate interest groups will be critical in determining the future form and shape that business representation takes. . . . In short, effective collective action may originate not from the desire of firms in these sectors to speak with a common voice on common interests, but from the desire of EU officials to create common collective interests from a multitude of private ones" (p 23).

itself as an organisation that is always open to external input and Commissioners welcome this input. The Commission has " . . . a reputation for being accessible to interest groups (because) it is in the Commission's own interest to do so since interest groups can provide the services with technical information and constructive advice" (OJ/C 63/02 author's brackets).

The Directorate-Generale XV (DG XV) considers the CEA to be the main representative of the insurance industry and was reinforced in a speech by Leon Brittan in 1989 ". . . the CEA has proved its worth . . . as a standard bearer for the insurance industry at the European level. I know that DG XV has come to rely greatly on the CEA and its officials . . . as an organisation which is fully representative of the insurance industry, which puts your views and concerns to us frankly and powerfully and defends them tenaciously" (Sir Leon Brittan, speech given to the CEA November 1989; cited in Camerra-Rowe, 1996; p 18).

These sentiments were supported by a number of interviews undertaken by the author (see below) and those provided by Mazey and Richardson (1996). Furthermore, they reflected agreement with a set of interviews undertaken by Camerra-Rowe (1996) in which a Commission official indicated that " . . . they (the Commission) have almost institutionalised corporatist - like relations with the CEA" (p 18 author's brackets)

THE INTERVIEW PROCESS

Through a series of interviews with EU decision-making institutions this chapter provides an investigation of where interest groups predominantly level their demands, and how they are dealt with by EU institutions.

The survey data illustrated the way the life insurance sector perceives the EU and how it attempts to mold a future regulatory environment (Life Insurance Regulation Matrices One and Two). These ideological preferences are provided by different cultural existence. The decision-making in the EU and the market to be formed out of such a process may tell us much about the way future trading in the EU was developed.

Interviews were undertaken with a number of key individuals concerned in the decision-making process at the European level. The interviews at the both the EU and UK level provide information that may allow the work to deduce a similar process among all Member States. Interview outlines (see below) and survey B (see below) were sent to other Member State interest groups and the responses allow some deduction of processes at work throughout the EU.

The key individuals interviewed by the author were representatives of the following institutions.

Directorate-Generale XV. (DG XV) (Finance).
The Council Permanent Representative for UK in Finance.
The Department of Industry and Trade (DTI).
Committee for European Assurance (CEA). Paris and Brussels.
Bureau International des Producteurs d'Assurance & de Reassurance (BIPAR).
Association of British Insurers (ABI).
British Insurers International Committee (BIIC)
Irish Insurance Federation (IIF).
Council Permanent Representative for France in Finance.

Each interviewee was an individual who dealt explicitly with the Third Life Assurance Directive and each illustrated interaction with other key individuals. The questions were codified so that each set of interview questions related to each other. This allowed a general perspective of the EU decision-making process and illustrated the interactions between the key players.

Formulating and Coding Semi-Formal Interview Questions

Grounded theory entails two basic analytical procedures. Firstly, one continually makes comparisons and secondly one asks questions. As noted above these processes have been adhered to in earlier parts of the study. However, at this point the study wishes to identify the process in relation to the interviews. Questioning opens up the data and the categories properties and dimensions constructed earlier in the study allowed the researcher to ask questions more precisely in the interviews. There are general questions that can be drawn from the data, which can stimulate a series of questions, which in turn " . . . lead to the development of further categories, properties and dimensions. The basic questions are "**Who? When? Where? What? How?** And **How Much?**" (Strauss and Corbin, 1990; p 77). The following questions build on the basic questions and the previous categories that were generated above. Indeed, the difficulties that were created through the categorisation of the European life insurance industry provide the basis and strategy of the interview questions. They emerge to deal with the problems that the study has uncovered.

The interviews were conducted on a semi-formal basis and centred around 10-12 core questions these were;

(1) What are the major functions of the CEA/BIPAR/ABI/the Commission/the Council/National Supervisors and how do these fit with each other at;
(A) The EU level.
(B) The national level.
(2) To what extent are decisions made with interest group/COREPER/Commission/National Supervisor in-put.
(3) Who defines decision parameters is it interest groups, national supervisors, the Council of Ministers or the Commission.
(4) Does the Council, the Commission, national legislatures and interest groups reach a compromise prior to a decision reaching the Council.
(5) Does an interaction exist between the Council/the Commission/national supervisors and specific interest groups at a national and European level.
(6) How does the Council/national supervisor know what to insist upon in respect of national interest.
(7) How much interaction exists between interest groups/Commission/Council/national supervisor and the Insurance Committee
(8) Were different Member States looking for specific types of life insurance regulatory environments for the SEM which is different from other member states.
(9) Were there differences between the;
(a) The French ideal
(b) The German ideal
(c) The Dutch ideal
(d) The UK ideal

(e) The Italian ideal
Please illustrate these differences.
How does your market ideal fit into these?

(10) How are compromises reached between the different national interest groups prior to the Commission initially drawing up draft legislation? Is there an interaction between the interest group at the European level and the Commission which takes into consideration a compromise reached by the member state interest groups i.e.. ABI through membership of the European interest group CEA/BIPAR.

(11) Where/When possible have compromises been reached between the Council, the Commission and Parliament before the final negotiations to enable a more efficient means of decision making?

(12) What takes precedence in the formulation of a Directive Member State or sector interests?

The questions were coded into categories so the same could be asked of each interviewee. This allowed the following categories to emerge from the interviews (see the interview results below). Overall the interviews identified the emergence of five categories, each built around the core category of European integration.

The Interview Results

In general, the interviews indicated agreement on a number of points. The Third Life Assurance Directive was unanimously perceived as a means of providing the environment that would allow mutual recognition to be achieved; it was also acknowledged that many influences went into the drafting of a directive. Since 1988 interaction between industries and the Commission has become more apparent at the EU level. The representative of DG XV considered that consistent contact with the life insurance industry was imperative in respect of legislative input.

Question One ***(Sub-Category = Understanding)***

What are the major functions of the Permanent Representative/ Commission/CEA/BIPAR/ABI/DTI and how do these fit in with the functions of other finance interest groups and governmental institutions at:

(A) The EU level?

(B) The national level?

DG XV primarily deals with the CEA and BIPAR. However, the impetus for legislation may come through the Member States or from the Commission itself. The CEA sees its role as bringing together a combined **understanding** of the direction negotiations should take. The CEA, BIPAR and DG XV representatives all considered that the Commission prefers to deal with a European-wide interest group. Both the ABI and BIIC agreed with this view and thought that the ABI and BIIC worked through the CEA as these days (post-SEA) it was easier to get **agreement** in the latter organisation. This they considered was due to the general acceptance of the UK's **understanding** of a regulatory structure. However, this was disputed in other interviews and by the results of survey A. Initially, the European life insurance industry was divided but through the treaties and the recognition of commonality compromise is now sought. Consequently, the importance of the CEA has continued to grow. This allows for negotiations to be appropriately targeted because individual company and national interest group involvement provided too much information and created turbulence. Turbulence is a concept initiated by Haas (1976) who argued that during the integration process there was too much information, which on made the situation unclear. In this context, European interest groups create wholes that enable shared belief systems and focal points and these enable co-operation (Haas, 1975; Garrett and Weingast, 1993).

Furthermore, the BIIC also relays common **understandings** to the national government (in the case of the UK) through the Department of Trade and Industry (DTI). This ensures that proposed legislation is acceptable to all of the parties concerned and successful at the Council level. Once the Commission and the industry are committed to a policy approach, the BIIC supports it with information and attempts to prevent backtracking (BIIC Representative). The ABI and the IIF do the same work as the CEA at the national level. In this context, the ABI through the BIIC interacts with the DTI on a regular basis to ensure that government fully **understands** what the industry needs. However, the DTI did point out that although it was also interested in the needs of the consumer, in general terms the **understanding** of the insurance directive is developed through the industry. At the EU level, the DTI is involved in Council working groups and gets involved in bilateral discussions on an *ad hoc* basis in an attempt to swing other Member States toward the UK's stance. The discussions pave the way for some kind of **consensus** in the working group. In this context, more of an intergovernmental perspective may be observed. However, this would incorporate "advice received from the industry" (DTI Representative) through the use of interest groups. The BIIC " . . . advises . . . on a regular basis and as the BIIC meeting precede the Council working group by two weeks, we go in broadly knowing what the industry wanted" (ibid). The IIF represented the Irish life insurance industry's interests at the EU level through lobbying. It would also have regard for other finance interest groups: these may be seen as allies or competitors. However, through the CEA **compromise** is usually reached. This illustrates more of a neo-functional rather than an intergovernmental perspective.

Questions Two and Three (Sub-Category = Negotiation)

To what extent are decisions made with interest group/ Commission/Permanent Representative/DTI input?

Who defines decision parameters it national/European interest groups, national supervisors the Council Ministers or the Commission?

The Commission aims to create a common **understanding** between the Member States. It will **negotiate** with Member State interest groups, e.g. the ABI or even directly with companies. But its main contacts are the European interest groups because they allow a European perspective and this is what the Commission wants (this was substantiated by the European interest group representatives). In this context, the CEA has little to do with national governments, leaving this area to national interest groups. As well as attempting to influence in this area, national interest groups will **negotiate** directly with Commission representatives occasionally, but will usually **negotiate** through European interest groups. National interest groups deal with MEPs at the European level. The IIF representative considered that " . . .

generally interest group input is taken fully on board". However, interest group input is not the only factor.

The creation of a **consensus** between Member States allows for successful legislation when it reaches the Council because it has been partially agreed in the initial stages. Of course, problems may occur once **negotiations** take place in the Council. However, successful legislation may be more apparent if there has been agreement in the initial stage, this was reinforced by the DTI representative.

The CEA representatives both considered that the CEA played an **interactive** part in the creation of European legislation, as did those representatives of the ABI, BIIC and BIPAR with reference to these organisations. Parameters in terms of decision-making are created through this process.

There are many influences that have an impact on proposal **negotiations**:

(a) The individuals in control, e.g. Delors, Brittan etc.
(b) The institutions in control, e.g. the Commission, Court of Justice, Parliament, Council.
(c) The economic sectors' perceptions of the legislation necessary.

However, it is the economic sectors that act as a stimulus and **interact** with the European political institutions. There is much input by trade associations who ensure their influence is part of **negotiations** as early as possible. In this respect, the insurance interest groups interact with the Commission at the following five levels of proposal formulation:

(1) The forming and influencing of ideas.
(2) Discussing the general problem.
(3) Having input into draft working papers.
(4) Having input into formal proposals.
(5) Lobbying Commission **negotiations**.

(DG XV, CEA and BIPAR Representatives). Overall, interest groups are an intrinsic element in the process of **negotiation**.

Theoretically, by level 5, the 'Commission discussions', agreement should have been reached. However, there could be minor disputes. At this point the proposed legislation is passed on to the European Parliament which gives its opinion as it would also have been lobbied by the given groups. In 1996 the "European Parliament indicated to CEA and several other large interest groups that it would prefer to deal specifically with them rather than the large number of institutions that currently attempted to lobby it" (CEA Representative).

The UK Permanent Representative thought it very likely that the Council would support the majority of proposals. However in some cases, it would not. Proposed legislation does not always totally reflect an industry's opinion in the way that the Commission's representative implied. However, legislation is easier to implement with **consensus**: yet if this is not possible, the proposal is still constructed. If the proposal is constructed without general **consensus** of the sector, further negotiation is necessary in the Council and implementation becomes more difficult and in some cases impossible. The DG XV representative cited the Insurance Contract Directive as an illustration of such a scenario. Indeed, the French Permanent Representative, who considered that interest group input into the decision-making process was intense and interactive, reflected a similar position. The role of the COREPER is to provide **consensus** and the more agreement there is prior to their involvement, the easier negotiations are in the Council.

The BIIC representatives thought that interest groups were extremely influential in the building of legislation and that this helps in the initiation of successful legislation (O'Leary). An ABI representative considered that the Commission was very open but had no programme: it also had to face a division of opinion throughout the EU. Interest groups at the European level have helped to overcome these divisions. Both UK interest group representatives considered that the trend these days was to seek **compromise**. However, in some cases Member States were reluctant to shift away from their preferred regulatory system, but she added that the UK has and will continue to shift when necessary.

Ultimately, the CEA is a pivotal body in the process of negotiation that allows an all-round or complete perspective of the sector's demands from the decision-making bodies. There was an increase in CEA activity in the mid-eighties following the Commission White Paper (1985) and the SEA (1987) which indicated the creation of the SEM. The CEA sees itself as a **facilitator** and a **negotiator** of turbulence (Haas 1976). European interest groups provide the means for an all-round European view and this allows for more successful legislation (CEA Representative).

Contract law provides for consumer protection. However, this is an area where harmonisation has proved difficult to achieve and allows an illustration of the difficulties involved in harmonisation when areas more sensitive to national sovereignty are broached. After fourteen years the insurance contract directive proved impossible to agree and finally it was abandoned. This does not provide the environment necessary to allow a SEM in life products because a Member State can theoretically block a product from crossing its border. The Commission Representative pointed out that a host country could not impose regulations in a "willy nilly" manner but only in the context of the 'general good'. Of course, one has to determine what is meant by this concept, as it is open to a number of interpretations. One Member State's 'general good' providing another Members State's trade barrier. However, he indicated that the Commission was continuing to monitor the situation.

It was apparent that it had been difficult to get agreement on the simplest parts of the insurance contracts directive. This gives an understanding of the problems the EU has if it does not undertake **consultation** with industries and interest groups. If it presses ahead alone difficulties are likely to be apparent at the Council level. A high level of **consensus** is necessary if proposals are to become legislation. It also illustrates the situation when the EU interferes with areas fundamental to the idea of Member State sovereignty e.g. contract law in general, taxation or pensions, etc. When the EU attempts interference in such areas it is tampering with civil systems and this ruffles nationalist feathers (for a further discussion see Chapter Six and the Spillover Model).

In general, decision parameters are defined by different organisations at different times during the creation of the legislation. Following discussions and **negotiations** with the national industries national interest groups inform national governments of the national industries preferences. However, these preferences are curtailed by other Member State industries and it is here that the European interest group comes into play. The Commission initiates the legislative process but needs the **input** of interest groups to develop successful legislation. It must also remain loyal to the spirit of the Treaty. Ultimately, the Council may drop certain areas but it cannot add anything without the assent of the Commission and Parliament. However, it may amend a proposal as long as the vote is unanimous.

Each organisation is involved in defining decision parameters because without the input of each Member State, the insurance industry and EU institutions legislation would not hold the essential ingredients to ensure its successful passage. This was emphasised by the French Permanent Representative who considered that interest groups define decision parameters regarding their area of interest. However, this is not the general interest and this is where the Commission and the Council provide a balance. The Council provide parameters once the legislation has reached them " . . . at the general level and often **negotiate** precise texts for validation" (French Permanent Representative). However, it is the Commission that has the "power of proposition and objection" (ibid).

The ideal is **consensus.** However, this is difficult to achieve without fundamental changes to the decision-making structures and an undermining of national sovereignty in the areas of legal structure and fiscal and monetary policy. 'General good or best practice' may be a means toward enabling this. A CEA representative argued that on a number of occasions Member States had not reached agreement and in these cases 'best practice' is brought into play. At the interest group level, they pursue unanimity: however this is always difficult and in some cases impossible.

In principle, the Commission defines the decision-making parameters. However, as illustrated above, one may argue that it does not do this alone. Because the Council provides the decisions it could be said that it is this institution that provides parameters. Additionally, if one takes into consideration interest group input, one may consider that these define parameters prior to the involvement of any institution or through an interaction with the Commission. "The Commission provides a framework for the CEA. Then the CEA undertakes negotiations with its membership" (CEA Representative).

Questions Four, Five , Six and Seven ***(Sub-Category=Interaction)***

Did the Commission/Council/Parliament, national legislatures and interest groups interact and reach a compromise prior to the Third Life Assurance Directive proposal reaching the Council?

Did an interaction exist between the Commission/Council/Parliament and the specific interest group on a national (ABI) and/or European level (CEA)?

How does the Commission/Council/Parliament know what to insist upon in respect of European interests i.e. in terms of insurance policy that is acceptable to all Member States?

How much interaction exists between Permanent Representatives, interest groups, the DTI and DG XV? Is this interaction undertaken through the Insurance Committee (if so how effective is the Insurance Committee)?

There is an **interaction** between the European and national institutions; the Council and Commission have college meetings where policy lines and strategies to pursue these policy lines are decided. Parliamentary opinions and assent are taken into consideration with a greater importance given to these since the Maastricht Treaty. However, this was minimal in respect of the Third Life Assurance Directive. As stated above, the Commission and Council acknowledged that there was an **interaction** with interest groups on a European and national level. Indeed, that the Commission would primarily go to European interest groups because such would provide an overall picture of the industry. The UK Permanent Representative considered that the Council does not really deal with interest groups directly but CEA papers are forwarded to both it and the Insurance Committee (Insurance Committee Directive 91/675/EEC). Whereas, the French Permanent Representative considered that they " . . . have contact with representatives of specific interest groups when there is a need of information". Of course, this could be similar to the UK position or more informal. However, the French Permanent Representative was quite clear on the extent of **negotiation** and **compromise** between the different groups before decisions reach the Council. To the question, " . . .do the Council, the Commission, national legislatures and interest groups **negotiate** a **compromise** prior to a decision reaching the Council" the French Permanent Representative answered " . . . yes, this is always the informal rule of procedure".

The Commission representative contended that DG XV knew what to insist upon in respect of what was necessary for a proposal by examining the green papers and treaties. However, he did admit that input from the specific industry or sector had to be seriously considered.

The representatives of the ABI/BIIC considered that normally the Council, Commission, national legislatures and interest groups **negotiate** a **compromise** prior to the legislation reaching the Council. It is unusual for something to reach the Council without a **compromise** being agreed (ABI Representative). The BIIC representative argued that the consensus was **negotiated** between the Commission and interest groups. However, there is no **interaction** between the Council and national interest groups. In this context, **interaction** is undertaken through the DTI. It is through this process that the Council identifies what the national industries will accept or prefer and the DTI is always willing to negotiate with national interest groups but they may also have their own agenda (but they know what is needed because they talk to interest groups).

It was generally agreed that the CEA and BIPAR both illustrated points where European **compromises** may be met which allows an easy **interaction** between the Commission, the Council, and Member States. Decision parameters are built up through four interacting areas:

(a) The Treaties' aims.
(b) The European institutions (i.e. through college meetings and decision-making procedures).
(c) Member States.
(d) Industries (interest groups and companies).

An indication of the need for interest group interaction is exemplified in the formation of the Insurance Committee Directive (91/675/EEC). This has allowed an expertise at the Commission level to ensure that there is an **understanding** between the industry and the Commission with reference to technical issues. The Insurance Committee is a new phenomenon which is being used to greater effect at an increasing rate.

The ABI/BIIC does **interact** with the insurance committee, as does the CEA. The Committee allows problems to be discussed and overcomes difficulties with interpretation. In this context, the EU institutions find the committee helpful. It also makes technical adjustments to financial instruments and provides a sounding board for the Commission (ABI Representative). However, the French Permanent Representative considered that although such a process did exist the interaction was informal i.e. through professional contact.

Questions Eight and Nine ***(Sub-Category=Difference)***

Were different Member States looking for specific types of life insurance market environments for the Single European Market (SEM) which were different from other Member States?

Could you clarify these differences, please.

In general, each interviewee agreed that different Member State industries wished the EU to create **conflicting** regulatory environments. A CEA representative contended that there were **different** concepts of what a regulatory environment entailed between the Member States and that this was due to **differing** normative and historical experiences. If it was accepted that there were **different** understandings of regulatory environments, it was agreed that European-wide interest groups were necessary to bring about consensus. He saw the necessity of best practice and how mutual recognition may overcome this. However, he agreed that a lack of contract legislation could undermine an SEM in life insurance.

The BIIC representatives agreed that there were **different** concepts of the regulatory environment in terms of products, cultural norms, and technical and product barriers. Each indicated that there were different preferences of market ideals pursued by separate Member States: these were agreed in general by all those interviewed:

French Ideal = Nationalised/Prescribed.
German Ideal = Prescribed.
Dutch Ideal = Liberal.
UK Ideal = Liberal.
Italian Ideal = Prescribed/Liberal.
Eire Ideal = Liberal/Prescribed.

The individual regulatory environments were considered to be very **different** from one another and as the Life Insurance Regulation Matrices One and Two illustrated (see Figs 4.1 and 4.2), each accepted that some form of **compromise** had to be reached if differences were to be overcome.

Questions Ten, Eleven and Twelve ***(Sub-Category=Compromise)***

How are compromises reached between the different national interest groups prior to the Commission initially drawing up draft legislation? Is there an interaction between the interest group at the European level, i.e. CEA and the Commission, which takes into consideration a compromise reached by the Member State interest groups i.e. ABI through membership of the European interest group?

Where/When possible have compromises been reached between the Council, the Commission and Parliament before the final negotiations? Would this allow a more efficient means of decision-making?

What took precedence in the formulation of the Third Life Assurance Directive, Member State, European (Commission) or life insurance industry interests?

To ensure successful legislation, **compromise** between differences need to be negotiated. Consequently this is pursued before the final **negotiations** to enable more efficient decision-making. "**Compromises** are achieved through working parties where agreements are reached and Member State and interest group policy lines merged" (UK Permanent Representative). "It occurs sometimes especially when there is a European organisation for a profession" (French Permanent Representative). However, " . . . the Commission never loses sight of the spirit of the proposal" (DG XV Representative). "**Compromises** are reached through IIF involvement in a European interest group" (IIF Representative).

The formulation of the proposal and consequent directive must take into consideration all input. However, precedence of input is difficult to distinguish. The Commission, as noted, concentrates on the "spirit of the Treaty" (DG XV Representative) or the EU interest; to do this it must take on board national interests and industries' interests and minimise the difference to ensure the passage of legislation through the Council. This can be achieved through the use of interest groups and more importantly European- wide interest groups.

In a post-SEA Europe, industry in general has recognised that it is in their interest to have input into forging the new market and have co-operated because they consider the SEM acceptable. Pre-1988, there was a **conflict** between the EU and industry: effectively, they seemed to be in **opposition**. It was the SEA that gave the impetus to the SEM, which forced the Member State industries to be involved in the formulation of their evolving home market.

Interest groups became more aware of what was necessary for creating European Union in a post-1986 scenario. Of course, there are a number of difficulties in attaining agreement continually and Member State interest groups and companies will continually attempt to influence the decision-making bodies themselves. However, the European decision-making bodies make it clear that negotiations should be undertaken through the CEA or other European interest groups i.e. BIPAR. The CEA interacts with many other groups at the EU level e.g. banking employers groups and trade unions. Indeed, the CEA attempts to become part of the process as early as possible and to this extent it has a good relationship with DGXV (ABI Representative).

When the proposal reaches the Committee of Permanent Representatives (COREPER), Permanent Representatives are urged to reach a **compromise** and formulate a decision. There are varying accounts of the extent to which a sector/industry may be listened to at Council level. Consequently, it is important for the sector/industry to have the support of its Member State in respect of the legislation being **negotiated**. However, the further the **negotiations** go in the Council process, the weaker the economic variables become.

A proposal is automatically despatched to Member State legislatures and relevant bodies, e.g. the DTI in the UK, and opinions on the proposal are sought. Interest groups also lobby at the national level. Consequently, legislation has support built into it through different avenues. The initiation of legislation is often a "blurred" (unclear in terms of initiation) activity. However, the industries/sectors are predominant in this initial area. When the proposal reaches the Council, concessions may have to be made to secure main points. The Third Life Assurance Directive was one where most difficulties seemed to be overcome in the initial stages. Germany pushed for more prescription but further **compromise** was reached (UK Permanent Representative).

It was accepted by the UK Permanent Representative that the move between the Member States trading situation and their **negotiating** positions indicate the changes the Member State wishes to bring about in its own regulatory environment. This allows the Member State to make changes without too much upheaval in respect of Member State legislation and regulation. It also provides the basis, which the Member State uses, when it approaches the **negotiation** process: it is listening to its sector/industry that has been lobbying at both the EU and national level. However, if it needs to ensure the legislation necessary it will negotiate with its sector's/industry's wishes. The Council representative identified this when he argued " . . . that political variables take precedence at the Council level".

The CEA does not only represent Member States but it does represent the fifteen Member States (then twelve) in its membership of twenty three. It deals mainly with national interest groups, which are its membership. However, it will also interact with individual companies. Once the EU has created a framework, discussions will be undertaken in a number of working groups, which are made up of national interest groups representatives and company representatives. Consequently, much **negotiation** is undertaken in the pursuit of a common **understanding** between the Member States regarding the most amenable legislation. Of course, the Commission pursues the spirit of the treaty but also needs to know what is workable at the EU level. However, **conflict** between Member States creates uncertainty in what is necessary to enable the SEM: if separate Member State sectors all lobby the EU with **different** ideas, difficulties will arise. Basically, the European interest groups are central to the creation of the SEM because they provide **understanding** of **difference** and through **interaction** allow **negotiation** and **compromise.** This enables successful legislation and illustrates the important role of European interest groups and the supranational bodies in the creation of the regulatory structure for the evolving SEM.

Under the emerged categories of **Understanding, Negotiation, Interaction, Difference** and **Compromise** a general understanding of **European integration** is identified. The interview coding illustrates the parts individual institutions play in the formulation and construction of legislation. Primarily, the coding categories were continually re-affirmed as the main processes of **European integration.** In each interview section the categories merged under the core category of European integration and supported a process of an interaction between self-interest and common good (this is further illustrated by the Decision-Making Model and Survey C below).

Survey B was initiated to provide a general understanding of what UK Members of the European Parliament Finance Committee and lobbying groups considered to be the situation regarding life insurance regulatory environments. However, the response was low and shed minimal light on the situation. There was little difference in how the UK political parties saw the situation. Each considered that the EU market in life insurance was liberal/prescribed and that was how it should remain.

SURVEY B

General Survey of Institutions involved in the Decision-Making Process

(1) How liberal or state controlled is your national life insurance industry?
(2) Where would your organisation's membership place the single European Market life insurance industry in respect of market freedom?
(3) What type of market would your organisation's membership consider that the Single European Market should be to allow the life industry its greatest profitability?
(4) What type of market would your organisation's membership consider that the Single European market should be to allow the greatest consumer protection?
(5) What type of market would your organisation's membership consider that the Single European Market should be to allow the greatest consumer choice?

THE DECISION-MAKING MODEL

One may consider that there are micro and macro elements to the model. The micro element concentrating on companies, national interest groups and national legislatures; and the macro aspect involved with European interest groups (or the meeting point of the national interest groups at the European level) and EU decision-making institutions. The macro model would pick up on the micro model output and attempt to illustrate the process within an EU context. However, the two areas are interactive.

At the European level, there is an **interaction** between the subjective interests of the different Member State industries and the objective interests of the European institutions. This work considers that a **compromise** is reached at the European interest group level through the industries **interacting** both with one another and with the Commission and Parliament. The **negotiated** legislation that goes through to the Council has been **compromised** by the Member State sectors/industries who either progressively or subsequently inform their own government of the situation in relation to the agreed legislation. During the process there may be **differences** between the Council and the other institutions.

Once the draft legislation is in the realms of the Council, certain agreements may be disposed of. However, one would expect the main tenets of the legislation to become law because the national industries would have **compromised** their positions at an earlier stage. Consequently, one would have expected them to lobby their governments to accept the proposed legislation: this is what the Council consists of representatives of the Member States. Indeed, it is the intergovernmental aspect of the EU decision-making institutions. If the Council, under the Co-decision procedures extensively interferes with the legislation, the European Parliament may intervene.

The interviews indicated agreement on a number of points: the Third Life Assurance Directive was unanimously perceived as a means of providing the environment that would allow mutual recognition to be achieved; it was also acknowledged that many influences went into the drafting of a directive. Since 1988, interaction between industries and the Commission has become more apparent at the EU level. The representative of DG XV considered that a ongoing contact with the life insurance industry was imperative in respect of legislative input. Most importantly, the interviews illustrate the **interaction** and **negotiation** in the creation of the Third Life Assurance Directive and the extent of the use of interest groups in the process. However, what is also clear is the intergovernmental aspects. The following **understanding** of the process and Decision-Making Model (see Fig 5.3) was accrued from the interviews and survey C (see below).

For the purpose of this study, the European Court of Justice (ECJ) is not discussed. There are a number of issues that need to be explained with regard to the model. Firstly, the survey regarding Member State interest group membership and the interviews illustrated that the majority of life insurance companies were members of national interest groups. Further interviews indicated that national interest groups were affiliated to interest groups at the EU level (mainly the CEA and BIPAR). Secondly, in the formulation of legislation (although Member State interest groups may approach the European institutions), the Commission and European Parliament preferred to deal with European-wide interest groups because these allow a European picture of the situation. Thirdly, because the sector understands what is necessary for the successful operation of the embryonic regulatory environment, it is highly likely that they will confer and reach some agreement prior to national, i.e. Council or intergovernmental interference. Finally, the interviews with the CEA, the ABI, the BIIC and members of EU decision-making institutions substantiated that other Member State insurance industries actively participated in the creation of EU legislation through interest groups.

Figure 5.2

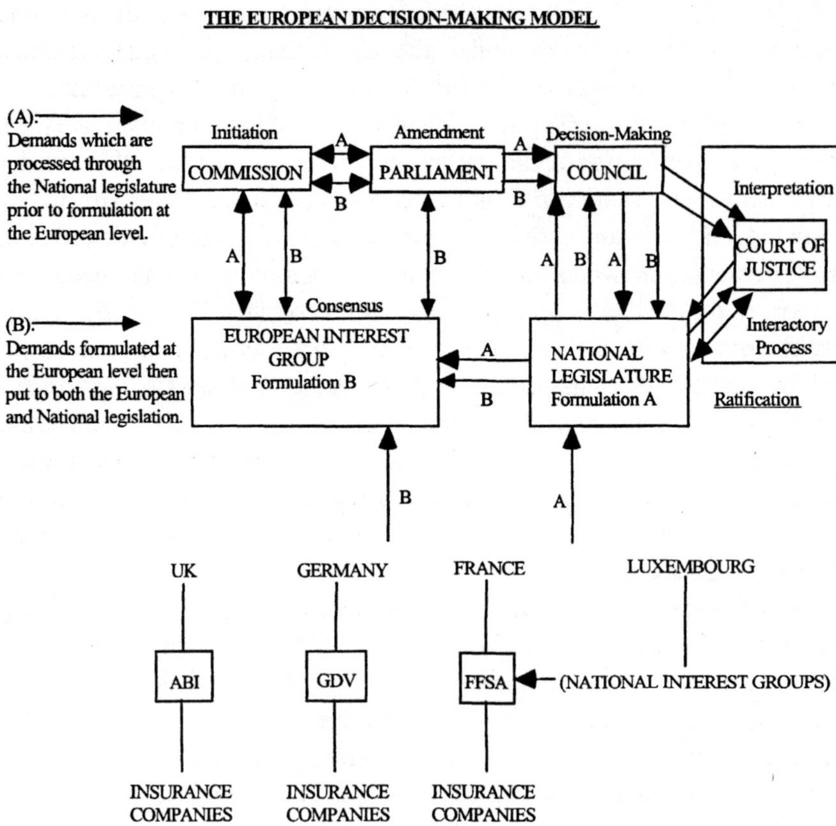

There are two general directions that could be taken regarding decision-making procedures identified on the model. These are indicated by arrows A and B; process A considers that demands are formulated through the national legislature prior to formulation at the EU level, whereas route B illustrates demands being **compromised** at the EU level prior to the involvement of the national legislature. Route A is a stronger intergovernmental or state-centric approach whereas route B illustrates more of a neo-functional process or multilevel governance. Of course the situation is not as clear-cut as depicted and elements of both routes were in use, but in general the interviews emphasised route B (see Fig 5.2). However, the European interest group rarely had any dealings with the national legislature and **interaction** between the two was undertaken between the national interest group and the national governmental departments (the DTI in the UK). Consequently, at this point there is intergovernmental involvement even though it is minimal and in most cases the DTI adheres to decisions already made at the EU interest group level. More importantly, there is intergovernmental involvement in the Council. However, since the SEA and QMV, this has been minimised because if a directive is to be successful it only needs a majority of Member States in this situation not unanimity.

The interviews illustrate that **compromise** is sought and usually accomplished at the European interest group level in tandem with the Commission and Parliament. Indeed, if the legislation is being **negotiated** by the industry through interest group involvement with a supranational institution (EU decision-makers) the research has uncovered elements of neo-functionalism. If a compromise is not reached at the EU level, then each Member State industry would pursue its own ideal market type (as indicated by the matrices see figs 4.1 and 4.2) and compromise would be difficult if not impossible to achieve. To enable successful acceptable legislation at the EU level, the interviews and surveys illustrate that both neo-functional and intergovernmental processes need to be at work. Even if neo-functionalism is not completely identified there is at least a form of multi-level governance. Indeed, earlier treaties have initiated the structures that determine the use of interest groups and supranationality. Further treaties will provide structures for future decision-making procedures and emphasise elements of the historical institutional approach.

Interest Group Usage in the UK (Survey C)

There is some debate about why companies join interest groups. Olson (1971) considered that collective goods were logically irrelevant to companies when they joined interest groups. He claimed that selective incentives were the reasons for group formation, not some collective good. However, Grant and Marsh (1977) and Marsh (1978) provided evidence that companies do not simply join interest groups for services or selective incentives, but for the collective good as well. Moe (1980) builds on Olson's model and replaces it with a " . . . broader perspective that links the decision to join with varying individual perceptions and indicates that members may join for political reasons if they think their contributions 'make a difference' in providing some of the collective good" (p 6). Furthermore, Moe (1980) argued that the pluralist model focused too much on the political elements of the debate, whereas Olson (1971) overemphasises the non-political.

To substantiate some reasons for interest group use, survey C (see below) investigated the extent to which the UK insurance industry used interest groups at the national and European level. For this survey 70 questionnaires were sent out and 36 (50%) were returned. When asked if they used a European interest group in their participation of the formulation of the Third Life Assurance Directive 81.4% said no. Yet, 81.5% considered that they used a national interest group in most cases, the ABI and BIIC. The BIIC negotiates on behalf of the ABI at the EU level and represents the views of the ABI's membership. The link between the European and national interest groups was further substantiated by questions three and four, 85.2% did not directly use European interest groups at all and 74.0% contended that they didn't even subscribe to one, whereas, 100.0% of respondents subscribed to a national interest group. Even when their European interests were threatened 77.7% of companies did not directly approach European institutions whereas 51.8% would approach their national government. However, 59.2% would usually use interest groups to lobby on their behalf at the European level and 89.9% at the national level. When asked if they prefer to use interest groups at the European level to enable European-wide industry compromises 81.5% of respondents rejected this idea. However, 85.2% used interest groups at the national level because this enabled nation-wide compromise. In general, national interest groups are members of European interest groups, which pursue national sector/industry compromises at the EU level; it is through this process that European-wide compromises are reached and the importance of European interest groups emphasised. Indeed, the survey results indicate that UK insurance companies do not lobby on their own behalf in the EU in the main they rely on interest groups.

Those respondents that indicated which interest groups they were members of, 28 were members of the ABI and 2 of the BIIC; these two considered that through their membership of the BIIC they were affiliated to the CEA. However, all 30 were affiliated to the CEA (the other 28 through their membership of the ABI). However, none of the respondents considered that they were direct members of any European interest group. One respondent did point out that his/her company was a member of other national interest groups in other Member States and would seek to influence their views on important matters.

A Survey of the UK Insurance Industry regarding Interest Group Use (Survey C)

(1) Your company used organised interest groups at the European level i.e. the CEA in the formulation of the third life directive.
(2) Your company used organised interest groups at the national level i.e. the ABI in the formulation of the third life directive.
(3) Your company uses organised interest groups at the European level for most European issues.
(4) Your company subscribes to a European interest group.
(5) Your company subscribes to a national interest group.
(6) Your company lobbies European institutions when its European interests are affected.
(7) Your company lobbies the national government when European interests are affected.
(8) Your company primarily uses interest groups to lobby on its behalf at the European level.
(9) Your company primarily uses interest groups to lobby on its behalf at the national level.
(10) Your company prefers to use interest groups at the European level because this allows European sector wide compromises.
(11) Your company prefers to use interest groups at the national level because this allows nation-wide sector compromises.

(Respondents were asked to give their answers on a Likert scale of 1-4)

The results of the survey indicated that in general the UK insurance companies seldom if ever, directly lobby at the EU level. At both the national and the EU level companies are prepared to allow interest groups to lobby on their behalf. In this context, on specific issues in certain sub-domains (Browne, 1990) there is a form of collective good even though self-interest is a strong driving force (Coleman and Grant, 1988; Grant and Marsh, 1977; Marsh, 1978; Moe, 1980). Of course, as Camerra-Rowe (1996) pointed out the reasons for the maximised use of interest groups could be the relative size of insurance companies. However, the UK industry is one of the largest in the EU. Consequently as the interviews suggest this could be the pattern in other Member States. This may indicate an interaction between self-interest and collective interest regarding interest group membership. As can be seen from survey B the UK industry has " . . . imperfect information and values other than economic self-interest (and in this context) rational behaviour is not inconsistent with the pursuit of common interests" (Moe, 1980, p 8 author's brackets). The problem is that the industry only considers that it is a member of the national interest group. Indeed, there is another dimension to membership in that the national interest group is a member of the European-wide interest group. Is the national interest group acting out of self-interests or is it ensuring the common interest at the EU level? Does the drive toward a SEM force a common interest through the self-interests of the national interest groups?

The evidence in this chapter suggests that the EU insurance industry relies on European-wide interest groups and the notion of collective action. Survey A identified the self-interest of individual companies in relation to the best regulatory environment for their company. Through the national interest group these individual preferences are compromised to form a common interest. Indeed, a common good is sought and reached at the national level. Finally, the national preferences are compromised at the EU level. Through interaction with a supranational institution, sub-national interests identify a common interest. However, it is argued that some companies are large enough to circumvent the interest group or control it. Allianz is capable of this at the national level and it is capable of lobbying the Commission directly. However, as identified by the Commission representative in the interviews, the

Commission prefers to deal with European-wide interest groups. This way it gets an overall perspective of Member State preferences.

Survey C provided some interesting insights into interest group membership in the UK. Most companies were unaware that they were members of a European interest group through ABI membership. If this is the case in other Member States, then the CEA is made up of national interest groups and in this context quite small. Being a small group Olson's logic would not apply (Olson, 1971). Survey B illustrates political goals at the national level and the interviews indicate political goals at the EU level. This has implications for Olson (1971) who emphasises the non-political elements of group membership and the pluralists who emphasise the political. Survey B identified a political basis for interest group membership but the author does not discount the non-political. Indeed, " . . . both political and non-political inducements now have a central logical role to play in explaining group membership" (Moe, 1980; p 6).

Furthermore, both self-interest and common interests have a bearing on interest group membership. Self-interest is obviously a contributory factor but collective interests also have a role to play (Moe, 1980). The EU life insurance industry uses interest groups at the EU level to serve both the self-interest of its membership (the national industries through national interest groups) and the collective interest of the EU industry as a whole when faced with an evolving SEM. However, at the national level few insurance companies realised that they were members of a European-wide interest group and this had implications for company involvement in the integration process. In general, lobbying is left to the national interest groups which as a member of the European interest group negotiates with EU institutions. The CEA is made up of national interest groups, which allows compromise to be easier reached in the EU domain. This ensures further European integration in insurance and other financial services industries.

CONCLUSIONS

This study considers that the interviews identify a process that is made explicit through the models. The Commission initiates legislation at the EU level. Further, " . . . the Commission is a critical actor in the policy initiation phase. . . . After surveying the evidence one cannot conclude that the

Commission serves merely as an agent of state executives" (Hooghe and Marks, 1997; p 28). Furthermore, " . . . if supranational policy-making institutions emerge there is an inherent 'logic' of interest group behaviour which will lead interest groups to re-target their lobbying strategies to take account of the new distribution of power. . . . If power has shifted to a new level of government, any sensible interest group is bound to attempt to influence at the new level. As one American interest group official put it, you need to shoot where the ducks are!" (Mazey and Richardson, 1996; p 200).

The empirical work identified that in the context of life insurance interest groups were central to the decision-making process. In the European Decision-Making Model route B was the one best supported by the interviews. **Compromises** are initially formulated at the national level which are then relayed to the European interest group. Through interaction and compromise a European perspective is sought and eventually put to the national and European decision-making institutions. Of course, there is also input from the national and EU legislatures while this European-wide stance is being created. Effectively, an all-round **understanding** and **compromise** is created which should enable successful legislation. Theoretically, once the Council level is reached, there should be general acceptance of the proposed legislation.

In general, the industry/sector creates an **understanding** of the preferred regulatory environment at the national interest group level: **difference** is consequently **compromised** through European interest groups. Through **interaction** with the Commission and Parliament, the institutions and the European interest groups come to an **understanding** on legislation that is acceptable to the majority of Member States. In some instances national interest groups and individual companies will attempt to **interact** with the Commission. However, the Commission does make it clear that it prefers to deal with European interest groups because this enables a European-wide perspective. This was made clear by all of those interviewed. Once the legislation has been agreed at this level it needs to go through the European legislative process. When the proposals reach the Council level, **differences** should have been minimised either because the Member State interest groups or the European interest groups would have informed governments of the industry's/sector's general acceptance of the directive. If there is no general agreement the directive will either fail or remain on the table. There are exceptions to this process and certain parts of proposed legislation may be discarded. However, in a post-SEA and SEM Europe there has to be a general means of reaching a compromise in terms of effective legislation.

This study considers that a means of reaching a compromise is illustrated here and that in the above context elements of a neo-functional process are observable. The work illustrates a supranational body toward which national organisations have partially shifted their allegiance. If European interest groups and supranationality are employed in the creation of legislation then neo-functionalism as well as intergovernmentalism is apparent in European integration. Indeed, if the above is considered to be the norm in a post-SEA EU, then one may posit that this process will also involve spillover in the financial services sector. The following chapter explores such a scenario.

Finally, the study indicates implications for the financial services sector in relation to participation in the EU policy-making process. Fundamentally, the analysis identifies a process that relates to life insurance and tentatively makes generalisations in respect of other industries within the financial services sector. Life insurance allows generalisations regarding other financial services industries in the EU because of its special nature in all Member States (it is culturally determined) and because of its similarity with other financial services products (regulation is a necessity because of its complex nature). This study generalises the processes identified through the interviews and surveys to other financial services sectors but recognises that this has limitations. However, industries and sectors are isolated entities concerned with their own situation in the wider market place. While at the same time they should be aware of what is happening in other industries and sectors, this in turn makes them initiators and reactors to the actions of other financial services industries and sectors. This provides for the pursuit of collective interests and the means by which generalisations can be made. Overall, through historical institutionalism Member States are being gently melded into multilevel and multi-tiered governance by the actions of numerous sub-national and supranational actors. And interest groups play an important role in this process.

Chapter Six

PROPOSING CASES OF SPILLOVER: TOWARD A SUBSTANTIVE THEORY

It is obvious that no matter how complete the theory may be, a middle term is required between theory and practice providing a link and a transition from one to the other. For a concept of the understanding, which contains the general rule, must be supplemented by an act or judgement whereby the practitioner distinguishes instances where the rule applies and where it does not (Kant, 1995; p 61).

INTRODUCTION

This chapter examines legislation currently in operation and the amount that is necessary to create a single market in financial services and capital movements. It accepts the previous chapter's conclusions about the EU decision-making process and argues that forms of spillover are identifiable regarding insurance and financial services legislation. It generalises the processes identified through the interviews and extends the model and its theoretical implications. A qualitative analysis generalises from one specific situation to another like situation, rather than from sample population to total population. Hence, this work argues that, the process identified by the European Decision-Making Model could be occurring in and impacting on other industries. The study recognises the limitations of such a generalisation and does so with these in mind.

Industries and sectors are isolated entities concerned with their own situation in the wider market place. However, this self-interest necessitates they be aware of what is happening in other industries and sectors; this in turn makes them initiators and reactors to the actions of other industries and sectors. In this context one may resurrect the concept of spillover. "Neo-functionalists such as Haas, purport to describe the mechanism of the linkage between integration in economic and political sectors through the concept of spillover. They use the concept to describe a dynamic and more or less automatic integrative process, gradually encompassing ever more functional sectors until, the final stage, a political union is reached" (Kirchner, 1976; p 2).

The objective of this chapter is to identify the links between legislation in financial services, discuss the concept of spillover and the implications this has for discovering the limits of European integration. "The current ascendancy of a qualified supranational style of decision-making is shown by the way in which, thanks to the Single Act, the Council now functions. . . . The revival of a supranational style of decision-making and the strengthening of European institutions in the Single Act resulted most immediately from decisions by governments to press in their own interests, for a removal of internal economic barriers and for institutional change that would permit such a policy to be carried out" (Keohane and Hoffman, 1991; pp 16-17)[1].

This argument is emphasised by Sandholtz (1994) who considers that 1992 " . . . increased the level of support, among publics and political leaders, for EC-level initiatives. Widespread enthusiasm for the 1992 project tilted preferences toward programs that could be seen as cementing the gains from the single-market program" (p 274). This was a case of spillover in that " . . . integration in one issue area would reveal functional linkages to other issue areas; as a result, the desire to obtain the full benefits of integration in the first area would lead to pressure for integration in a second, linked sector" (ibid, pp 274-275). However, spillover, as deterministic process toward greater integration was criticised and " . . . theorists wrote about 'spill-backs' and 'spill-arounds.' What was not refuted was the notion that spillovers could

[1] At the time of writing, an impasse was apparent regarding pensions, taxation and capital markets, because they come under the unanimity rule. However, these one may assume, will have to be overcome now EMU is operating.

occur; indeed, if issues are linked, then the potential for spillovers always exists. The process is simply not automatic or one directional" (ibid, p 275).

This study agrees with the argument that spillover is neither deterministic nor one directional. However, it does argue that a form of spillover is identifiable in the process of European integration. Indeed, it argues that spillover can be divided into two areas: intergovernmental and neo-functional. Intergovernmental spillover provides the Treaties and decisions made at intergovernmental conferences, e.g. the creation of the ECSC, EEC, the SEA, Maastricht and Amsterdam. Whereas neo-functional spillover can be broken down into two areas: vertical spillover (within the same industry); horizontal spillover (within the same sector). Through an interaction between intergovernmental and neo-functional spillover integration is intensified (for an illustration of this see the Spillover Model). Consequently, the study argues that intergovernmental processes are at work within the creation of the single market, i.e. in the guise of the SEA and the Maastricht and Amsterdam Treaties. Fundamentally, it is considered that " . . . spillover requires prior programmatic agreement among governments, expressed in an intergovernmental bargain. Such a bargain is clearly important in accounting for the Single European Act" (Keohane and Hoffman, 1991; p 17). Furthermore, it is argued that neo-functional processes are providing an impetus for harmonisation and integration. In this context, the work contends that intergovernmental spillover provides the environment for neo-functional spillover to take place i.e. through the ECSC, the EEC, the SEA, the Maastricht and Amsterdam Treaties. However, it also considers that the Member States are pushed in this direction by the dynamics of neo-functional spillover. Indeed, as it becomes more difficult to pass further directives/regulations in an area, further amendments to the Treaties are identified. This was apparent with regard to the SEA, the Maastricht and Amsterdam Treaties and may become even more explicit with the actuality of EMU. The accumulation of legislation as Europe moved toward monetary union, overcame a number of difficulties and as an element of intergovernmental spillover adds impetus to further harmonisation. Finally, this chapter overviews elements of intergovernmental and neo-functional spillover in respect of: the Cecchini Report (1988), the White Paper (1985), freedom of establishment and services, harmonisation, mutual recognition, the SEA, the SEM, the Maastricht Treaty, EMU, and relevant European Court judgements.

There have been two major judgements regarding financial services. The first was made in 1979 in the Cassis de Dijon case which allowed *mutual recognition*. The second was made in 1986 in response to four Member States (Denmark, Eire, France and Germany) that were imposing Non-Tariff Barriers (NTBs) to prevent insurance companies in other Member States from entering their markets. The judgement in the second case considered that the NTBs were partially illegal but partially justified. The judges felt that they were justified with regard to consumer protection which in the field of insurance is particularly important. However, the judges excluded from this all those risks for which such protection was not necessary i.e. large scale risks whose expertise would not necessitate special consumer protection. The benefits of this judgement were included in the insurance directives of the following years.

SPILLOVER, FINANCIAL SERVICES AND EUROPEAN INTEGRATION

The Cecchini Report (1988) put forward a rational argument for the provision of an actual SEM. Following the White Paper (1985), the report illustrated the rationale for the SEA (1987) if the impasse that European integration had reached was to be overcome. If a common market was to be realised then further European integration would be necessary. Cecchini (1988) proposed that national standards and regulations were what European businesses perceived as the second most important NTB to be removed (Cecchini, 1988; p 5). The importance of the service sector was not underestimated in the report, although the extent to which the figures may now be relied upon are debatable. The work does not wish to give a prognosis on the validity of Cecchini's calculations. It does, however, wish to draw on certain qualitative conclusions that the report displayed.

Cecchini (1988) argued that the role of the service sector in Europe was one of " . . . growing importance . . ." and that " . . . the potential for much more significant growth is being artificially pinned back by regulations which significantly inhibit the free flow of services and thus the free play of competition between companies" (ibid, p 37). Cechinni spoke of the pivotal role that financial services would have in the creation of the single market. "Basing its figures on a survey conducted on the three main areas of financial services activity . . . the report forecasts gains of ECU 22,000 million for the eight Community countries Belgium, France, Germany, Italy, Luxembourg, Netherlands, Spain and the UK . . . the value-added generated by the credit and insurance sectors alone accounted for some 6.5% of the Community's gross domestic product in 1985. . . . The benefits would be even greater if the freedom to provide within a European financial common market could be linked immediately to a common currency, since exchange costs would disappear and businesses and individual consumers could achieve substantial savings" (European Document, 4/1989; p 7).

Additionally, the freedom to provide cross-border financial services in tandem with liberalised capital movements would create a more attractive environment for financial business and an efficient means of channelling savings into investment projects. The difficulties created by national capital markets in the EU were highlighted in a Commission report dated April 1983. The Commission report identified that gross savings in the EU amounted to ECU 430,000 million and in the USA, ECU 340,000 million. However, the amount mobilised for investment in the EU's five leading markets (France, Germany, Italy, the Netherlands and the UK) was less than in the USA (ECU 212,000 million in the USA, ECU 142,000 million in the EU). This illustrated the difficulty of mobilising capital in smaller national financial markets (ibid). "Financial services such as banking and insurance will be among those to benefit most from the removal of all barriers and the completion of a large internal market" (ibid, p 18).

By the early 1980s it had become clear that the EEC was far from a common market: fundamentally it was an uncommon market. This term is taken from Holland (1980) who considered that in 1980 the void between theory and practice regarding the EU was immense: that the Common Market was not such at all but an uncommon market in terms of national self-interest. Effectively, it encapsulated no more than a Custom Union. Additionally, thc idealism of integration has been misplaced in that " . . .the Community is essentially a capitalist market, uncommon and unequal" (ibid, p 8).

NTBs were ensuring that a real common market could not develop. In 1985, the Commission put forward plans to remove physical, technical and fiscal barriers between Member States by 1992. "Financial services . . . including insurance, were to be governed by three major principles, i.e. minimum co-ordination of individual national rules, mutual recognition and home country control" (ibid). This indicated the need for Treaty amendments and these were encapsulated in the SEA.

The SEA necessitated a number of amendments concerning the free movement of services and capital that are displayed in Articles 43-60 of the consolidated version of the Treaty (Foster, 1999). These illustrate intergovernmental spillover and are the basis from which further neo-functional spillover could take place:

(1) Right of Establishment
(2) Services
(3) Capital

The programme of a SEM is a continuous process of change that is built on the basic tenets of the (Treaties of Rome, 1988; Arts 2 and 3) and one that will evolve as further treaties come into effect. This process of change had already begun and has carried on in a post-SEM Europe.

Along with supranationality and sub-national interests spillover is central to the concept of neo-functionalism. In general spillover is indicated when integration in one industry/sector creates its own impetus and necessitates further integration both in the same, and in other industries/sectors. "Specifically, the term spillover describes the accretion of new powers and tasks to a central institutional structure, based on changing demands and the expectation on the part of such political actors as interest groups, political parties and bureaucracies" (Haas, cited in Kirchner, 1976; p 3). Effectively, there is an interplay between spillover and supranationality in that the " . . . establishment of supranational institutions designed to deal with functionally specific tasks will set in motion economic, social and political processes which generate pressures towards further integration" (Tranholm-Mikkelsen, 1991; p 4).

Spillover can be identified as a means by which co-operation in one sphere spills into another. Legislation in one sector creates the need for legislation in other sectors and/or further legislation in different areas of the same sector. In this context, the establishment of a SEM was not an end in itself but a stage in the spillover process. Haas (1958) argued that spillover was the result of " . . . swapping concessions from a variety of sectors" (p243). That spillover was the expansive logic of sector integration through a variety of sectors swapping concessions, which provided the motor of political integration (ibid). However, spillover is not automatic and the extent to which changing incentives created by spillover allowed an explanation for European integration has been a point of contention. Nye (1971) argued that the functional linkage of tasks has been a less dynamic aspect of European integration than it was originally believed. Lindberg and Scheingold (1970) wished to deny spillover, whereas Keohane and Hoffman (1990) provided a more sophisticated understanding of spillover one that interacts between domains and sectors. They argue that successful spillover needed prior agreement among Member States in terms of intergovernmental agreements.

This study supports Keohane and Hoffman (1990) and argues that intergovernmental bargains provide the bases for spillover in and between sectors and industries. That " . . . successful spillover requires prior programmatic agreement expressed in an intergovernmental bargain" (p 287). In the 1980s Member State positions regarding further integration changed. The UK pursued deregulation, France changed its economic policy, Spain wanted economic modernisation and Germany wished for monetary stability. Each was changing policy in relation to global competitive pressures (primarily the USA and Japan) and internal pressures that called for a true common market and cross-border trade in the EEC. For instance when Margaret Thatcher was asked in 1989 why she had agreed to the SEA she argued that the UK " . . . wished to have many of the directives under majority voting because things which we wanted were being stopped by others using a single vote. For instance, we have not yet got insurance freely in Germany as we wished"(cited in Keohane and Hoffman, 1990; p 287). However, as well as self-interest, European integration and spillover depend on shared objectives. In the 1950s and 1960s these shared objectives revolved around Keynesian economic policies and in the 1980s and early 1990s around deregulation or re-regulation.

Industries and sectors are isolated entities concerned with their own situation in the wider market place. However, it is through this self-interest that they must be aware of what is happening in other industries and sectors this in turn makes them initiators and reactors to the actions of other industries and sectors. Sectors and industries need to involve themselves in the European integration process. They need to ensure their competitive advantage and this means participating in the European decision-making process. Fundamentally, they are the instigators of changes in legislation in both their own and similar industries/sectors. Indeed, on occasion they pressure their Member State governments to bring about new treaties.

As outlined in Chapter Three there are two main understandings of spillover outlined in this study:

(S1) Spillover occurs because of the impact it has on differentiated actors, including multinationals, interest groupings, the Commission and national organisations. These actors form coalitions to increase EU decision-making in new sectors and enhance integration in sectors where agreements have already been reached.

(S2) Spillover is a result of past policies created by Member States. They remain central to the integration process and continue to make crucial policy decisions in the EU. (Member States remain central actors but they are dictated to by past actions) (see Keohane and Hoffman, 1990; p 286).

As noted this work to builds on the above definitions of spillover and devises a model to illustrate how it is an element in the process of European integration. Spillover may be observed in the legislation specific to the insurance industry (vertical neo-functional spillover); between legislation in the services sector e.g. between insurance, banking, pensions etc. (horizontal neo-functional spillover). The work also argues that an intergovernmental process of spillover is at work within European integration in the guise of the treaties and there outcomes. Indeed, ". . . spillover requires prior programmatic agreement among governments, expressed in an intergovernmental bargain. Such a bargain is clearly important in accounting for the Single European Act" (Keohane and Hoffman, 1991; p 17). This is spillover from treaty to treaty, which may be labelled intergovernmental spillover and is indicated by definition (S2) above. However, wider transnational processes are also providing an impetus for European integration. In this context, the study argues that intergovernmental spillover is usually confined to providing the environment for further neo-functional spillover (vertical or horizontal) to take place. This is illustrated by definition (S1) above. Fundamentally, one may argue, that there is an interaction between neo-functional and intergovernmental spillover, which widens and deepens European integration. Again a move toward an intensification of multi-level governance and historical institutionalism. Indeed, multilevel governance indicates the processes at work whereas historical institutionalism identifies the direction to be taken.

The Spillover Model (Figs 6.1 and 6.2) outlines the above interactions: intergovernmental spillover is indicated in the left hand column and is made up of intergovernmental agreements and neo-functional spillover is illustrated on the right hand side of the model. The crosses on the model represent legislation that has been passed in relation to the treaties that existed at that time e.g. X1 relates to the Reinsurance Directive and X2 the Co-insurance Directive etc.

The liberalisation of insurance, banking and capital markets is tied closely to the free movements of capital. The treaties indicate that the liberalisation of the banking and insurance sectors " . . . shall be effected in step with the progressive liberalisation of the movement of capital" (Foster, 1999; Art 51). This could be seen as part of the impetus for intergovernmental spillover which provides an opportunity for horizontal neo-functional spillover (industry to industry or banking to insurance) and vertical spillover (within the same industry i.e. insurance). This could be seen as an example of intergovernmental spillover providing the initial environment for further neo-functional spillover.

In its proposal for a the Third Life Assurance Directive, the Commission emphasised that " . . . the internal market in insurance represents a primary goal . . . in view of the importance of this strongly expanding sector"[2]. The insurance industry considered that it needed priority treatment because it lagged behind the liberalisation of the other economic sectors within the financial services sector (omitting pensions). Directives in securities and banking had already been implemented and as a consequence the insurance industry had been left at a competitive disadvantage in relation to these industries. Indeed, an example of horizontal neo-functional spillover (within the same sector; banking to insurance).

In terms of vertical neo-functional spillover, the adopted insurance directives from the early 1970s have taken form in three generations, these are briefly overviewed below. Directives concentrating on more specific areas include the Council directive on measures to facilitate the effective exercise of freedom of establishment and freedom to provide services in respect of the activities of insurance agents and brokers (ex ISIC group 630) and in

---

[2] Com 91 57 final SYN 329 p 2

particular, transitional measures in respect of these activities (77/92/EEC)[3]. Further directives providing the infrastructure for the second generation included the Co-Insurance Directive (78/473/EEC)[4], the Credit and Suretyship Assurance Directive amending Directive (87/343/EEC)[5], and the Legal Expenses Directive (87/344/EEC)[6]. The infrastructure directives for the third generation include the Council Directive on the Annual Accounts and Consolidated Accounts of Insurance Undertakings (91/674/EEC)[7] and the Council Directive setting up an Insurance Committee (91/675/EEC)[8]. The former of these Directives (91/674/EEC) proposed the harmonisation of EU insurance accounting practices, which is necessary if valuation and solvency indicators are to be uniform. Indeed, such is necessary if an integrated capital market is to be achieved. Furthermore, Directive (91/675/EEC) provided a committee to act as an intermediary between the industry (sub-national interests) and the Commission and to assist in implementation procedures. The committee also examines any questions relating to the application of existing directives and the preparation of new legislation proposals in the insurance sector. Indeed, this could be seen as an example of interaction between spillover and supranationality (Kirchner, 1976; Tranholm-Mikkelsen, 1991).

NEO-FUNCTIONAL SPILLOVER, MUTUAL RECOGNITION AND HOME COUNTRY CONTROL

One may consider that one person's protective legislation is another's trade barrier and it is from such a premise that the EU undertakes a harmonisation process under a tripartite system:

- the harmonisation of essential standards.
- the mutual recognition of other Member State standards
- (based on the above) home country control and supervision.

[3] OJ L 26, 31/06/77
[4] OJ L 151, 07/06/84
[5] OJ L 185, 04/07/87
[6] OJ L185, 04/07/87
[7] OJ L 374, 31/12/91
[8] OJ L 374/31/91

The treaties determine that the EU should be attempting to create a functioning SEM. However, it may be argued that intervention in legislative processes should be limited to the domains in which mutual recognition cannot ensure the protection of essential requirements. To assist in the convergence of legislation, the EU could take measures to promote the transparency of transposing legislation at the national level through exchanges of information and allowing the national courts a greater capacity for ensuring the adherence to EU legislation. A legislative framework should respond to the objectives of free movement and the respect of essential requirements immediately. However, at the same time, it must also adhere to the objectives of a balanced social and economic development.

To enable the achievement of a SEM, the Commission concluded that the regulatory framework could be achieved through mutual recognition and home country control. The White Paper (1985) proposed that the minimum of essential standards should be harmonised. The difficulty is how to interpret 'essential' and 'minimum' in respect of the proposed regulatory framework. Member States will have a different interpretation of these terms, which will be reflected in its existing legislation and consequent regulatory environment. The work has proposed that norms of a legal nature must differ from state to state; consequently, a process of compromise may be discerned through the construction of the legal framework that will indicate both the future and present state of the SEM regulatory structure. Indeed, chapters Four and Five concluded that national legislation is compromised by Member States through the use of interest groups and supranational authorities (see the European Decision-Making Model, Fig 5.2). Mutual recognition encapsulates an important mechanism in the pursuit of the SEM as it gives a framework for compromise. However, as this study has indicated where diversity is so great, there will be a need for greater rather than less harmonisation of Member State legislation. "The principle of mutual recognition . . . pre-supposes agreement on a number of basic rules . . . these minimum harmonisation requirements . . . are only possible because common interest, mutual confidence and a high degree of economic convergence exist between EEC member states" (Loheac, 1991; p 409).

One has to question if "minimum harmonisation requirements" were met in respect of the life insurance market. The achievement of such requirements is extremely rare and even if there is a " . . . high degree of economic convergence" in the life insurance market, the practical realities of achieving an SEM through mutual recognition alone are apparent (ibid). A convergence process must be undertaken prior to the actions of mutual recognition coming into play (see Figs 4.1 and 4.2).

The idea behind mutual recognition suggests spontaneous legislative adaptation. However, it does not deal with all regulation and as a convergence point is necessary for mutual recognition to be effective it could be conceived as an impetus that encourages legislative change and compromise.

Following intergovernmental spillover, the convergence process illustrates neo-functionalism because agreement between Member State industries has to be reached, as does agreement between the Commission and the industry in general. This allows the formulation of legislation that is agreeable to both the Member State industries and the EU and increases the chance that the legislation will be successful at the Council of Ministers' stage. Directives allow Member States to build legislation into their own legal frameworks and to allow this, they are quite broad in character. At this point, mutual recognition comes into play and the theory is that this will allow convergence through market forces. However, mutual recognition usually requires prior compromise and convergence. This work argues that it is such a process as this that indicates neo-functional spillover in the creation of the legislation that underpins regulatory structures.

European Banking Legislation

Two co-ordination directives have affected the European banking sector. The First Banking Directive (77/780/EEC)[9] cleared most obstacles to the freedom of establishment for banks and other credit institutions, introduced home country supervision and a common position for the granting of banking licences. However, problems were still apparent and certain obstacles needed to be removed before a genuine single market in banking could be achieved.

[9] OJ L 322 17/12/77

The Second Banking Directive (89/646/EEC)[10] aimed at the removal of authorisation problems i.e. 12 different supervisors, a definition of banking activities and cross-border trade. Consequently, the second directive enabled a single banking licence, a list of banking activities and minimum capital levels (5m ECU laid down for new banks). The directive also provided supervisory rules in terms of internal management, audit systems and the amount of control of major shareholders.

The directive on Investment Firms and Credit Institutions (CAD) provides the framework for the Investment Services Directive (ISD) (93/22/EEC)[11]. The two directives engender an internal market in respect of investment services and give all institutions, whether credit or investment firms, the ability to offer investment services throughout the EU. This illustrates horizontal neo-functional spillover (industry to industry in the financial services sector).

In December 1992, the Council adopted the Directive on Monitoring and Controlling Large Exposures of Credit Institutions[12]. As part of the legislation necessary to create an SEM in the banking sector, it deals with the prudential treatment of large exposures with a single client. Large exposures are defined in the Own Funds Directive (89/299/EEC) [13] in which an exposure is considered large if it exceeds 10% of the credit institution's own funds. The Directive states that companies should make known the existence of all large exposures and none should exceed 25% of the credit institution's own funds.

At the ECO/FIN Council on 23 Nov 1992, the Commission's approach to the BCCI affair was outlined by Sir Leon Brittan. He argued that the system of home country control and consolidated supervision did not need major reforms. However, he contended that in certain respects supervision may be strengthened and clarified, particularly with reference to: the transparency of group structures; greater exchange of information between supervisory authorities; the role of external auditors; and intensified co-operation between international prudential supervisors. The 35th meeting of the Banking Advisory Commission was consulted in respect of the draft proposals of the Commission. This concerned a directive to amend the Council directive on

[10] OJ L 386 30/12/89

[11] OJ L 141 11/06/93

[12] OJ L 29 05/02/93

[13] OJ L 124 05/05/89

strengthening the supervision of credit institutions following the discussions on BCCI at the ECO/FIN meeting. The Banking Advisory Committee also discussed a broad outline by the Commission on amending the Council Directive concerned with the re-organisation and winding-up of credit institutions.

In general, during the nineties, there have been numerous decisions made by the Commission and Council as well as further directives with regard to the banking sector. For instance, Council Directive (96/13/EC)[14] amends article 2 (2) of (77/780/EEC)[15] in respect of the list of permanent exclusions of certain credit institutions. Indeed, directive (96/10/EC)[16] amends directive (89/647/EEC)[17] regarding contractual netting by competent authorities; directive (95/15/EC)[18] and (94/7/EC)[19] amend the directive regarding solvency ratios. Effectively, the last directive in terms of banking that was not an amendment to a previous directive was (93/6/EC)[20] which covered both investment firms and credit institutions and subsequently both security markets and insurance as well. Fundamentally, banking legislation and its consequent regulation spills over and necessitates legislation in other financial services industries. This process is illustrated by the interaction between security markets and banking. Indeed, one may consider that this is an example of neo-functional horizontal specific spillover; or spillover from industry to industry.

EUROPEAN SECURITY MARKET LEGISLATION

The objective of an SEM in security markets is one in which companies are free to raise capital and be admitted to stock exchange trading in other Member States, as easily as they may in their own. The directive (80/390/EEC)[21] was the first step in the process and it indicated the

[14] OJ L 066 16/03/96
[15] OJ L 322 17/12/77
[16] OJ L 085 03/04/96
[17] OJ L 125 05/05/89
[18] OJ L 125 08/06/95
[19] OJ L 089 06/04/94
[20] OJ L 141 11/06/93
[21] OJ L 100 17/04/80

harmonisation of conditions for stock exchange listings and agreed mutual recognition in respect of any listing that met 1980s particulars. In 1993, a proposal to amend this Directive was posted[22]. The aims of the proposal were to simplify cross-border listing requirements for established companies and to facilitate the listing of companies on junior markets. The amendments are an extension of Article 6 and are based on the assumption that most of the information needed by investors already exists in the market. Therefore, its duplication to ensure consumer protection is no longer justified.

The proposed amendments of (80/390/EEC) should create more efficiency in the securities market because the proposed legislation is more beneficial to the realities of the existing market. The measures relating to cross-border listing would also assist the implementation and completion of the EUROLIST project which is to be launched by the Federation of Stock Exchanges at some point in the future.

Directive (85/611/EEC) on undertakings for collective investment in transferable securities (UCITS)[23] from October 1990 allowed an investment fund authorised in its home Member State to be sold anywhere in the EU. In December 1989 the Commission adopted an amended proposal for a Council directive[24], which complemented the Second Banking Directive and provided for the liberalisation of security-related services provided by non-banking intermediaries (spillover between industries). It introduced cross-border provisions in respect of broking, dealing and portfolio management. The directive also allowed anyone authorised by their home country to be a member of their national stock exchange to be a member of any other Member State stock exchange. This is a major difficulty as there should be no dictate on how Member States administer their own stock exchange. Discussions with Member States are at an early stage and progress is very slow. One may consider that this is because further changes are necessary and these can only be realised through monetary union (intergovernmental spillover through the Treaty of Maastricht).

---

[22] OJ C 23 27/01/93

[23] OJ L 1995 375/3

[24] Com (89) 629 final-SYN 176

EUROPEAN INSURANCE LEGISLATION

Insurance legislation is an example of vertical neo-functional spillover or spillover within the same industry. Initially, there were two general programmes proposed to ensure that both the freedom of services and establishment would be realised in life insurance by the beginning of 1970. This was indicated through five main bi-annual target dates.

1964 Reinsurance. Freedom of establishment and services.
1966 Indemnity insurance. Freedom of establishment.
1968 Life insurance. Freedom of establishment.
1968 Indemnity insurance. Freedom of services.
1970 Life insurance. Freedom of services.

As may be observed, life insurance was to be harmonised in two stages, which would have corresponded with the initial plans for EMU. However, decision-making was difficult and the timetable too crowded. The programme was an over-ambitious attempt to align substantive law. During the 1970s, this was replaced with equivalence and mutual trust between Member States and the harmonisation of substantive law kept to a minimum.

EU legislation has primarily taken a three dimensional approach to insurance. Following Council directive (64/225/EEC) that abolished restrictions on freedom of establishment and freedom to provide services concerning reinsurance and retrocession, insurance has been broken down into non-life and life. Reinsurance was the easiest to harmonise because it was international by nature. Consequently, the harmonisation of different national legislation in this area was less of a problem. The life and non-life areas of insurance have had to deal with differing national regulations conceptualised in historical normative ideas of what constitutes insurance products, consumer protection and choice. These problems have affected non-life insurance. However, the most difficult problems to be overcome have been those that pertain to the life insurance market.

In its proposal for a the Third Life Assurance Directive, the Commission made clear that " . . . the internal market in insurance represented a primary goal . . . in view of the importance of this strongly expanding sector"[25]. The

---

[25] Com 91 57 final SYN 329 p 2

insurance industry considered that it needed priority treatment because it lagged behind the liberalisation of the other economic sectors within the financial services sector (omitting pensions). Directives in the securities and banking industry had already been implemented and as a consequence the insurance industry had been left at a competitive disadvantage in relation to these industries, an example of horizontal neo-functional spillover.

In terms of vertical neo-functional spillover, the adopted insurance directives have taken form in three generations dating from the early 1970s: these are briefly overviewed below. Directives concentrating on more specific areas include the Council directive on measures to facilitate the effective exercise of freedom of establishment and freedom to provide services in respect of the activities of insurance agents and brokers (ex ISIC group 630) and in particular, transitional measures in respect of those activities (77/92/EEC)[26]. The Co-Insurance Directive (78/473/EEC)[27], the Credit and Suretyship Assurance Directive amending Directive (87/343/EEC)[28], and the Legal Expenses Directive (87/344/EEC)[29]. The latest, more specific, directives include the Council Directive on the Annual Accounts and Consolidated Accounts of Insurance Undertakings (91674/EEC)[30] and the Council Directive setting up an Insurance Committee (91/675/EEC)[31]. The former of these Directives proposes the harmonisation of EU insurance accounting practices which is necessary if valuation and solvency indicators are to be uniform. The latter directive provided a committee to act as an intermediary between the industry and the Commission and to assist in implementation procedures. The committee also examines any questions relating to the application of existing directives and the preparation of new legislation proposals in the insurance sector. The Insurance Committee met in Brussels on 24-25 May 1993 to discuss a directive, which would take into account the BCCI experience; the problem of Member State legislation implementation; the proposal for an EC Co-operative Company and its effects on insurance supervision. All of this legislation is not depicted on the spillover model because this would make it

[26] OJ L 26, 31/06/77
[27] OJ L 151, 07/06/84
[28] OJ L 185, 04/07/87
[29] OJ L185, 04/07/87
[30] OJ No L 374, 31/12/91
[31] OJ No L 374/31/91

unclear. However, elements could be included as each has an influence on the other and provides an illustration of neo-functional spillover (see the Spillover Model, Figs 6.1, 6.2).

Also under discussion during the early nineties was the proposal for a Council directive on the co-ordination of laws, regulations and administrative provisions relating to insurance contracts[32]. This was discontinued in 1993. As discussed above protection against divergent contracts may be used as an NTB because unfair contract protection is different in separate Member States. However, the implementation of the EC Unfair Contract Terms Directive in 1993 has reduced the extent that insurance contracts can be used as NTBs. Indeed, " . . . by converting common law self regulatory Statements of Insurance Practice into statutory codes applying to all insurance companies trading in consumer risks within the UK market" (Ellis, 1995; p 54). This in itself could be seen as an aspect of spillover, where a general piece of European legislation overcomes difficulties in specific sectors. Even though this does not completely deal with the difficulties that emerge from the lack of an Insurance Contracts Directive. It does, however, allow a benchmark for contract terms that may be acceptable in the European Union. This illustrates spillover and provides a starting point for harmonisation in the European life insurance industry. Still under discussion is the proposal for a Council directive on the co-ordination of laws, regulations and administrative provisions relating to the compulsory winding up of direct insurance undertakings[33].

Each of these proposals relates to consumer protection, while at the same time they attempt to ensure consumer choice and a competitive market. However, Member States find difficulty in reaching a compromise with the EU in these areas because of both sovereignty and market environment issues. These directives are more generally known as the Contracts and Liquidation Directives. The first Council discussion on the contracts proposal was in 1980[34] with the latest taking place in 1988. Council discussions on the liquidation amendment[35] began in the first six months of 1993. The problems

[32] OJ No C 71, 28/07/79

[33] OJ No C 71, 19/03/87

[34] OJ No C. 355 31/12/80

[35] OJ No C. 235 06/10/89

in these areas reflect those experienced by the third generation life and non-life insurance directives.

Finally, in respect of further spillover, it is worth noting the overlap with regard to the legislation between these three areas: much of it will lay the basis for future legislation in areas not sufficiently touched upon, i.e. pensions and taxation. Financial services legislation has created difficulties for other sectors which has necessitated further legislation. This is horizontal neo-functional spillover when there is task expansion from one sector to another, e.g. from services to capital and from one area of financial services to another, e.g. from banking to insurance. Additionally there is vertical neo-functional spillover and this is illustrated by legislation in one area of the sector, e.g. insurance, creating the necessity for further legislation in the same area (see below). The non-life insurance directives are, on the one hand, tied closely to the life insurance directives, while on the other, like their life insurance counterparts, they border banking and security services legislation. Effectively, there has been a task expansion throughout the sector and one may consider that this encompasses a form of spillover.

The Life Assurance Directives

As mentioned above, the life assurance directives illustrate vertical neo-functional spillover in its most simplified form with each generation creating the need for the next. However, each generation also created the need for further legislation, both in insurance and other areas of financial services. The first generation of directives allowed for the freedom of establishment as long as the Member State in which the company wished to establish approved conditions of contracts and tariffs. The First Life Assurance Directive dealt with the need for licensing and the means by which an insurance establishment would be approved and standardised. Additionally, the supervisory responsibility in respect of establishment competence was transferred to the Member State where the principal place of business was situated. However, there was little legislation regarding freedom of services in this directive.

Figure 6.1 The Spillover Model

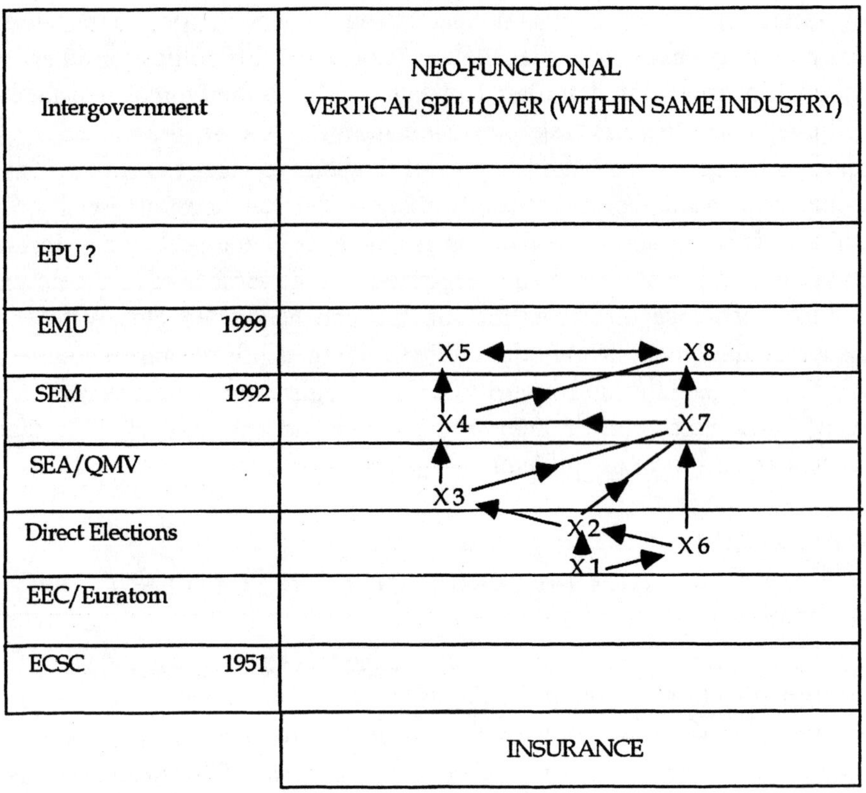

Neo-Functional Vertical Spillover (Within Same Industry)

1. Re-insurance Directive 64/225/EEC
2. Co-insurance Directive 78/473/EEC
3. First Life Insurance Directive. 79/267/EEC
4. Second Life Insurance Directive. 90/ 619/EEC
5. Third Life Insurance Directive. 92/96/EEC
6. First Non-Life Insurance Directive. 73/239/EEC
7. Second Non-Life Insurance Directive. 88/357/EEC
8. Third Non-Life Insurance Directive. 92/49/EEC

Figure 6.2 Neo-Functional Horizontal Spillover (Industry to Industry Within the Same Sector)

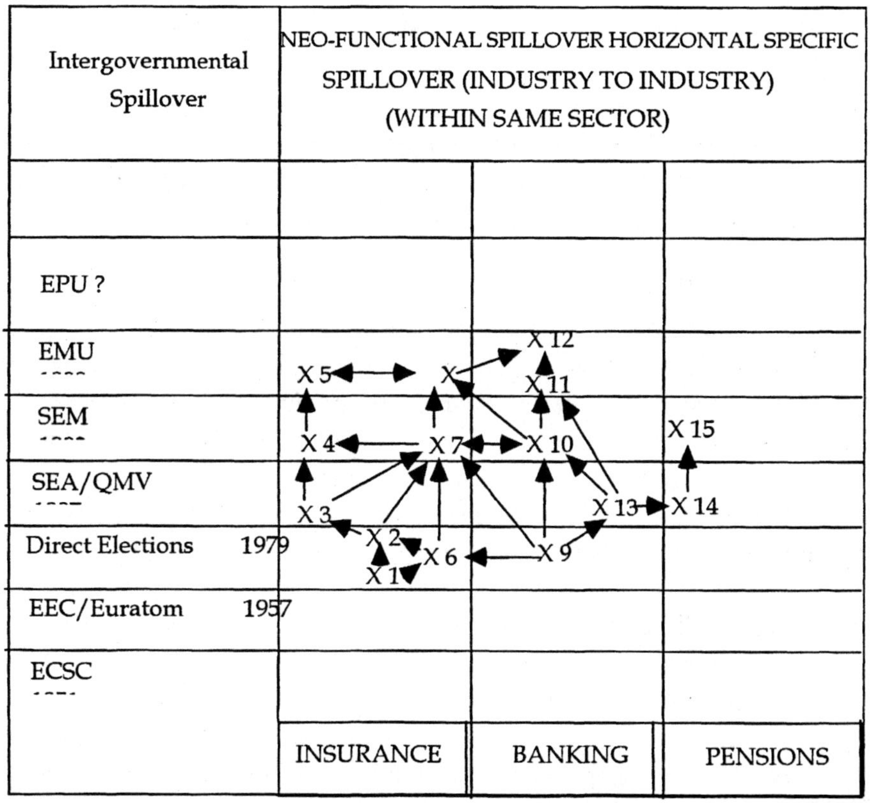

Neo-Functional Horizontal Spillover (Industry to Industry Within the Same Sector)

X1. Re-insurance Directive 64/225/EEC
X2. Co-insurance Directive 78/473/EEC
X3. First Life Insurance Directive. 79/267/EEC
X4. Second Life Insurance Directive. 90/ 619/EEC
X5. Third Life Insurance Directive. 92/96/EEC
X6. First Non-Life Insurance Directive. 73/239/EEC
X7. Second Non-Life Insurance Directive. 88/357/EEC

X8. Third Non-Life Insurance Directive. 92/49/EEC
X9. First Banking Directive. 77/780/EEC
X10. Second Banking Directive. 89/646/EEC
X11. Capital Adequacy Directive. 93/6/EEC
X12. Solvency Ration Directive. 94/7/EEC
X13. Accounts Directive for Banks and Other Credit Institutions. 86/635/EEC
X14. Directive Concerning Equal Treatment for Men and Women in Occupational Social Security Schemes. 86/378/EEC
X15. Directive Concerning the Rights of Residence for Self-Employed Persons Who have Ceased Occupational Activity. 90/365/EEC

The Second Life Assurance Directive (90/619/EEC)[36] provided the means for cross-border business and distinguished between active and passive provisions of services. The directive takes the consumer as its starting point and provides for free movement through two regulations. Firstly, if policyholders approach an insurer from another Member State, the legislation of the Member State where the insurer has its majority of business applies. However, secondly, if the insurer attempts to persuade the policyholder to take out a policy, the legislative code of the Member State in which the insurer performs a service applies. This denied cross-border trade in life insurance and necessitated further harmonisation. This led to the Third Life Assurance Directive and vertical neo-functional spillover.

The Third Life Assurance Directive (92/96/EEC)[37] was adopted on 10 November 1992 and implemented on 1 July 1994. Fundamentally, it created a uniform system of control in that insurers need only be granted approval where they have their headquarters, their own Member State should administer control. It amends both former directives and specifically removes the passive/active clause from the Second Life Assurance Directive. In general terms, host Member State legislation only applies if it is considered to be for the general good - this incorporates the permitted application of host country rules where there is no duplication in the country. The general good should

[36] OJ No L 330 29/11/90
[37] OJ No L 360 09/12/92

also be applied without national discrimination and proportionate to the objective being pursued.

The main provisions are as follows. Firstly, there is the single licence, this shifts responsibility for financial supervision (in terms of all business) to home country or head office supervision. This is whether policies are written through:

(a) A head office; or
(b) A branch in another Member State; or
(c) A service basis. There is no need to seek authorisation.

The undertaking should simply notify the authorities. Secondly, the directive pursues uniformity in terms the assets to be used to represent the solvency margin in respect of:

(a) Accounts of Mutuals.
(b) Preferential share capital.
(c) Subordinated loan capital; and undated securities.

Thirdly, the directive indicates actuarial principles governing the calculation of technical provisions. It also requires premiums for new business, on reasonable actuarial assumptions, to enable insurers to establish adequate technical provisions.

Fourthly, regulations on matching and localising assets representing the technical provisions are provided. This is done with regard to:

(a) The currency matching of the asset representing the technical provision.
(b) The extent that assets must be both adequately spread and diversified.
(c) How far and which assets may be used to represent technical provisions.
(d) Limitations regarding certain assets.

It is also stated that Member States are not allowed to determine insurers investment categories. Additionally, the directive deals with qualifying holdings, composite insurers, contract cancellations and disclosure. Qualifying holdings are demarcated as 10%-plus of capital or voting rights; or that which enables significant influence over the management of the given undertaking. The competent authorities need to be notified about existing qualifying holdings and if there are any changes to them. No new composite insurers are permitted. However, those already in existence may continue to write both life insurance and non-life insurance as long as each activity is separately managed. Contracts will be subject to a 14-30 day cancellation period and all relevant information should be provided both prior to and during the term of the contract.

Finally, once the directive was in place, Member States no longer needed to require prior approval or give systematic notification of rates or policy conditions. However, the home Member State may ask for some systematic notification of the technical bases used for calculating scales of premiums and technical provisions, but only to verify compliance with Member State provisions concerning actuarial principles. Host Member States will be allowed to require non-systematic notification of policy conditions and other printed documents, but not scales of premiums. However, insurance contracts must adhere to the national legislation of the host Member State and to this end it could forbid the contract if it is contrary to national rights or public interest. Subsequently, the Member State has a means of disallowing an insurance company the right to provide a cross-border service. To create a European market in insurance products, particularly life, further directives will be necessary and the bulk of Member State legislation harmonised. Each piece of legislation necessitated and created the next, and this process has formed the basis of the SEM's regulatory structure in insurance and financial services.

CONCLUSIONS

Neo-functional spillover alone cannot bring about European integration it is limited without the impetus of intergovernmental spillover (this can takes the form of further political treaties). However, the need for further treaties is created through neo-functional spillover and the realisation of the four freedoms. In these terms, neo-functional spillover is a functional variable within the integration process. It could be argued that the attainable legislation in financial services ha been reached in the period of integration prior to EMU and if further neo-functional spillover was to be achieved greater intergovernmental spillover was necessary. This analysis argues that intergovernmental and neo-functional spillover interact and that further intergovernmental spillover was realised in the Maastricht Treaty. Indeed, the actuality of the SEM and the environment for EMU allows neo-functional spillover to take place. However, further treaties (intergovernmental spillover e.g. the Treaty of Amsterdam) will be necessary to create the environment for further harmonisation (neo-functional spillover) in the process of European integration.

The Spillover Model outlines this process: intergovernmental spillover is indicated in the left-hand column and is made up of intergovernmental agreements and neo-functional spillover is illustrated on the right hand of the model. As explained above neo-functional spillover constitutes three processes and each figure attempts to clarify these. The crosses on the model represent pieces of legislation that have been passed in relation to the treaties that existed at that time e.g. X1 relates to the Reinsurance Directive and X2 the Coinsurance Directive. Indeed, the model, in line with this chapter, attempts to clarify if spillover is part of the process in European integration. It does not rule out spillbacks etc, but does identify the existence of task expansion.

A SEM in financial services is intrinsically tied to the need for a single currency. However, whether EMU will be consolidated is debatable. One may only draw tentative conclusions about what the future situation will entail. The Germans and French believe that EMU is still on course and there are those who are making the transference to the euro. Yet there are those who are either unready or unwilling. In this context a two-speed Europe is not difficult to envisage. How the difference between being in the 'slow lane' or the 'fast lane' will affect the financial service sectors in the specific Member States remains to be seen. However, one cannot help thinking that the 'fast lane' may be more advantageous. To this end, it could be envisaged that a Member State financial services industry would want its government to ensure early entry.

Delors and the Commission " . . . portrayed EMU as functionally linked to the internal program and necessary for its success. . . . The August 1990 EC Commission document, Economic and Monetary Union . . . declares: A single currency is the natural complement of a single market. The full potential of the latter will not be achieved without the former" (Sandholtz, 1994; p 274). Indeed, " . . . the argument is that complete capital liberation . . . and exchange rate stability (in the EMS) are incompatible with divergent national monetary policies. It is illogical to expect that the EU can have; a single market, a fixed exchange rate, liberal capital movements and autonomous national monetary policies" (ibid). Something must give because the " . . . first three bring about gains in efficiency . . . the submersion of national monetary policy autonomy in a European monetary policy" (ibid, p 276) becomes imperative. However, there are two major problems with the spillover hypothesis. Firstly, the functional link is not clear, a SEM could function without a single currency. Effectively, there is little consensus on the desirability of EMU let alone its necessity. Secondly, if the neo-functional theory of spillover is to hold, then " . . .once an integrative step has been taken, actors discover that they must integrate further in order to realise benefits. In the case of EMU, that kind of learning cannot have taken place . . . The learning process postulated by neo-functionalists has not had time to occur" (ibid).

These are valid points. However, it would be unthinkable to consider that the initiation and pursuit of a SEM had nothing to do with EMU. "The 1992 programme produced a . . . positive attitude toward the EC, was fertile soil for the EMU initiative . . . It bears remembering that the goal of monetary union had been established at the Hague summit in 1969, yet the EC made no real progress in that direction in the 1970s. The member states reaffirmed monetary union as their objective at the creation of the EMS in 1979, but in succeeding years they failed to take any of the steps foreseen to achieve it. In 1988 and 1989, however, EMU became a movement. What had intervened was the 1992 project" (ibid, 277).

Without the SEA and SEM, EMU would not have reached the agenda. The SEM gave EMU credibility. Sectors realised the potential of the market which together " . . . increased the credibility of the community as a source of solutions to common problems" (ibid, p 276).

One may contend that economic sectors and political institutions perceive regulatory structures as externality's that affect their behaviour. However, it can be argued that a sector's and institution's behaviour both affect the regulatory environment and that they are subsequently affected by it; that there is a constant interaction between the two. Indeed, as illustrated above, this work has analysed the differing regulatory environments within the individual Member States and the legislation that displays how such differences may be discerned (see Life Insurance Regulation Matrices Figs 4.1 & 4.2).

It may be argued that by the early 1980s financial services legislation had reached an impasse and that without the impetus of greater integration that the

SEA allowed, the harmonisation process would have slowed down considerably. However, even with the Treaties of Maastricht and Amsterdam and the implementation of the euro, it is now apparent that only the lesser problematic areas of harmonisation have been achieved in the existing phase of European integration. If a SEM in financial services is to be realised, further harmonisation will be necessary. As the Treaties point out, single markets in banking and insurance are closely linked to the free movement of capital. However, to achieve the free movement of capital, one may contend that a single currency is essential and until this exists the idea of free capital movement is unrealistic. Indeed now monetary union has been realised taxation and pension issues can be discussed in detail and compromises pursued; through the realisation of the Maastricht Treaty (intergovernmental spillover) neo-functional spillover be intensified.

This study argues that there are two processes of spillover at work; one at a state level and one at a supranational, sector and interest group level. The former may be identified as intergovernmental spillover, the latter as neo-functional spillover. The latter may be broken down into two further categories, horizontal spillover (services to capital or insurance to banking) and vertical spillover (within insurance i.e. industry bound).

Finally, the difficulties outlined above may be perceived in the pursuit of creating a single market in financial services and particularly in life insurance. Chapters Four and Five discussed the problems involved in the negotiations that created the Third Life Assurance Directive and showed how agreement may have been impossible without QMV and the SEM. The need for interest groups, supranationality and both forms of spillover in the integration process suggests that integration is not simply driven by intergovernmental processes, but by neo-functional processes as well. Through a generalisation of the European Decision-Making Model Chapter Six has proposed an extension of spillover (that incorporates aspects of both intergovernmentalism and neo-functionalism) and provides further understanding of European integration.

Chapter Seven

CONSTRUCTING A SUBSTANTIVE THEORY

What, then, is Europe? It is a kind of cape of the old continent, a western appendix to Asia. It looks naturally toward the west. On the south it is bordered by a famous sea whose role, or should I say function, has been wonderfully effective in the development of the European spirit with which we are concerned (Valery, 1962; pp 311-312).

INTRODUCTION

This work has heeded the calls for empirical studies regarding European integration theory. Through an analysis of the European life insurance industry, it has attempted to build a substantive theory in a bid to discover the limits of European integration. A substantive theory has been created which joins the hierarchy of substantive/formal theories in the area of integration. It is a theory, which mainly investigates neo-functionalism and intergovernmentalism, and ultimately identifies elements of both in the process of European integration. Indeed, it adds to the formal theories and posits that certain parts may be fused to further our comprehension of European integration limitations. The work pursued a grounded theory understanding of theory, which considers that a theory's only replacement is another theory, that theories are modified rather than proved. In this context, the work's ontology was *critical realist* (taking the view that reality does exist beyond human construction but the human intellect is flawed and unable to comprehend it perfectly). Indeed, the inquiry paradigm was *postpositivist* (Guba and Lincoln 1994).

THEORY BUILDING

Grounded theory techniques have been employed in the following ways. Firstly, the *open coding* of *concepts* was undertaken through the *categorisation* of individual Member States' life insurance legislation and regulatory regimes. This allowed *properties* and *dimensions* to be identified which provided the basis of a regulation table and matrix. Categories emerged through the *open sampling* of the data. Further coding and sampling through a survey of Member State insurance industries refined the matrix. Coding at this point was primarily open, however, *axial coding* had begun to relate the *categories* and *sub-categories* more specifically and indicate possibilities of *process*. In this context, sampling began to focus on the *validation* of the *categories* and the relationships between them. The validated table and matrix raised questions with regard to how legislative differences between Member States may be resolved. Through *axial coding* and *selective coding*, further interaction and *process* were identified and illustrated through the European Decision-Making Model. Initially the sampling was *relational and variational*, however it soon became more *discriminate* and pin-pointed those individuals that needed to be interviewed and determined a further survey. Each part of the *theoretical coding* and *sampling* added to the tables, matrix and models, which provide the building blocks of the substantive theory. Indeed, further sub-categories emerged through the interviews, which provided further comprehension of process and European integration. **Understanding, Negotiation, Interaction, Difference** and **Compromise** identified aspects of process e.g. the amalgamation of self-interest and common interest, and assisted in making this explicit through the construction of the European Decision-Making Model.

The *selective coding* process is specifically illustrated by the matrix and the model fitting together around the core category of European integration through the creation of the *sub-categories*. Axial coding draws all parts of the analysis together and it is the pivot or the axis of theory building. Selective coding identifies the *core category* and develops it in relation to *sub-categories*. Indeed, *open, axial* and *selective coding* interact in the process of theory building. This is illustrated through the Spillover Model, which generalises the process of legislation formulation identified in the European Decision-Making Model and postulates both neo-functionalism and intergovernmentalism in the process of European integration. The generalisation is one usually employed in qualitative methodology i.e. from one setting to others. This provides high validity but low reliability. Indeed, the four central criteria *(fit, comprehendability, generality and control)* of substantive theory are met in the theory building process. The theory draws on diverse data and attempts to be true to the reality under scrutiny (it should *fit*). Secondly, the *fit* should be made understandable. This has been achieved through using matrices, models and diagrams to make the findings of the research process explicit. Thirdly, from the diverse data certain *generalisations* are made. However, the research makes clear the limitations of these generalisations and clarifies when the conditions apply to specific situations, there is *control*.

In this context, substantive theory is formulated in relation to the formal theories of intergovernmentalism, as well as neo-functionalism, state-centricism, multilevel governance and historical institutionalism. Through grounded theory techniques a substantive theory is constructed to give an understanding of integration theory and allow a greater comprehension of European integration and from this attempt to discover its limitations.Through grounded theory techniques a substantive theory is built to give an understanding of European integration and allow a greater comprehension of European governance, the SEM, and the European Union. Through open coding and comparative analysis the need for a survey is initiated (induction) this provides a deduction which considers that to create an SEM Member States need to compromise their normative regulatory environments; this provides selective coding which indicates further induction through axial coding. These procedures illustrate the need for a further survey which allows for data saturation and an in-depth understanding of the phenomenon. Throughout the analysis induction and deduction go hand-in-hand. One is continually analysing the data in the process of building theory. One is continually challenging theory through collecting and analysing data.

The substantive aspects of the theory have built up an understanding of the processes of integration through an analysis of decision-making. This illustrated how the Member States as political units were losing control over the creation of legislation and their subsequent sovereignty. The benefits of being a member of the EU are illustrated against these losses in terms of greater profitability and the consequent necessity of ensuring regulatory structures to maximise this. In this way, a calculation of benefit or loss may be posited. Ultimately, one may determine the rationale behind membership of the EU and the extent to which sovereignty may or may not be surrendered. Neo-functionalism (a formal theory) is one of incremental integration through the transfer of allegiance to a supranational body, the use of interest groups and the concept of spillover. On the other hand, intergovernmentalism (another formal theory) considers that the nation-state is the main impetus behind the European integration process. The substantive element of the theory formulated in this work assesses to what extent the formal theories are supported by the evidence.

If the sector/industry (in this case, the insurance industry) is involved in the construction of the SEM and furthering European integration, then the process is not purely intergovernmental (or state-centric): other actors are involved. However, as the Council of Ministers passes legislation, an intergovernmental element still remains quite strong. But even at this level, ". . . state executives do not determine the European agenda because they are unable to control the supranational institutions they have created at the European level. The growing diversity of issues on the Council's agenda, the sheer number of state executive principals and the mistrust that exists among them, and the increased specialisation of policy-making have made the Council of Ministers reliant upon the Commission to set the agenda, forge compromises, and supervise compliance. . . . Policy-making in the EU is characterised by mutual dependence, complementary functions and overlapping competencies" (Marks *et al,* 1996a; p 372)

The substantive theory developed here considers that industries/sectors compromise their own interest at the EU level (this is achieved through national interest groups, e.g. the ABI, and European interest groups, e.g. the CEA). This too illustrates aspects of neo-functionalism as the use of interest groups, particularly European interest groups, is central to a neo-functional understanding of European integration. Compromise between the EU-wide sector/industry and the Commission is reached primarily through European interest groups. The use of EU-wide interest groups is emphasised in the interaction and compromises that are reached between the EU legislative bodies and the EU-wide interest groups in the creation of European legislation. However, the national interest groups still play an important role in the process by reporting back to national governments. In general, the substantive theory concludes that there has been a shift in allegiance from the national legislature to the EU with regard to certain issues. However, the Member States still played an important role in the decision-making process. Indeed, through multilevel governance, there has been a shift toward joint sovereignty in the creation of EU legislation. This is illustrated through the concepts of intergovernmental and neo-functional spillover; the former creates the environment through the treaties and Member State agreements whereas, the latter adds impetus to this through industries/sectors to ensuring their advantage in the evolving EU. This process initiates a shift away from economic interdependence toward an intensification of integration, a move away from intergovernmental process of integration toward neo-functional. Not simply state-centric governance, but governance of a multilevel nature governance that illustrates a shift in sovereignty. "In practice, the erosion of national sovereignty means the erosion of the power of the Member State's to decide exclusively much of their public policy. . . . Empirically, it is beyond dispute that the EU level is now the level at which a high proportion (possibly 60 per cent) of what used to be regarded as purely domestic policy-making takes place . . . therefore power has shifted. A much more complex structure of policy-making has developed" (Richardson, 1996a; p 3).

FORMAL THEORIES

Neo-functionalism is grounded in Kantian political thought and considered peace-oriented in terms of a specific region. It is a peaceful process directed at a peaceful end and wishes to ensure a 'civil constitution' under the auspices of perpetual peace (Kant 1995). Furthermore, there is a propensity for Hegelian 'recognition'. Member States need to adhere to human rights, they need to be democratic entities if they are to become members of the EU (Ringmar, 1994).

Neo-functionalism proposes that the EU is a supranational entity, which through its expanding authority encourages the transferal of allegiance from national to the European institutions. The main body of the research in this work investigated the extent of intergovernmentalism and neo-functionalism in the creation of the European Union. It considers that, unlike federalism, the neo-functional supranational entity is a step towards functional ends, i.e. that supranationality is a process and an element in a transformation away from the nation-state toward an international entity. The study argues that the part of the dynamism in this process is spillover and the enhancement of supranationality.

On the other hand, intergovernmentalism argues that the nation-state is central to the process and will remain so. "The intergovernmentalist argument implies that states form their preferences via some hermetic national process, then bring those interests to Brussels. The implication is that EC institutions have no impact on the formation of state interests" (Sandholtz, 1994; p 260). Indeed, the interviews and the European Decision-Making Model illustrate that " . . . national interests of EC states do not have independent existence; they are not formed in a vacuum then brought to Brussels. . . . States define their interests in a different way as members of the EC than they would without it" (ibid). This again allows an extension in supranational decision-making.

The empiricism is bound up in the changes that are take place as the EU evolves, especially now that the process has intensified. The idea of neo-functional transformation has re-emerged in the aftermath of the SEA, the SEM and the plans for EMU and the evolving EU is where the process may be identified and best observed. As Haas (1958) pointed out, ". . . for the political scientist the unification of Europe has a peculiar attraction quite irrespective of merits and types. He may see it, as I do, an instance of voluntary 'integration' taking place before his eyes, as it were under laboratory conditions. He will wish to study it primarily because it is one of the very few current situations in which the decomposition of old nations can be systematically analysed within the framework of the evolution of a larger polity, perhaps, to develop into a nation of its own" (p xxxi).

This work proposes that through the political impetus of the SEA (1987) the harmonisation of legislation and regulation, as pointed out by Cecchini (1988), is being reformed to meet what is considered the normative conception of the evolving SEM. However, it also proposes that the normative concept of the SEM is tempered by the ideas that the industries have of their own trading structures and that these will differ from one Member State to the next, because each is acclimatised to trading in a specific regulatory environment. "Two features of the 1992 programme in particular suggested that there might still be explanatory force in neo-functionalism: the role of the Commission as a central bureaucratic actor manipulating circumstances to further integration; and secondly, the role played by multinational business interests in pressurising governments to complete the internal market. . . . Ironically it was politicians who in 1957 first conceived the idea of a common market, often over objections from the business community. Now the situation has been reversed; it is entrepreneurs and corporations who are keeping the pressure on politicians to transcend considerations of local and national interest" (George, 1994; p 7)

Such has been indicated by the results of the European survey and is explicit in the Third Life Assurance Directive, with reference to both the process of formulation and the end result (as indicated through the interviews). This allows the author to suggest that both supranational and sub-national interests are at work.

Overall, the study has identified a number theoretical propositions suggested by neo-functionalism through an empirical analysis of the Member States life insurance industries and the EU's decision-making processes. The survey proposes that differences exist between the Member state concepts of the best regulatory environment. At some point, if the European life insurance industry was to be unified in what was considered to be the best regulatory environment, these differences needed to be resolved. In its negotiations with the Commission some common ground was necessary. If the legislation being formulated was not supported by enough of the Member State industries, it could be blocked at the Council level. In this context, there is a need to negotiate with the supranational body through the use of European interest groups to ensure successful legislation and, through compromise, the most comfortable trading conditions. Through the need to be involved in the decision-making process, one may consider that supranationality and spillover are at work. The need to ensure preferred regulatory conditions force Member State industries/sectors and governments to become further involved in the European integration process. In some contexts industries and sectors that as social entities construct the future playing fields define the limitations of European integration.

As the free movement of services is being attempted and monetary union is realised it becomes ever more necessary for Member States to negotiate mutual concessions. Compromise becomes a central factor and national assertion in the face of the need for pragmatism slows up or destroys the process. However, as integration intensifies, agreements are harder won. "There is no paradox between the progress of economic integration in the

Community and sharpening political disagreement; indeed, the success of economic integration can be a cause of political disagreement. The Member States are engaged in the enterprise for widely different reasons, and their actions have been supported or instigated by elites seeking their own particular goals. Therefore, conflicts would seem endemic as the results of joint activity come to be felt and as the pro-integration consensus shifts" (Lindberg, 1963; p 80).

These conflicts may be illustrated through the intergovernmental role in the integration process. As international difficulties with regard to European competitiveness became paramount, pressure was put on governments by industries/sectors to further a common market in Europe. This created the necessity to agree the SEA and the Maastricht Treaty at the Member State level, and indicated the part played by industries/sectors in pursuing self-interest. However through this self-interest in terms of joining the EU or interest groups a common interest is formed.

The SEA, the SEM and the Maastricht Treaty create clarity of objectives and what is necessary if these objectives are to be realised. It also becomes necessary for each area to be looked at in the context of its own specifics and this necessitates the involvement of interest groups and sectors. The sword is double edged: what needs to be changed becomes clearer but winning these changes becomes harder. However, clarity negates Haas' "turbulence" and creates "wholes" (Haas, 1976). Both treaties and sub-national interests provide "focal points" and "shared belief systems" (Garrett *et al,* 1993; p 176).

Understanding different national trading structures and what is necessary to negotiate harmonisation (focal points) negates turbulence. The actors involved draw up working parameters and, through the spillover and supranationality, compromise is reached and integration intensified. However within the process, there is an intergovernmental element, i.e. the Council of Minister's and the sectors' interaction with national governments, but as integration intensifies this aspect of the process diminishes and the realist understanding that political change will be linked to its historical circumstances is verified (Morganthau 1973). Indeed, the process of integration is neither purely intergovernmental nor totally neo-functional, but as has been illustrated, an amalgamation of both and in this context it carries elements of realism and functionalism. Indeed is defined by historical institutionalism and characterised by multilevel governance.

Neo-functionalist and intergovernmental tendencies are apparent in the process of European integration. The European Union is a peaceful process looking toward a peaceful future and its limits cannot easily be forecast. Can any end be categorically stated? With regard to European Union one may question what Europe actually is? What are its boundaries? (Valery, 1964). Neo-functionalism could be seen as a step in the direction of an international civic constitution and could be seen as a means of attaining a functional end. The step could be seen as Hegelian recognition through an amalgamation of neo-functional and intergovernmental processes in the form of historical institutionalism and multilevel governance. Through recognition Member States form an understanding of self and their place within the growing European structure. Through mutual recognition, understanding and peaceful co-existence are enhanced. On the other hand it may be the European Union and European integration may be perceived as the means of creating nation-state structure that will become progressively more state-centric. The former of these outcomes indicates a neo-functional slant and the latter an intergovernmental.

The Substantive Theory

The substantive theory is built through coding, categorisation and process. The regulation table and matrices provide the basis of the substantive theory in that they acknowledge that separate Member States pursue different regulatory environments. This sets up the problem of understanding how compromise is reached. The interviews, observations and survey C further construct the substantive theory with regard to the EU decision-making process. This substantive theory has implications for the formal theories of intergovernmentalism, state-centric governance, neo-functionalism and multilevel governance in terms of spillover, supranationality and interest group utilisation. Furthermore, one is also able to detect elements of historical institutionalism in terms of governments being unable to predict the preferences of combined sectors and industries. Fundamentally liberal-intergovernmentalism, state centicism, multi-level governance and historical institutionalism can be seen as substantive theories of the formal theories i.e. intergovernmentalism and neofunctionalism. Which themselves are substantive theories in relation to functionalism and realism. Finally, these may be considered substantive theories in relation to Hegel and Kant.

"A substantive theory generated from the data must be formulated, in order to see which of diverse formal theories are, perhaps, applicable for furthering additional substantive formulations" (Glaser and Strauss, 1967; p 34). This illustrates that theories are never complete but processes in themselves.

The substantive theory is illustrated by the table, scale, matrices and models that were built by the on-going research (see below) from which a number of conclusions may be drawn. Diagrams are a fundamental aspect of grounded theory, they allow a visual representation of the substantive theory and illustrate the relationships between the concepts and how different parts of the research relate to one another.

Regulation and Legislation Table (Table 4.1).
Regulation Scale (Table 4.2).
Life Insurance Regulation Matrix One (Figure 4.1).
Life Insurance Regulation Matrix Two (Figure 4.2).
The European Demand Model (Figure 5.1).
The European Decision-Making Model (Figure 5.2).
The Spillover Model (Figures 6.1 & 6.2).

Indeed, the substantive theory itself, may be summarised in the following way:

(a) Sectors/industries (in this context the life insurance industry) ***negotiate*** *the construction of the SEM and consequently further and intensify* ***European integration.***

(b) Sectors/industries ***interact*** *in the decision-making process in a number of ways but primarily through the use of national and European interest groups.*

(c) Each Member State's sector/industry ***compromises*** *it's own interest at the EU level (this is achieved through national interest groups, e.g. ABI, and European interest groups, e.g. CEA).*

(d) ***Compromise*** *between the EU wide sector/industry and the Commission is reached primarily through* ***interaction*** *and* ***negotiation*** *between European interest groups and European decision-making institutions.*

(e) ***Compromise*** *of* ***difference*** *between the EU legislative bodies, national legislatures and interest groups takes place throughout the creation of European legislation.*

(f) There is a shift in allegiance (by the national sector industry) from the national legislature to the EU with regard to certain issues. However, the Member States still play an important role in the decision-making process. Indeed, there has been a shift toward joint sovereignty in the creation of EU legislation. Through this process European ***integration*** *is intensified.*

(g) ***Difference*** *is overcome through sub-national interests, supranantionality and spillover. This creates an impetus for further integration.*

(h) ***European integration*** *is given impetus by economic industries/sectors pursuing their self-interest in the creation of EU legislation. However, this allows welfare for Europeans in terms of greater prosperity and peaceful co-existence. Through* ***understanding difference European integration*** *is intensified.*

The substantive theory takes into consideration the special nature of life insurance and other financial services products. Indeed, this work considers that products such as life insurance and pensions are closely linked to individual cultures. "Differences in the way distinct countries subjectively value insurance products have not come into being by chance. They have evolved out of historically developed differences in values between one national society and another" (Hofstede, 1995; p 423). This situation exists between the separate Member States and relates to financial services products other than insurance. From this starting point, it is assumed that a study of the life insurance industry can allow generalisations about the EU regarding other financial services industries and sectors. Life insurance allows generalisations in respect of the EU because of its special nature in each of the Member States and its similarity with other financial services products. Through spillover generalisation is identifiable with regard to insurance and financial services legislation. This study generalises the processes identified through the interviews and extends the model and its theoretical implications. Indeed, a qualitative analysis generalises from one specific situation to another like situation, rather than from a sample of population to the total population. Consequently, this study argues that the process taking place regarding life insurance is likely to be happening from industry to industry and from sector to sector. The work recognises the limitations of such a generalisation and does so with these in mind. Indeed, industries and sectors are, on the one hand, isolated entities concerned with their own situation in the wider market place. However, it is through this self-interest that they must be aware of what is happening in other industries and sectors this in turn makes them initiators and reactors to the actions of other industries and sectors. In this context, there is *fit, comprehendibility, generalisation* and *control*.

As mentioned above, the substantive theory was constructed through an induction/deduction process. The inductive element encompassed the creation of a matrix through coding and categorisation. This was added to by a survey, this led to a number of deductions. These initiated further inductive research through a series of semi-formal interviews. Once again, this created further deductions, which were verified by another survey. In practical terms, this meant that through the construction of the matrix, we discover that different Member States pursue different concepts of a regulatory environment. Which led the work to the question: do Member States compromise their differences and if they do how is this achieved? From the interviews emerged a comprehension of how **Understanding, Negotiation, Interaction and Compromise** are pursued and **Difference** overcome. Indeed, they provided some generalisations that linked with the formal theories.

Finally, the substantive theory considers that a multilevel or multi-tiered understanding of governance is apparent at the EU level. This does not mean that the Member State is not involved, but it does indicate the difficulties with a purely intergovernmental or state-centric view. "Multilevel governance does not confront the sovereignty of states directly. Instead of being explicitly challenged, states in the European Union are being melded gently into a multilevel polity by their leaders and by the actions of numerous sub-national and supranational actors. State-centric theorists are right when they argue that states are extremely powerful institutions that are capable of crushing direct threats to their existence. The organi(s)ational form of the state emerged because it proved an effective means of systematically wielding violence. . . . One does not have to argue that states are on the verge of political extinction to believe that their control of those living in their territories has been significantly weakened" (Hooghe and Marks, 1997; p 38 author's bracket).

The interviews suggested that in some cases state executives are unable to hold onto sovereignty. Indeed, collectively they are unable to define the agenda " . . .because they are unable to control the supranational institutions they have created at the European level" (ibid). Sectors and interest groups (sub-national actors) circumvent the national legislature and directly lobby the EU institutions. It is apparent that decision-making at the European level " . . . is characterised by mutual dependence, complementary functions, and overlapping competencies" (ibid). Thus, there is an interaction between intergovernmental and neo-functional processes at the EU level. During the 1960s and the 1970s, an intergovernmental system was in ascendence and this provided the environment for intergovernmentalism and the state-centric model. However, with the advent of the SEA in the 1980s and the added authority of the EU institutions " . . . a system of multilevel governance arose, in which the activities of supranational and sub-national actors diluted national government control" (ibid, p 39). The interviews illustrated that the Member States were " . . . no longer . . . the exclusive nexus between domestic politics and international relations" (ibid). Indeed, sub-national actors were making " . . . direct connections . . . in diverse political arenas. Traditional and formerly exclusive channels of communication and influence are being side-stepped" (ibid). Multilevel governance allows interest groups to be involved at both EU and national levels. However, as the interviews and subsequent European Decision-Making Model illustrated, when we speak of European legislation, the shift is toward the supranational.

The SEA the Maastricht and Amsterdam Treaties have led to discussions around the concept of sovereignty. "Several member-state governments, are themselves deeply riven on the issues of integration and sovereignty. States and state sovereignty have become objects of popular contention - the outcome of which is as yet uncertain" (ibid, p 40).

Since its inception the EU " . . . has mainly been studied as an example of . . . supranational integration or intergovernmental co-operation between, (previously) sovereign nation-states" (Hix, 1994; p 1). Indeed, Hix (1994) pointed out that, even though they had the same ontological and methodological basis, there were distinctions between the way international relations and comparative politics theories analysed the EU. Indeed, he considered that theories of international relations were limited when analysing the internal politics of the community. "The international approaches may be appropriate for the studies of European integration. However, comparative politics are more appropriate for the analysis of European Community politics" (p 23). This work considers that both are applicable when analysing the EU. However, as European integration intensifies the debate will move away from politics between states and turn toward European governance and politics within states. This slight shift may be identified through the governance arguments initiated by Hooghie and Marks (1997), Keohane and Hoffman (1991), Marks (1993), Marks (1995), Marks *et al* (1996) and Marks *et al* (1996a). As well as the shift toward debates around governance, this change has also been realised through the study of specific sub-national interests and their interactions with EU policy-making institutions. (see Camerra-Rowe, 1996; Coen, 1997; 1998; Greenwood *et al*, 1992; Greenwood and Cram, 1996; Greenwood, 1995; 1997; Mazey and Richardson, 1996; McLaughlin *et al*, 1993; McLaughlin and Greenwood, 1995; McLaughlin, 1995). Within the international relations tradition there have been attempts to synthesise pluralist and realist theories like neo-functionalism and intergovernmentalism through multilevel governance (Hooghie and Marks, 1997). Furthermore, some commentators have considered that historical institutionalist arguments indicate that the EU " . . . is no longer simply a multilateral instrument, limited in scope and firmly under the control of individual member states" (Pierson, 1996; p 158). That Member State " . . . governments are not the only important decision-makers in the EU" (Garrett and Tsebelis, 1996; p 294). And the EU illustrates ". . . an emergent multitiered system of governance" (Pierson, 1996; p 158).

This work argues that there is an amalgamation of international relations approaches to European integration processes in the form of multilevel and multi-tiered governance. Indeed, it concludes that through an empirical study of the EU life insurance industry, insurance interest groups and EU policy-making institutions it has provides some generalisations regarding both governance and European integration. Fundamentally, through the Hegelian concept of 'recognition' we are moving toward a Kantian 'civil constitution'. Hegelian recognition could be perceived as a means of transferring between realist and functional understandings of integration, between the realist interpretation of Hegel and the Kantian civil constitution. Hegelian recognition is a mechanism that could bring about perpetual peace and the just civil constitution. Fundamentally for this study, recognition determines the limits of European integration.

REFERENCES

Ainsworth, S. (1993) Regulating Lobbyists and Interest Group Influence. *The Journal of Politics*. 55/1. pp 41-56.

Andersen, S. S. and Eliassen, K. A. (1991) European Community Lobbying. *European Journal of Political Research* 20: 173-187.

Annells, M. (1996) Grounded Theory Method: Philosophical Perspectives, Paradigm of Inquiry, and Postmodernism. *Qualitative Health Research*. Vol. 6, No. 3, August pp 379-393.

Aristophanes. (1970) *Plays One, The Peace*. Oxford Paperbacks.

Aristotle. (1983) *Ethics*. Penguin Classics.

Aron, R. (1985) (Trans T. Kilmartin) *The Opium of the Intellectuals*. University Press of America.

Bishop, M. Kay, J. Mayer, C. (eds). (1995). *The Regulatory Challenge* . Oxford University Press.

Blau, J. L. (1952) *Men and Movements in American Philosophy*. New York Prentice Hall.

Blumer, H. (1962) *Symbolic Interaction* in *Human Behaviour and Social Process Rose*, A. M. (ed) Houghton-Mifflin pp 179-184.

Blumer, H. (1969) *Symbolic Interaction*. Prentice Hall: Englewood Cliffs NJ.

British Insurers' International Committee Bulletins (various).

Browne, W. P. 1990 Organized Interests and Their Issue Niches: a Search for Pluralism in a Policy Domain. *Journal of Politics* Vol 52 No 2 May pp 477-509.

Bulmer, S. J. (1994) The Governance of the European Union: A New Institutional Approach. *Journal of Public Policy*. Vol 13 No 4 pp 351-380.

Calfruny, A. W. and Rosenthal, G. G. (eds) (1993) *The State of the European Community Vol 2. The Maastricht Debates and Beyond.* Lynne Rienner. Longman

Camerra-Rowe, P. (1996) *Firms and Collective Representation in the European Union.* The American Political Science Meeting. The San Francisco Hilton and Towers. Aug 29-Sept 1. The American Political Science Association.

Carlson, R. E. (1984) *The Nurses Guide to Better Communication.* Glenview Ill; Scott Forstman and Co.

Cawson, A. (1995) *Public Policies and Private Interests: The Role of Business Interests* in *Determining Europe's Future Television System in European Casebook on Business Alliances* (ed) Greenwood, J. Prentice Hall. Hemel Hemstead.

Cecchini, P. (1988) *The European Challenge. The Benefits of a Single Market.* Wildwood House.

Charmaz, K. (1983) *The Grounded Theory Method: An Explication and Interpretation.* In *Contemporary Field Research. A Collection of Readings.* ed R. M. Emerson. University of California L. A.

Club De Bruxelles. (1994) *Lobbying in Europe After Maastricht.* Club De Bruxelles.

Coase, R. H. (1995) *Essays on Economics and Economists.* University of Chicago Press. Chicago and London.

Coen, D. (1998) European Business Interest and the Nation State: Large Firm Lobbying in the European Union and Member State. *Journal of Public Policy,* 18 1, pp 75-100.

Coen, D. (1997) The Evolution of the Large Firm as a Political Actor in the European Union. *Journal of European Public Policy.* 4:1 March pp 91-108.

Coleman, W. and Grant, W (1988) The Organisational Cohesion and Political Access of Business: a Study of Comprehensive Associations. *European Journal of Political Research.* 16: pp 467-487.

Comite Europeen Des Assurances (CEA). (1990) *Note on the Proposal for a Third Life Assurance Directive*(October).

Comite Europeen Des Assurances (CEA). (1990) *Doc. MC 093* 09/90.

Comite Europeen Des Assurances (CEA) Position Papers (various).

Comite Europeen Des Assurances (CEA). (no date) *Codification of European Insurance Directives*

Comite Europeen Des Assurances (CEA INFO). (1994) November and December.

Commission of the European Community. (1985) *White Paper on Completing the Internal Market.* Brussels.

Commission of the European Community Report. (1992) *Completing the Internal Market.* European Commission Jan.

Corbin, J. and Strauss, A. (1990) Grounded Theory Method. *Qualitative Sociology.* Vol 13 pp 3-21.

Cottingham, J. and Hussey, R. (1996) *A Grounded Theory Study of Related Party Transactions.* Conference paper, Portsmouth University.

Cox, R. W. (1981) Social Forces States and World Orders: Beyond International Relations Theory. *Millennium,* 10: 2, pp 126-55.

Cram, L. (1997) *Policy-Making in the European Union. Conceptual Lenses and Integration Processes.* Routledge London.

De Gucht, K. (1991) *Report on the Commission's Proposal for a Third Non-Life Directive.* Committee on Legal Affairs and Citizens Rights. Doc EN/RR/112339.

Dehousse, R. (1992) Integration v. Regulation? On the Dynamics of Regulation in the European Community. *Journal of Common Market Studies (JCMS).* Vol 30 No 4 December pp 383-402.

Derrida, J. (1992) *The Other Heading. Reflections On Todays Europe.* Trans Brault and Naas. Indiana University Press

Deutsch, K. W. (1953) *Nationalism and Social Communication.* Cambridge Mass MIT Press.

Dewey, J. (1950) *Art as Experience.* Capricorn New York.

Dicey, A. V. (1962) *Law and Public Opinion in England during the Nineteenth Century* (ed) Wade E.

Diesing, P. (1972) *Patterns of Discovery in the Social Sciences.* Routledge and Kegan London.

Directorate General XV. *News From DG XV* (various).

Directorate General XV (1993) *Community Measures in the Field Of Insurance and Pension Funds.* July XV C. 2.

Drabbe, H. (1994) The Internal Market for Insurance: A Reality? *The Geneva Papers on Risk and Insurance* 19 No 71 April pp 135-143.

Easton, D. (1953) *The Political System: An Enquiry into the State of Political Science.* New York Knopf.

Easton, D. (1965) *A Systems Analysis of Political Life.* John Wiley and Son Inc.

Easton, D. (1965a) *A Framework for Political Analysis.* Engelwood Cliffs N.J.: Prentice Hall, Inc.

Ellis, T. H. (1995) *Policyholder Protection in the Single European Market* in *The Law and Practice of Insurance in the Single European Market* (eds) McGee, A and Heusel, W. Trier Academy of European Law.

Ellis, T. H. (1994) *The Single European Market and Insurance Law and Practice.* London Witherby and Co.

Ellis, T. H. (1990) *European Integration and Insurance. (Creating a Common Insurance Market).* London Witherby and Co.

EUR OP (1992) *Treaty on European Union.* Council of the European Communities and Commission of the European Communities. Brussels.

European Documentation (1989) *The European Financial Common Market* Periodical Vol 4.

European Parliament (1991) *Europeanisation of the Insurance Industry in the Internal Market After 1992.* Legal Affairs Series W 3 DG for Research.

European Parliament Working Paper (1992) *European Court of Justice, (ECJ) Judgement. 4/12/86.*

Financial Times. May 19 1989. Editorial.

Financial Times Management Report. (1992) *Insurance in the EC and Switzerland Structure and development towards harmonisation* .

Fitchew, G. E. (1990) *The European Regulatory and Supervisory Framework* in Fair & Boissieu (eds) *Financial Institutions in Europe Under New Competitive Conditions.* pp 27-37 Kluwer.

Galtung, J. (1968) A Structural Theory of Integration, *Journal of Peace Research* 5 (4) .

Garrett, G. (1992) International Cooperation and Institutional Choice: the Eurpean Community's Internal Market. *International Organisation.* 46, 2, Spring pp 531-560.

Garrett, G. and Weingast, B. (1993) *Ideas, Interests, and Institutions: Constructing the European Community's Internal Market* in *Ideas and Foreign Policy: Beliefs, Institutions, and Political Change.* Cornell Universiy Press.

Garrett, G. and Tsebelis, G. (1996) An Institutional Critique of Intergovernmentalism. *International Organisation,* 50, 2, pp 269-99.

Gehring, T. (1996) Integrating Integration Theory: Neo-functionalism and International Regimes. *Global Society. Journal of Interdisciplinary International Relations.* Vol 10 No 3.

George, S. (1994) *Supranational Actors and Domestic Politics: Integration Theory Reconsidered in the Light of the Single European Act and Maastricht.* Sheffield Papers in International Studies No 22. (University of Sheffield).

George, S. (1995) *Politics and Policy of the European Community.* Oxford: Oxford University Press.

Glaser, B. and Strauss, A. (1967). *The Discovery of Grounded Theory.* Sage New York.

Glaser, B. (1978) *Advances in the Methodology of Grounded Theory. Theoretical Sensitivity.* University of California. San Francisco.

Glaser, B. (1992) *Emergence vs Forcing. Basics of Grounded Theory Analysis.* Sociology Press Mill Valley CA.

Grant, W. (1995) *Pressure Groups, Politics and Democracy in Britain.* London P. Allen.

Grant, W. (1990) *Organised Interests and the European Community.* Paper presented to Fetrinelli Foundation; Cortona Italy May.

Grant, W. and Marsh, D. (1977) *The Confederation of British Industry.* Hodder and Stoughton London.

Greenwood, J. (1997) *Representing Interests in The European Union.* The European Union Series. Macmillan London.

Greenwood, J. (1995) (ed) *European Casebook on Business Alliances. European Casebook Series on Management.* Prentice Hall International (UK).

Greenwood, J and Cram, L. (1996) European Level Business Collective Action: The Study Agenda Ahead. *Journal of Common Market Studies.* Vol 34, No 3.

Greenwood, J. Grote, J. and Ronit, R. (Eds) (1992) *Organized Interests and the European Community.* Sage.

Guba, E. G. and Lincoln, Y. S. (1994) *Competing Paradigms in Qualitative Research* in Denzin, N. and Lincoln, Y. S. *Handbook of Qualitative Research.* pp 105-117. Sage: Thousand Oaks.

Haas, E. B. (1958) *The Uniting of Europe.* Stanford University Press.

Haas, E. B. (1964) *Beyond the Nation State. Functionalism and International Organization.* Stanford University Press.

Haas, E. B. (1964a) *Technocracy, Pluralism and the New Europe* in *A New Europe* ed Graubard S. R. Boston

Haas, E. B. (1971) *The Study of Regional Integration: Reflections on the Joy and Anguish of Pretheorizing* in *Regional Integration. (eds)* Lindberg & Scheingold. Harvard.

Haas, E. B. (1976) Turbulent Fields and the Theory of Regional Integration. *International Organization* 30 part 2 pp 173-211.

Haas, E. B. (1975) Is there a hole in the whole? Knowledge, technology, interdependence and the construction of international regimes. *International Organization.* Vol 29 part 3 pp 827-875.

Hammersley, M. (1990) *The Dilemma of Qualitative Method. Herbert Blumer and the Chicago Tradition.* Routledge. London.

Hampsher-Monk, I. *A History of Modern Political Thought.* Blackwell. Oxford.

Heathcote, N. (1966) The Crisis of European Supranationality. *Journal of Common Market Studies*. Vol 5 December no 2 pp 140-171.

Hegel, G. W. F. (1967) *Philosophy of Right*. Trans T. M. Knox, Oxford University Press.

Hegel, G.W. F. (1977) *Phenomenology of Spirit.* Trans A. V. Miller Foreword J. N. Finlay. Clarendon Press Oxford

Heidegger, M. (1978) *Being and Time.* Blackwell Oxford.

HMSO. (1988) *Treaties Establishing the European Communities.* London.

Hofstede, G. (1995) Insurance as a Product of National Values. *The Geneva Papers on Risk and Insurance*, 20 No 77 October pp 423-429.

Holland, S. (1980) *Uncommon Market.* Papermac.

Hooghe, L. and Marks, G. (1997) *Contending Models of Governance in the European Union* in (eds) Calfruny, A. W. and Lankowski, C. *Europe's Ambitious Unity. Conflict and Consensus in the Post Maastricht Era.* Lynne Reiner. London.

Hurwitz, L. (ed) (1980) *Contemporary Perspectives on European Integration.* Aldwych London.

Jordan, G. (1993)*The Pluralism of Pluralism,* in *Pressure Groups* (ed) Richardson J. J. Oxford University Press.

Jur, Ing, E. H. and Schmidt, R. (1989). The First Geneva Lecture. The Practical Consequences for Insurers of the Freedom of Services throughout the European Community.*The Geneva Papers on Risk and Insurance Supplement No 51 April.*

Kant, I. (1995) *Political Writings* (ed) Hans Reiss. (Trans) Nisbet, H. B. Cambridge Texts in the History of Political Thought. Cambridge University Press.

Keohane, R. and Nye, J. (1977) *Power and Interdependence*. Little Brown and Co.

Keohane, R. and Hoffman, S. (1990) *Community Politics and Institutional Change* in *The Dynamics of European Integration* (ed) Wallace, W. The Royal Institute of International Affairs. Pinter. London and New York.

Keohane, R. and Hoffman, S. (1991) *Institutional Change in Europe in the 1980s* in *The New European Community: Decision Making and Institutional Change.* Westview.

Kimber, R. and Richardson J. J. (1974) *Pressure Groups in Britain* . Dent. London

Kirchner, E. J. (1976) *An Empirical Examination of the Functionalist Concept of Spillover.* Case Western Reserve University.

Kirchner, E. J. (1980) *Interest group Behaviour at Community Level* in *Contemporary Perspectives on European Integration* (ed) Hurwitz, L. Aldwych London.

Kirchner, E. J. and Schwaiger, H. (1981) *The Role of Interest Groups in the European Community.* Economic and Social Committee of the EC. Gower Aldershot.

Kirchner, E. J. (1992) *Decision-Making in the European Community: the council presidency and European integration.* Manchester University Press.

Lieber, R. J. (1974) *Interest Groups and Political Integration in British entry into Europe* in *Pressure Groups in Britain* Kimber & Richardson pp 27-56 Dent London.

Lindberg, L. (1967) The European Community as a Political System: Notes Toward the Construction of a Model. *Journal of Common Market Studies* Vol 5 June no 4 pp 344-387.

Lindberg, L. and Scheingold, S. A. (1970) *Europe's Would-Be Polity: Patterns of Change in the European Community.* Englewood Cliffs NJ Prentice Hall.

Lindberg, L. and Scheingold, S. A. (eds) (1971) *Regional Integration: Theory and Research.* Cambridge Mass: Harvard University Press.

Lindberg, L. (1963) *The Political Dynamics of European Economic Integration.* Stanford University Press.

Loheac, F. (1991) Deregulation of Financial Services and Liberalization of International Trade in Services. *The Geneva Papers on Risk and Insurance Issues and Practice* . No 61 October pp 406-413

Luchner, J. E. (1992) *International Relations Theory and European Integration: The Political Economy of the European Monetary System and the SEA.* Ph.D. Work. The Pennsylvania State University.

Mally, G. (1973) *The European Community in Perspective* . Lexington Mass.

Majone, G. (1990) *Introduction* in*Deregulation or Re-regulation? Regulatory Reform in Europe and the United States.* pp 1-2.

Majone, G. (1996) A European Regulatory State? in European Union Power and Policy-Making (ed) Richardson J. J. Routledge London and New York.

Marks, G. (1993) *Structural Policy and Multilevel Governance* in*The State of the European Community. The Maastricht Debate and Beyond Vol 2* (eds) Calfruny, A. W. and Rosenthal, G. G. Lynne Rienner. Longman.

Marks, G. Hooghe, L. and Blank, K. (1995) *European Integration and the State.* European University Institute Working Paper No 95/7.

Marks, G. Scharpf, F. W. Schmitter, P. C. and Streeck, W. (eds) (1996) *Governance in the European Union.* Sage London.

Marks, G. Hooghe, L. and Blank, K. .(1996a) European Integration from the 1980s: State-Centric *v.* Multi-level Governance. *Journal of Common Market Studies* Vol 34, No 3.

Marsh, D. (1978) More on Joining Interest Groups. *British Journal of Political Science.* Vol 8 pp 380-384.

Mayer, C. (1995) *The Regulation of Financial Services: Lessons from the UK for 1992* in *The Regulatory Challenge* eds Bishop, M. Kay, J. and Mayer, C. pp 227-253 Oxford University Press.

Mazey, S. P. (1992) British Pressure Groups in the European Community: The Challenge of Brussels. *Parliamentary Affairs* Vol 45 Pt 1 pp 92-107.

Mazey, S. P. and Richardson, J. J. (1993) *Interest Groups in the European Community;* in *Pressure Groups* (ed) Richardson J. J. Oxford University Press.

Mazey, S. P. and Richardson, J. J. (1996) *The Logic of Organisation. Interest Groups* in *European Union Power and Policy-Making* (ed) Richardson, J. J. European Public Policy Routledge London.

McGowan, F. and Seabright, P. (1995) *Regulation in the European Community and its Impact on the UK* in *The Regulatory Challenge* eds Bishop, M. Kay, J. and Mayer, C. Oxford University Press.

McLaughlin, A. M. (1995) *Automobiles: Dynamic Orgainisations in Turbulent Times?* in Greenwood, J. *European Casebook on Business Alliances.* pp 172-183. Prentice Hall International UK.

McLaughlin. A. M. and Greenwood, J. (1995) The Management of Interest Representation in the European Union. *Journal of Common Market Studies* Vol 33, No 1. March pp 143-146.

McLaughlin, A. M. *et al.* (1993) Corporate Lobbying in the European Community. *Journal of Common Market Studies* Vol 31 No 2. June. pp 192-213.

Mead, G. H. (1962) *Mind, Self, and Society* (Morris, C. ed) University of Chicago Press.

Melia, K. M. Rediscovering Glaser. *Qualitative Health Research.* Vol. 6 No, 3, August pp 368-378.

Mitrany, D. A (1943) *Working Peace System* London; Royal Institute of International Affairs.

Mitrany, D. A. (1944) *The Road to Security.* Peace News Pamphlet No 29 London NPC.

Mitrany, D. A. (1965) The Prospect of Integration Federal or Functional. *Journal of Common Market Studies.* Vol 4 December pp 119-149.

Mitrany, D. A. (1970) *The Functional Approach to World Organization* in Cosgrave, C. A. and Twitchett, K. *New International Actors: The United Nations and the EEC.* London Macmillan. pp. 65-75.

Mitrany, D. A. (1975a) *A Political Theory for a New Society* in Groom, P. and Taylor, A. pp 25-37.

Mitrany, D. A. (1975b) *Functionalism: Theory and Practice in International Relations* in *Functionalism* Groom and Taylor (eds) University of London Press.

Mitrany, D. A. (1975c) *The Functional Theory of Politics* . LSE. London.

Moe, T. M. (1980) *The Organisation of Interests.* University of Chicago Press. Chicago and London.

Moravcsik, A. (1991) *Negotiating the Single European Act* in Keohane, R. and Hoffman, S. (eds)*The New European Community: Decision-Making and Institutional Change.* Westview.

Moravcsik, A. (1993) Preferences and Power in the European Community: a liberal intergovernmentalist approach. *Journal of Common Market Studies* Vol 31, pp 473-524.

Morgenthau, H. J. (1973) *Politics Among Nations. The Struggle for Power and Peace.* Alfred Knopf New York

Munich Re: (1992) *Life Insurance in the EC and EFTA Countries.* Eurofolder.

Munich Re: (1988) *A Series of Notes on Insurance in the EC .*

Nye, J. S. (1971) *Comparing Common Markets: A Revised Neo-Functionalist Model* in *Regional Integration: Theory and Research.* Lindberg, L. & Scheigold, S. A. (eds) Cambridge Mass: Harvard University Press.

Nye, J. S. (1971a) *Peace in Parts. Integration and Conflict in Regional Organisation.* Little Brown & Company. Harvard.

Official Journals of the European Community (various).

Official Journal of the European Community. (1993) *An Open and Structured Dialogue Between the Commission and Interest Groups* (OJ 93/C63).

Ogus, A. (1994) *Regulation Legal Form and Economic Theory.* Clarendon Oxford.

Olson, M. (1993) *The Logic of Collective Action* in *Pressure Groups* (ed) Richardson, J. J. Oxford University Press.

Oyen, E. (ed) (1990) *Comparative Methodology Theory and Practice in International Social Research* Sage.

Parkinson, F. (1977) *The Philosophy of International Relations; a Study in Political Thought.* Sage Library of Social Research 52.

Patton, M. (1980) *Qualitative Evaluation Methods.* Sage.

Pedersen, T. (1992) Political Change in the European Community. The Single European Act as a Case of System Transformation. *Co-operation and Conflict.* Vol 27 Pt 1 pp 7-44.

Pentland, C. (1975) *Functionalism and Theories of International Political Integration* in Groom, P. and Taylor, A. J. R. (eds) *Functionalism.* University of London. London.

Petersen, J. (1995) Decision-making in the European Union: towards a framework for analysis. *Journal of European Public policy.* 2:1 March pp 69-93.

Pool, W. E. (1990) *The creation of the internal market in insurance. Commission of the European Communities.* The Commission of the European Communities Document.

Pool. W. E. (1992). Insurance and the European Community. *The Geneva Papers on Risk and Insurance Issues and Practice.* No 63 April 1992 PP 338-402.

Rees, N. A. G. (1992). *The Politics or Regional Development in the European Community: An Inter-Organisational Perspective.* Ph.D. Work University of South Carolina.

Richards, D. (1996) Elite Interviewing: Approaches and Pitfalls. *Politics.*Vol 16, No 3, September.

Richardson, J. (ed) (1996) *European Union. Power and Policy-Making.* European Public Policy. Routledge.

Richardson, J. (1996a) *Policy-Making in the EU. Interests, Ideas and Garbage Cans of Primeval Soup* in *European Union. Power and Policy-Making* (ed) Richardson, J. European Public Policy. Routledge.

Ringmar, E. (1995) The Relevance of International Law: a Hegelian interpretation of a peculiar 17th century pre-occupation. *Review of International studies* 21 pp 87-103.

Russell, A. (1988) *The UK Supervisor's view.* Up-date '88 Conference 1992 - The EEC & Insurance.

Salafatinos, C. (1996) *Applying Grounded Theory in Management Accounting Research: A Case Study of ABC Implementation.* Conference paper Portsmouth University.

Sandholtz, W. (1994) Choosing Union: Monetary Politics and Maastricht in Neilsen, B. F. and Stubb, A. C-G. (Eds) *The European Union. Readings on the Theory and Practice of European Integration.* Lynne Rienner London.

Sandholtz, W. and Zysman, J. (1989) 1992: Recasting the European bargain. *World Politics* Vol 42, pp 95-129.

Sarantakos, S. (1993) *Social Research.* Macmillan.

Schmitter, P. C. *Examining the Present Euro-Polity with the Help of Past Theories* in Marks, G. Scharpf, F. W. Schmitter, P. C. and Streeck, W. *Governance in the European Union*. Sage. London.

Schneider, V *et al.* (1994) Corporate Actors Networks in European Policy-Making: Harmonizing Telecommunication Policy. *Journal of Common Market Studies* Vol 32 No 4.

Sen, A. (1992) *On Ethics and Economics.* Blackwell Oxford.

Sloane, B. (1988) *Chairman's Introduction.* Up-date '88 Conference 1992 - The EEC and Insurance.

Smith, A. (1985) *The Wealth of Nations* . Penguin.

Smith, H, W. (1981) *Strategies of Social Research*. Prentice-Hall.

Stern, N. P. (1994) *Eroding Grounded Theory* pp 212-223 in Morse, J. M. (ed) *Critical Issues in Qualitative Research Methods.* Sage: Thousand Oaks.

Strauss, A. (1987) *Qualitative Analysis for Social Scientist.* New York Cambridge University Press.

Strauss, A. and Corbin, J. (1990) *Basics of Qualitative Research. Grounded Theory Procedures and Techniques.* Sage.

Strauss, A. and Corbin, J. (1994) *Grounded Theory Methodology An Overview* in Denzin, N. and Lincoln, Y. *Handbook of Qualitative Research* pp 273-285. Sage: Thousand Oaks.

Swiss Re (UK). (1989) *Sigma* no 2.

Swiss Re (UK). (1990) *Sigma* no 1.

Swiss Re (UK). (1990) *Sigma* no 4.

Swiss Re (UK). (1991) *Sigma* no 2.

Swiss Re (UK). (1992) *Sigma* no 1.

Taylor, P. (1968) The Functionalist Approach to the Problem of International Order. *Political Studies* Oct pp. 393-410.

Taylor, P. (1980) Interdependence and Autonomy in the European Communities: The Case of the European Monetary System. *Journal of Common Market Studies*.Vol XVIII no 4 June.

Ugur, M. (1997) State-Society Interaction and European Integration: A Political Economy Approach to the Dynamics of Policy-Making of the European Union *Review of International Studies.* 23 pp 469-500.

Valery. (1962) *The European in History and Politics* (Trans) Folliot and Matthews. Bollingen N.Y.

Vipond, P. (1995) European Banking and Insurance. Business Alliances and Corporate Strategies in *European Casebook on Business Alliances* (ed) Greenwood, J. Prentice Hall UK.

Wallace, H. Wallace, W. and Webb, C. (1983).*The European Community* John Wiley and Son. London.

Wallace, H. (1990) *Making Multilateral Negotiations Work* in *The Dynamics of European Union* Wallace, W. (ed). Royal Institute of International Affairs. Pinter. London.

Wallace, W. (ed) (1990) *The Dynamics of European Union.* Royal Institute of International Affairs. Pinter. London.

Webb, C. (1983) *Theoretical Perspectives and Problems in Policy Making* in *The European Community* (eds) Wallace, W. Wallace, H. and Webb, C. John Wiley & Son. London.

INDEX

A

B

C

D

E

F

G

H

I

K

L

M

N

O

P

Q

R

S

T

U

V

W